Oasis of Wisdom

The Worlds of the
Desert Fathers and Mothers

David G. R. Keller

LITURGICAL PRESS
Collegeville, Minnesota

www.litpress.org

Cover design by Ann Blattner. Photo by Marv Hiles.

Scripture quotations, unless otherwise noted, are from the New Revised Standard Version Bible: Catholic edition, © 1989, 1993, Division of Christian Education of the National Council of the Churches of Christ in the United States of America. Used by permission. All rights reserved.

Other acknowledgments begin on page ix.

1   2   3   4   5   6   7   8

Library of Congress Cataloging-in-Publication Data

Keller, David G. R., 1937–
 Oasis of wisdom : the worlds of the desert fathers and mothers / David G. R. Keller.
 p. cm.
 Summary: "Introduces readers to the wisdom of the desert elders in the context of their daily lives, presenting their background (historical, cultural, and religious) and describing the environment of solitude, ascetic disciplines, labor, and interactions with other people that was the source of their wisdom"—Provided by publisher.
 Includes bibliographical references and index.
 ISBN 13: 978-0-8146-3034-1 (pbk. : alk. paper)
 ISBN 10: 0-8146-3034-0 (pbk. : alk. paper)
 1. Spiritual life—Christianity—History of doctrines—Early church, ca. 30–600. 2. Desert Fathers   3. Monastic and religious life of women—Egypt—History—Early church, ca. 30–600. I. Title.

BR195.C5K45 2005
271'.009'015—dc22

2004021179

The desert waits,
ready for those who come,
who come obedient to the Spirit's leading;
or who are driven,
because they will not come any other way.

The desert always waits,
ready to let us know who we are—
the place of self-discovery.

And whilst we fear, and rightly,
the loneliness and emptiness and harshness,
we forget the angels,
whom we cannot see for our blindness,
but who come when God decides
that we need their help;
when we are ready for what they can give us.

—Ruth Burgess

Oasis of Wisdom
is dedicated with gratitude and delight to
my parents,
David Gardiner Ross Keller, Sr.,
and
Elizabeth Benjamin Keller Dee
Two generous lovers of souls.

and

my step-parents,
Ruth Thierry Parkes Keller
and
John Alyn Dee
who were a blessing to me.

and

Marguerite Buchanan, R.S.M.
and
Suzanne Toolan, R.S.M.
Whose desert is the bay area of San Francisco,
and in whose lives the Spirit sings a continuous prayer
for prisoners, youth, seekers and the Liturgy of the Church.

and

The Rev. René Astruc, S.J.
in thanksgiving for his life and ministry in Alaska;
an ecumenical colleague and soul friend for thirty-nine years.
He was the best Jesuit Eskimo dancer in the world.

Contents

Acknowledgments

I am grateful to Drevis Hager, whose passion to learn more about the desert fathers and mothers led to the formation of a group of nineteen persons who studied the desert elders with me. We met for six months in 2003 at St. Mark's Episcopal Cathedral in Minneapolis, Minnesota. My presentations to that group of pilgrims led to the chapters that formed *Oasis of Wisdom*. Their desire to learn about the experiences and environments that produced the wisdom of the abbas and ammas, their honest and searching questions about the sayings, and their awareness of the implications of this wisdom for their own lives inspired and guided my writing. I am obliged to these companions in the desert.

My primary mentor in early monastic history is Fr. Columba Stewart, O.S.B., professor of theology at St. John's School of Theology/Seminary and Director of the Hill Monastic Manuscript Library at St. John's Benedictine Abbey, Collegeville, Minnesota. His extraordinary gifts as a teacher led me into a unique and rich world I had never experienced before. I encountered the desert elders as persons, not historical figures, and soon discovered that their spiritual path includes transformation of the whole person and is related to living an authentic human life. For the first time I saw the psychological wisdom of these desert elders. I am grateful for Father Columba's challenging teaching, research and writing, especially his definitive study *Cassian the Monk* and its insights into early monastic life. He has given me a background and some personal confidence to share this tradition. I am grateful, also, to Sr. Mary Forman, O.S.B., of St. John's School of Theology/Seminary who first opened my eyes and heart to the wisdom of the desert mothers, especially Mary of Egypt and Amma Syncletica. Sister Mary is a modern amma and a weaver of wisdom who challenged me to learn from these early monastic women whose lives and influence on the formation of Christian spirituality have been overshadowed far too long by males.

I am indebted to three other scholars whose understanding of desert monasticism has substantively influenced my thought and writing. Sr. Benedicta Ward's English translation of the sayings of the desert elders has been a primary source for *Oasis of Wisdom*, along with her biographical sketches of the elders and her introduction to the patterns of desert monasticism in *The Lives of the Desert Fathers*. Her work has made the sayings accessible.

Douglas Burton-Christie has deepened my understanding of the use of the Bible in desert monasticism and given me a window through which I have been able to view the lives and oral teaching of the desert elders with great detail. His thorough study *The Word in the Desert* has provided data and commentary that have, with other sources, enabled me to construct a picture of the daily lives of the desert elders. Burton-Christie has helped me identify the Bible and the life of Jesus as the central authority for the desert elders' teaching and praxis. He has given me a clearer understanding of the essential role of humility in desert monasticism.

There are key words that constantly reappear in desert monastic sayings and lives. These words relate the heart of the desert elders' experiences of God and summarize their lives of prayer. The Greek Orthodox monastic scholar Stelios Ramfos uses twelve of these words as chapter headings in his inspired study of the teaching of the desert elders, *Like a Pelican in the Wilderness*. Following his pattern, six chapters in *Oasis of Wisdom* use monastic words that I believe form the core of desert spirituality and at the same time provide essential guidance for humane and authentic human life today: cell, patience, praxis, labor, silence and humility. My understanding of desert monastic renunciation, solitude, discipline, time, labor, self-knowledge, repentance and transformation has been enriched by Professor Ramfos's insights. My writing and conclusions would be much less complete without his influence. I am indebted to these wise mentors, but assume responsibility for my own research, synthesis and conclusions. Errors or limitations in this work are my own.

I thank The Rev. Linda Maloney, academic editor, and Fr. Cyril Gorman, O.S.B., pastoral editor at the Liturgical Press for encouraging me to submit this manuscript. Father Cyril has given constant editorial advice and has, as always, been a valued soul friend. I am grateful, also, to the friendly and competent production staff of Liturgical Press who helped form and improve *Oasis of Wisdom,* much like the desert elders challenging and supporting a novice monk.

The monks of Saint John's Abbey, Collegeville, and the sisters of Saint Benedict's Monastery, Saint Joseph, Minnesota, were my close neighbors for eight years. We shared our work, worship, and lives, mostly in the ordinary things of life. But their greatest gift, through their faithfulness to the Rule of Saint Benedict, was and is the wisdom of the desert fathers and mothers made tangible in their work, inclusive hospitality, love of learning, creativity, humor, and love of their neighbors.

I could not have completed *Oasis* without the loving and patient support of my wife, Emily Wilmer, who was always there with humor when I reappeared from my monastic writing cell. I thank Emily for her ideas, questions and proofreading the final draft. We walk this path together.

I am grateful for permission to use material from publishers whose works have made the research for *Oasis of Wisdom* possible and who provide access to the words and lives of the desert elders. Excerpts from the following works published by Cistercian Publications are used with permission:

The Syriac Fathers on Prayer and the Spiritual Life. Trans. Sebastian Brock. Kalamazoo: Cistercian Publications. © 1987.

Dorotheos of Gaza: Discourses and Sayings. CS 33. Trans. Eric P. Wheeler. Kalamazoo: Cistercian Publications. © 1977.

Evagrius Ponticus: The Praktikos and Chapters on Prayer. CS 4. Trans. John Eudes Bamberger, O.C.S.O. Kalamazoo: Cistercian Publications. © 1972.

The Lives of the Desert Fathers. Norman Russell and Benedicta Ward, S.L.G. Kalamazoo: Cistercian Publications. © 1980 by Norman Russell and Benedicta Ward.

Pachomian Koinonia, 1, The Life of Saint Pachomius and His Disciples. CS 45. Armand Veilleux. Kalamazoo: Cistercian Publications. © 1980.

Harlots of the Desert. CS 106. Benedicta Ward, S.L.G. Kalamazoo: Cistercian Publications. © 1987 by Benedicta Ward.

The Sayings of the Desert Fathers. Trans. Benedicta Ward, S.L.G. Kalamazoo: Cistercian Publications. © 1975 by Sister Benedicta. Foreword © 1975 by The Sisters of the Love of God.

Excerpts from works published by Paulist Press are used with permission:

Excerpts from *The Forgotten Desert Mothers: Sayings, Lives and Stories of Early Christian Women,* by Laura Swan. © 2001 by Saint Placid Priory, Paulist Press, Inc., New York/Mahwah, N.J.

Excerpts from Athanasius: *The Life of Antony and the Letter to Marcellinus,* translated and introduced by Robert C. Gregg; preface by William A. Clebsch, from The Classics of Western Spirituality. © 1980 by Paulist Press, Inc., New York/Mahwah, N.J.

A Study of Gregory Palamas, by John Meyendorff. Crestwood: St. Vladimir's Seminary Press, trans. © 1964 by George Lawrence.

Excerpts and adaptation of one map from the following work published by University of California Press are used with permission:

Pachomius: The Making of a Community in Fourth-Century Egypt, by Philip Rousseau. Berkeley: University of California Press, © 1985 The Regents of the University of California.

Excerpts from the following work published by Orbis Books are used with permission:

Desert Wisdom: Sayings from the Desert Fathers, translation and art by Yushi Nomura and with an introduction and epilogue by Henri J. M. Nouwen. Maryknoll: Orbis Books, © 1982/2001 by Yushi Nomura. Introduction and Epilogue © 1982/2001 by the Estate of Henri J. M. Nouwen.

Excerpts from the following work published by Holy Cross Orthodox Press are used with permission:

Like a Pelican in the Wilderness: Reflections on the Sayings of the Desert Fathers, by Stelios Ramfos, trans. and abridged by Norman Russell. Brookline: Holy Cross Orthodox Press. © 2000 by Holy Cross Orthodox Press.

Excerpts from the following work published by Upper Room Books are used with permission:

Making Life a Prayer: Selected Writings of John Cassian. Selected, edited and introduced by Keith Beasely-Topliffe. Upper Room Spiritual Classics-Series One. Nashville: UpperRoom Books. © 1997 by Upper Room Books.

Short excerpts from the following works have been used with permission of the publishers cited:

To Love as God Loves, by Roberta Bondi. Philadelphia: Fortress Press. © 1987 by Augsburg Fortress Publishers.

Paths to the Heart: Sufism and the Christian East. Edited by James C. Cutsinger. Excerpts from "How Do We Enter The Heart?" by Kallistos Ware. Bloomington: World Wisdom Inc. © 2002 by World Wisdom, Inc.

Purity of Heart in Early Ascetic and Monastic Literature. Edited by Harriet A. Luckman and Linda Kulzer, O.S.B. Collegeville: Liturgical Press. © 1999 Order of Saint Benedict, Inc.

The Ground of Being: Foundations of Christian Mysticism, by Joseph Milne. London: Temenos Academy. © 2004 by James Milne.

The Lausiac History of Palladius. Willits, Calif.: Eastern Orthodox Books. No copyright cited.

I am grateful to Ruth Burgess, copyright holder, for permission to use her poem "The Desert Waits" that was originally printed in *Bread of Tomorrow,* ed. Janet Morely. London: SPCK/Christian Aid, ISBN 0-281-04459-3. "The Desert Waits" also appeared in *Women Pray: Voices Through the Ages, from Many Faiths, Cultures, and Traditions,* ed. Monica Furlong. Woodstock, Vt.: SkyLight Paths, 2001. Used with permission.

Introduction

In the fifth century the desert mother Syncletica said, "Just as it is impossible to be at the same moment both a plant and a seed, so it is impossible for us to be surrounded by worldly honor and at the same time to bear heavenly fruit."[1] She also said,

> My children, all of us—male and female—know about being saved, but through our own negligence we stray away from salvation. First of all we must observe the precepts known through the grace of the Lord, and these are: "You shall love the Lord your God with all your soul, and your neighbor as yourself" (Matthew 22:37 and 39). Whatever people say by the grace of the Spirit, therefore, that is useful springs from love and ends in it. Salvation, then, is exactly this – the two-fold love of God and of our neighbor. . . . Well, what do we need for the present conflict? Obviously, austere asceticism and pure prayer.[2]

Syncletica was an intelligent, well-educated, and beautiful woman. She lived sometime between the mid-fourth and mid-fifth centuries and died in her mid-eighties. Her parents had moved from Macedonia to the cosmopolitan Nile delta city of Alexandria. They were devout Christians, wealthy, and well-known in Alexandria's large Christian community. Syncletica, her sister and two brothers were influenced by the environments of their parents' faith and virtues and a larger faith community dominated by Alexandria's great Christian Catechetical School, the Didaskaleion. It was a center of biblical, theological, and philosophical learning and debate, dominated by the influence of two of its great leaders, Clement and Origen. Alexandria was so large it was sub-divided into four "corporations" based on nationality. It was a thriving meeting place of cultures, religious traditions, learning, and commerce. There was a large Jewish community known for its biblical scholars such as Philo, famous for his allegorical interpretation of the Hebrew Scriptures. For centuries Alexandria had influenced the

Roman world through its great library and schools of rhetoric, philosophy and science. Leaders and teachers who mastered rhetoric and intellectual skills were held in highest esteem. Alexandria's Hellenistic and Roman culture, learning and religious life influenced local Egyptian, Christian, and Jewish thinking and practice.

Egypt was Rome's bread basket with a steady flow of ships from Alexandria's harbor to Italy. The city's commerce and rich society were fertile ground for fame, fortune, and political power. Its Roman homes were elaborate with floors and walls decorated with colorful mosaic art and low tables and couches designed for rich banquets. Along with its substantive cultural and religious life Alexandria was also an icon of materialism and hedonism. Scholars, poets, politicians, and theologians vied for reputation and influence while further east the Empire disintegrated and in 412 C.E. fell when the Visigoths sacked Rome. The face of the Roman world was changing in the midst of chaos, terrorism, and threats to the stability of hallowed institutions. There were threats, also, to Christian communities scattered throughout the Mediterranean world. Following official recognition under Constantine in 312 C.E. the church experienced an enculturation that enabled it to influence Roman culture but at the same time made it vulnerable to the materialism and power struggles of the surrounding culture. This threatened the stability of indigenous expressions of Christian life in favor of the need to establish more universal patterns of church life and thought. Liturgy, theology and church structures were in transition.

Syncletica lived in a city and a church in the midst of frenzy and changes that scattered the human soul. The dysfunctions, pride and vices of her society constricted its vision of wholesome freedom and authentic human abundance. Syncletica desired a more extended vision of reality and early in her life began a disciplined life of prayer in her parents' home.[3] During that period both her brothers died, one as a youth and the older brother at twenty-five. After her parents' death Syncletica distributed the family wealth among the poor of Alexandria and as an act of committing her life totally to prayer cut off her hair in the presence of a priest. She moved, with her blind sister, to a family tomb on the outskirts of Alexandria. Her intent was to seek God in solitude, but gradually other women came to her for advice and inspiration. A small community of women formed around Syncletica, and her wise teaching forms the major portion of *The Life of The Blessed and Holy Syncletica* written within fifty years of her death in the mid-fifth century.

It is tempting to interpret Syncletica's actions as a renunciation of the natural goodness of earthly life and human relationships. Indeed, during her lifetime some Greek philosophers and Christian theologians characterized human life as a lesser form of existence that should be transcended for a more enlightened spiritual realm. Syncletica's teaching indicates that this was not her intent. She did not abandon human life. Her withdrawal from the futile conventions of Alexandrian society was motivated by an intentional desire for a more **authentic human life** grounded in a disciplined life of prayer, self-knowledge, humble dependence on God and love of neighbor. Some twenty-first century voices would tell Syncletica to "get real." That is precisely what she did. She left a society that was content with living on the surface of life and took the risk of directing her energy and heart to what she believed is the root of human life: our relationship with God. Syncletica's fifth-century voice speaks clearly to our twenty-first century's reliance on rational solutions, material pleasures and power-based security. Perhaps her voice will open our minds and expand our hearts to the inner movement of divine love and wisdom.

The church historian Irénée Hausherr, S.J., comments: "If you study the history of spirituality or the spiritual life of the Church, you will find that each time that there is a spiritual renewal in the Church, the desert fathers are present."[4]

The Sources of Desert Wisdom

Who were these desert fathers and mothers? Where did they live? What were their lives like? What is the significance of their experiences and wisdom for our lives today?

There are no easy answers to these questions. In recent decades many scholars of Christian monasticism have focused their attention on a formative period in early Christianity known as the "desert tradition." Although its presence and influence continues to this day, its origins lie in the late third century and it flourished at least until the late seventh century. It was a major influence on the formation of Celtic and Benedictine monasticism in the West and monasticism in the Eastern Orthodox churches.

The wisdom of the desert fathers and mothers had its roots in the life and teaching of Jesus of Nazareth, his Jewish heritage, especially the Psalms, and the communal life and writings of the earliest Christian faith communities. Our knowledge of the lives and teachings of the desert elders comes from collections of their sayings, some of which include incidents from their lives, and from longer written biographies of influential desert saints.

Beginning in the third century, thousands of men and women left the sophisticated, anxious and materialistic society of the Roman Empire and went to live in the deserts of Arabia, Egypt, Palestine, and Syria. Although a small minority fled for economic or political reasons, the primary motive, like Syncletica's, was to seek experience of God and conversion or purification of life. Their eyes were cast toward heaven and the distractions of the inhabited world made the solitude and silence they desired difficult or impossible. Gradually, their lives of prayer formed the roots of Christian monasticism. Some lived as hermits; others in informally connected groups of disciples, each gathered around a single wise teacher; and the remainder lived in formally organized monastic communities, each guided by its own rule of life. Although all these men and women had withdrawn from conventional society, word about their lives and wisdom spread rapidly. Others came to join them or to seek guidance and spiritual wisdom.

In 394 C.E. seven monks from Palestine visited monks who had settled in the Egyptian desert. They wanted to see with their eyes what they had only heard with their ears. They visited eleven monastic sites and listened to some of the wisest and most experienced desert elders. The account of their visit, *The History of Monastic Life in Egypt*, while acknowledged as generally accurate, is more like a portrait than a narration of facts.[5]

> We also put in at Nitria (an isolated and desolate region west of the Nile delta), where we saw many great anchorites (hermits). . . . Some applied themselves to contemplation, others to the active life. When a group of them saw us approaching from a distance through the desert, some came to meet us with water, others washed our feet, and others laundered our clothes. Some of them invited us to a meal, others to learn about the virtues, and others to contemplation and the knowledge of God. Whatever ability each one had, he hastened to use it for our benefit. Indeed, how can one relate all their virtues, since one is totally unable to do them justice?[6]

Other accounts of the life and wisdom of these wise mentors of early Egyptian ascetic life are *The Life of Antony* by Athanasius of Alexandria, *The Lausiac History* by Palladius, the *Conferences* by John Cassian, and the *Apophthegmata Patrum*, an early collection of sayings and incidents from the lives of the desert fathers and mothers.[7] The primary collection of sayings in the Christian East is called the *Gerontikon*, the Book of the Elders, and contains 1,202 sayings of 127 desert fathers and three desert mothers. It was compiled around the seventh century and includes wisdom handed down "in simple and unaffected speech."[8] Refer to endnote number eight for details about English translations of these collections. I have used these and other primary sources to provide a glimpse of the lives of these early monastic elders so that they may make an impression on our twenty-first century lives. A collection of stories and sayings of the desert mothers existed also, but its earliest versions are lost. It was called the *Materikon*. A partial edition in English is cited in the Bibliography on page 168.

Desert Wisdom in Context

An Experiential Approach

The substantive treasure of the desert tradition is largely unknown in the modern church beyond schools of theology and monastic communities. It is my hope that *Oasis of Wisdom* will make the lives and wisdom of the desert fathers and mothers available to a wider constituency, especially persons who have little or no background in the history of Christian spirituality or theology. Drawing from study and synthesis of primary sources and some of the best scholarship of this period, I will present the environment of solitude, ascetic disciplines, work and charity that became the sources of the wisdom of the desert fathers and mothers.

My goal is to present the wisdom of the desert elders in the context of their daily lives and demonstrate that cultural, political, economic, and ecclesiastical issues in the society that surrounded them influenced their spiritual formation and way of life. Readers will be challenged to look into and reflect on the experiences of the desert fathers and mothers and discover how their ascetic manner of life became the source of their wisdom. I hope readers will catch the spirit of these men and women who were intoxicated with God and be confronted with the realism, psychological wisdom, and spiritual richness of their lives.

It is tempting to read the *Sayings* for personal edification and theoretical knowledge. This may be edifying and enjoyable, but it would result in an incomplete encounter with the desert elders and possibly lead to romanticized or cynical conclusions about their way of life. The authenticity of the wisdom of the *Sayings* will be missed unless an effort is made to discover the personal experiences that produced them. By exploring the lives of the fathers and mothers of the desert, we will be able to absorb their wisdom. Patience will be required to discover the contexts of their lives and the literary methods that convey their wisdom. It will be difficult to understand their lives and teaching if we use our own culture and experience as the benchmark. We must look with the eyes of our heart as well as the rational activity of the head. The challenge is to seek a binding of head and heart. The reward will be great. We may discover the implications of the *Sayings* for our own lives.

Reading Desert Wisdom in Context

Before we enter the lives of the desert fathers and mothers, a word of caution is necessary. The desert elders lived an intensely austere monastic life. Although it was a life they chose freely, its environment and disciplines will be foreign to the social and religious cultures of most modern readers. Their language, behaviors, and teaching methods may seem strange, unappealing, and sometimes repulsive. Yet we must not allow our reactions, however motivated, to lock the door to the desert elders' wisdom. I invite readers to risk a pilgrimage into unfamiliar territory. Be willing to look through the austerity and discover the passion of the desert fathers and mothers that enabled them to be transformed by the God they experienced in prayer.

Learning from the Desert Fathers and Mothers

Although the wisdom of the desert elders transcends time and place, we should avoid trying to live vicariously through them. Our lives can be informed by their experiences and learning, but they cannot live for us. Perhaps their wisdom can help us see ourselves more clearly and inspire us to seek God in a way that leads to our own transformation. They walked the desert before us and can help us discern our paths today. They can be faithful companions along the way, but we must do our own walking.

As you encounter the lives and sayings of the desert elders, you will discover that their austere life was not an end in itself. They entered the desert in order to seek God, unencumbered by the influences, distractions and futility of the inhabited world of their day. Like Syncletica, their renunciation of the futile aspects of society was not a judgment on human society *per se*. In fact, they formed their own societies in the deserts and towns of Arabia, Egypt, Palestine, and Syria. They withdrew from the misuses of human relationships, material goods, power, and labor that they judged as inhumane and a desacralization of life. In order to restore life's original goodness they chose a life of intentional awareness of God's presence and a limitation of worldly pleasure. Through the development of easily satisfied needs, they discovered the most fundamental values and realities of human life. Their goal was to experience God's presence in each moment and activity through a disciplined pattern of prayer, reflection on Scripture, and labor. This awareness released them from a dependence on the limited and narrow desires of the ego and widened their horizons to see the sacred dimension of labor, food, relationships, time, prayer, and their neighbors. The monastic communities they created became the context for a sacred society in which the individual practice of each monk contributed to the community and was at the same time formed and supported by the community. Their primary goal was love of God and their neighbor.

I am convinced that the oasis of wisdom formed by the desert elders is crucial far beyond their ancient world because it manifests what is fundamental for Christian living. This wisdom, while conveyed through sayings, is not about words. It is about the struggle to find and live authentic human lives. Three essential aspects of this struggle in the desert were the development of an open and pure heart, humility, and charity. Conventional wisdom of the twenty-first century tries very hard to discredit these fundamental human virtues and replace them with self-interest, arrogant self-confidence and self-preservation. These are the demons of the modern world that narrow our vision and harden our hearts. They are the most dangerous weapons of mass destruction. Our world of technology, vast resources, unparalleled military power, and sophisticated institutions seems unable to resolve our frenzy to learn how to live together in justice and peace. These great towers of modern self-confidence stand tall but powerless.

The peace we desire requires a change of consciousness. A transformation is necessary in the way we see and value each other within our vast array of cultures, races and religious paths, as well as our attitude toward the earth. The wisdom of the desert elders will not solve our problems. That is not our most important need. These ancient teachers will help us **see ourselves** as we truly are and exhort us to **rely on God** to transform our lives. They will become companions along the way, challenging us to embrace the hard work of becoming authentic human beings whose primary desire is love of God and our neighbors, including our enemies. The life of the world depends on our commitment to walking this path.

A Path into the Desert

Oasis of Wisdom will present seven fundamental aspects of desert monastic life as windows for looking into the lives of the desert fathers and mothers. After two preliminary chapters describing their worlds, a chapter will be devoted to each of the following windows:

- Sunrise to Sunrise: the prayerful rhythm of daily life.
- The Cell: an environment for seeking God and one's true self.
- Patience: learning not to run from God or self.
- Praxis: the ascetic disciplines that form, nourish and guard the soul.

• Labor and Time: the sanctification of work, time and community life.
• Solitude and Silence: letting go of self and being present to God, self and others.
• Humility: the embodiment of love of God through love of neighbor.

These aspects of desert monastic life appear repeatedly in *The Sayings of the Desert Fathers* and other primary sources. They are thoroughly **interdependent** in the lives of the desert elders, even though they receive separate attention in *Oasis of Wisdom*. Readers will note repetition of these and other key words, phrases and themes of the abbas and ammas. This is intentional to help readers form an internal awareness of this unique wisdom and was a common teaching method of the desert elders, themselves.

A Rationale for Entering the Desert

The desert elders did not teach that everyone must live as they lived. They taught, by their actions, that purity of heart, humility and charity are virtues that lie at the heart of **all human life.** Their renunciations, practical wisdom, and prayerful living taught people from all walks of life in their day to see themselves and the way they lived in the context of God's love and desires for human life. Perhaps the desert elders will evoke a change of consciousness in us as well. They exhort us to practice an interiorized monasticism whether or not we are monks. From its earliest days Christianity has proclaimed that the heart of monastic life is for all Christians. The early Eastern Churches resisted any distinction between the monastic and lay vocations.[9] One of its greatest leaders, St. John Chrysostom, said,

> When Christ orders us to follow the narrow path, he addresses himself to all. The monastics and the lay person must attain the same heights. . . . Those who live in the world, even though married, ought to resemble the monks in everything else. You are entirely mistaken if you think there are some things required of ordinary people, and others of monks.[10]

In an age when many Christians seek wisdom outside our own faith communities, it will be good news to find great treasure, also, very close to home that will challenge, transform, and nurture our lives.

Finding the Oasis

It is time to visit the desert elders yourself. Consider the remainder of this book a guide for a pilgrimage into a way of life much different from your own. You are entering a desert. Let go of expectations and try to be as open as possible. The desert is a place where we are stripped of power and are not in charge. This does not mean being passive and without emotions or reactions. You will probably see ways in which the wisdom of the desert elders applies to your life and to situations in the modern world. On the other hand you may be repelled by some teaching or ascetic behavior you encounter. Try to observe the lives of the desert elders without using your personal experience as a benchmark for judgment. It will take time to enter this world. If you listen with an open heart, your life will never be the same. Take the risk to be changed; it is the challenge of wisdom.

Here are some suggestions to help you along the path:

- Read each chapter twice. Avoid consulting the endnotes during the first reading. During the first reading allow the chapter to guide you into a new aspect of the lives of the desert fathers and mothers. During the second reading, stop from time to time to reflect on parts of the desert elders' lives and teaching that become attached to you.

- Keep a journal as you read this book. Record your reactions, questions and insights. It may be helpful, also, to enter into a written conversation with one or more of the desert elders. This is an ancient practice, and you may be surprised at what you write.

- When a particular saying of one of the elders sticks in your mind, take time to reflect on that saying in silence. Read the saying aloud three times, and then continue to listen to it in silence without mental analysis (2 to 5 minutes). Read the saying three more times and listen again in silence (2 to 5 minutes). This time try to hear what the saying may be telling you personally. Read the saying three more times, followed by five minutes of silence in which you simply give the saying and yourself into God's presence.

- Consider buying a copies of Benedicta Ward's translation of *The Sayings of the Desert Fathers* and Laura Swan's *The Forgotten Desert Mothers* so that you may refer to more sayings and incidents in the lives of the desert elders than could be included in *Oasis of Wisdom*. (See the bibliography for information.)

Notes

1. Laura Swan, *The Forgotten Desert Mothers: Sayings, Lives, and Stories of Early Christian Women* (Mahwah, N.J.: Paulist Press, 2001) 60.

2. Pseudo-Athanasius, *The Life of Blessed and Holy Syncletica*, trans. Elizabeth Bryson Bongie (Toronto: Peregrina, 1999) vv. 22, 29.

3. For more details about Syncletica's life see Bongie's trans. of the *Life* and Mary Schaffer, *The Life of Blessed Syncletica by Pseudo-Athanasius, Part Two: A Study of the Life* (Toronto: Peregrina, 2001). I recommend Mary Schaffer's study as an indispensable guide to Syncletica's life and teaching and as a resource demonstrating the substantive influence of a woman on the early development of Christian monastic life.

4. I. Hausherr, S.J., "Pour comprende l'orient chrétien: La primauté du spiritual," *Orientalia Christiana Periodica* 33 (1967): 359.

5. For an English translation of the *Historia Monachorum In Aegypto*, see *The Lives of the Desert Fathers*, trans. Norman Russell, introduction by Benedicta Ward, S.L.G. (Kalamazoo: Cistercian Publications, 1981).

6. Russell and Ward, *Lives*, 20, "On the Monks of Nitria," 5, 6; 105.

7. See Athanasius, *The Life of Antony and the Letter to Marcellinus*, trans. Robert C. Gregg, (Mahwah, N.J.: Paulist Press, 1980); *The Lausiac History of Palladius* (Willits: Eastern Orthodox Books); John Cassian, *The Conferences*, trans. Boniface Ramsey, O.P. (New York: Paulist Press, 1997). For English trans. of the *Apophthegmata Patrum* see *The Sayings of the Desert Fathers*, trans. Benedicta Ward, S.L.G. (Kalamazoo: Cistercian Publications, 1975); *The Wisdom of the Desert Fathers*, trans. Benedicta Ward, S.L.G. (Oxford: SLG Press, 1975); and *The World of the Desert Fathers*, trans. Columba Stewart, O.S.B. (Oxford: SLG Press, 1986).

8. Stelios Ramfos, *Like a Pelican in the Wilderness*, trans. Norman Russell (Brookline: Holy Cross Orthodox Press, 2000) 1. In the Christian West the collections are called the *Patrilogia Latina*, compiled in 1849 by J. P. Migne and the *Patrilogia Graeca*, compiled in 1858, also by Migne. These collections are dated and have been supplemented through subsequent research by C. J. Guy in *Recherches sur la Tradition Grecque des Apophthegmata Patrum* (Subsidia hagiographica no. 36. Brussels, 1962). Two modern collections in English are Ward, *Sayings*, cited in endnote 7, and a collection compiled by the Orthodox priest John Anthony McGuickin, *The Book of Mystical Chapters: Meditations on the Soul's Ascent from the Desert Fathers and Other Early Christian Contemplatives* (Boston: Shambala 2002). A third and smaller collection suitable for meditation is by Yushi Nomura, trans. with an introduction by Henri Nouwen: *Desert Wisdom: Sayings from the Desert Fathers* (Maryknoll, N.Y.: Orbis Books, 2001).

9. For documentation see Paul Evdokimov, *Ages of the Spiritual Life* (Crestwood, N.Y.: St. Vladimir's Seminary Press, 1998) 135–39.

10. As quoted in Evdokimov, *Ages: Epist. Ad Haeb.*, 7, 4; 7, 41 and *Adv. Oppugn. Vitae monist.*, 3, 14.

1 Politeia

The Monastic World of the Desert Fathers and Mothers

For in Egypt I saw many fathers living the angelic life as they advanced steadily in the imitation of our divine Savior. . . . For they are true servants of God. They do not busy themselves with any earthly manner or take account of anything that belongs to this transient world. But while dwelling on earth in this manner they live as true citizens of heaven.[1]

Amma Theodora said, "Let us strive to enter by the narrow gate. Just as trees, if they have not stood before the winter's storms cannot bear fruit, so it is with us; this present age is a storm and it is only through many trials and temptations that we can obtain an inheritance in the kingdom of heaven."[2]

Who Were the Desert Fathers and Mothers?

The desert elders were people from all walks of life, with names like Mary, John the Dwarf, Theodora, Antony, Moses the Robber, Arsenius, Syncletica, Talis, Poemen, Amoun, and Evagrius. Some were sophisticated city dwellers and others were farmers, seamstresses, camel-drivers, released slaves, traders, weavers, former criminals or local village craftsmen. They came from wealthy, middle-class, and poor families. Arsenius was a scholar and of senatorial rank, a tutor to the princes of the Emperor Theodosius I. He left Rome in 360 C.E. and traveled to the desert of Egypt and placed himself under the guidance of John the Dwarf, the son of poor parents from the town of Tese, Egypt. Theodora lived in the desert, also in the fourth century and according to Palladius was "the wife of a tribune who reached such a depth of poverty that she became a recipient of alms and finally died in the monastery of Hesychas near the sea."[3] She consulted with Archbishop Theodophilus of Alexandria and was a wise mentor to many monks. Antony was the son of peasant farmers. After his parents' deaths, he became the disciple of a local holy man. Eventually he went deep into the desert and remained a hermit for most of his life. Monks, bishops and peasants sought his guidance, and his example and wisdom became a major influence in the development of Christian monastic life. Talis spent eighty years in disciplined prayer and became the mother of a community of sixty women in the upper Nile city of Antinoe where, according to Palladius, there were twelve convents. The love of her by the women in her community was legendary.

The Lure of the Desert: An Overview

In the midst of such diversity, the desert elders shared a common goal: the transformation of their lives through experience of God in prayer. It was a difficult life that denied unnecessary pleasures in order to experience a knowledge of self that would direct their hearts and wills away from a false self-centeredness toward love of God and their neighbors. Some desert monks settled in or near towns, and others went deeper into the desert. A smaller number attracted visitors and disciples seeking discernment for their lives. They became known as *abbas* and *ammas,* the Aramaic words for fathers and mothers. Through their experience of God and a letting go of unrestrained self-will, a pattern of prayerful discipline and practice formed in their lives, independently or with knowledge of each other's practice and teaching.

This *ascetic* vocation may be described as "training undertaken in order to practice a certain way of life."[4] Derived from the Greek word *askesis,* it recognized that, like athletes, seeking God required conditioning and training. The ascetic life of the desert elders united head and heart in prayer and combined manual labor with work that fed the soul. It required *hesychia,* a physical solitude and quietness, that became an environment for solitude of the mind, heart and soul and the possibility for transformation of self. Although the abbas and ammas chose to live apart from the rest of society, what they learned about themselves had much to say about authentic human life wherever it is lived. The monastic communities they formed in the desert influenced the formation of monasticism in both the eastern and western Christian church which, in turn, has helped form the piety, teaching and practice of Christian faith communities all over the world. The legacy of the desert elders is a life of prayer that requires discipline and integrates the physical, psychological, intellectual, and spiritual dimensions of human life. Their goal was the embodiment of God's love.

Two Complimentary Worlds

In order to get to know the desert fathers and mothers as persons, we must explore the various "worlds" that influenced their lives. There were two primary worlds they described with the Greek words *politeia* and *oikoumene*. In Greek culture, politeia referred to a person's way of life in secular society. The desert elders used politeia to describe their alternative society of prayer and virtuous living. Politeia also referred to a monk's individual environment of prayer and spiritual discipline. This chapter will describe the formation and features of a unique desert politeia that led to the transformation of their lives. Chapter 2 will explore oikoumene, referring to *the inhabited world*, that surrounded and influenced their lives in a myriad of ways. This background is essential for persons who may not have had the opportunity to study this important period in early Christianity.

Politeia: An Evolutionary Approach

The desert fathers and mothers did not appear in the deserts of Arabia, Egypt, Palestine, and Syria in a vacuum; nor was the evolution of their monastic manners of life part of a centralized strategy of the early Christian church. The phenomenon of desert spirituality was the work of God's spirit within a complex mosaic of life during the late Roman Empire. Beginning in the third century C.E., it surfaced independently in a myriad of cultures present in the eastern Mediterranean world. Its origins shared some common roots:

- The life, teaching, death and resurrection of Jesus of Nazareth (ca. 4 B.C.E.–30 C.E.)
- The spiritual heritage of Jesus present in the Hebrew Scriptures, especially the Psalms (1000 B.C.E.–150 B.C.E.)
- The responses to Jesus' life, death and resurrection that formed the earliest Christian faith communities
- The traditions and literature of the early Christian communities recorded in the New Testament and other texts not included in the New Testament
- The political, social, philosophical, and religious influence and control of the late Roman Empire on indigenous cultures and the Christian church

- The tensions and challenges present in the formation of liturgy, theology, biblical interpretation, leadership, prayer and political structures of the evolving Christian churches
- The materialism, power struggles, immorality, and anxiety present in late Roman society
- The imperial persecution of Christians that often led to martyrdom, perceived as the ultimate offering to God
- The eventual acceptance of Christianity as an official religion and its enculturation into Roman life

These major roots created a variety of motives and circumstances that led men and women to withdraw from their conventional relationships and responsibilities in their local cities, towns, or villages to seek a separate life of prayer and complete devotion to God. Although they withdrew from society, complete isolation was practiced by only a minority of the desert elders.

A Common Call to the Desert: Listening and Responding to an Inner Voice

The roots of Christian monasticism during this early period share a common tap root. It includes three fundamental interior and exterior "events":

- **Oikoumene:** Oikoumene is an interior awareness that the *inhabited world* is a distraction from a deep personal longing to seek God and live the Gospel without distraction. This leads toward . . .
- **Anachoresis:** Anachoresis is a physical separation from the usual patterns of a person's relationships, activities, responsibilities and the conventional values of society through a *withdrawal* to the desert. (Anachoresis is the Greek root for **"anchorite,"** referring to a person who lives in solitude apart from their community.) The place of anachoresis is . . .
- **Heremos:** Heremos is the Greek for *desert.* It may be experienced within or on the periphery of the inhabited world or in a more desolate and uninhabited location. A physical desert or wasteland became both the image of and often the locus for separation from society to seek complete dedication to and dependence on God. (Heremos is the root for **"hermit,"** a person who seeks God in isolation from others and for **"eremitic,"** referring to that manner of life.) It is the desert, whatever its physical location, that provides the hesychia or solitude for prayerful transformation.

Four Evolving Patterns of Desert Monastic Life

The wisdom of the desert fathers and mothers emerged from the crucible of their daily lives and spiritual disciplines. Their primary method of teaching was by example. Succeeding chapters of *Oasis of Wisdom* will provide a glimpse of the rhythms, spiritual practices, relationships and labor that formed their lives. It is beyond the scope of this book's length and purpose to document the desert tradition in its entirety. Decisions about what to include or omit have been difficult. Therefore, *Oasis of Wisdom* will focus on the evolution of the desert tradition in Egypt. This is not to infer that its presence and personalities in Arabia, Palestine, and Syria are less important. These three areas made integral and unique contributions to this tradition and references will be made to their monastic communities and the lives and teaching of their desert elders. There was regular sharing of example and wisdom, often through visitations, but there were also significant differences between theological perspectives and monastic practices. I have included many sayings from a variety of the ammas and abbas so that readers may hear them speak for themselves. Readers should consult the bibliography for further study of this rich tradition.

During a period of about 150 years, four patterns of monastic life developed as people responded to the call of anachoresis. These patterns were not part of a master plan. The need for each pattern emerged informally influenced by:

- local culture and society
- individual preference for more or less austerity and solitude
- basic needs for lodging, food, and self-support
- varying desires for involvement with the surrounding society, including caring for the poor
- differing preferences for ways to become formed in and live the monastic life
- the desire to give one's life totally to God

Just as Christian martyrs had given their lives under Roman persecution (red martyrdom), leaving the inhabited world for the desert became a new form of martyrdom after Christianity became a religion endorsed by the empire (white martyrdom).

The Four Patterns

The following patterns of desert monastic life developed gradually and complemented and influenced each other:

APOTAKTIKOI: THE VILLAGE ASCETICS

Apotaktikoi refers to men and women in Egyptian cities, towns, and villages who set themselves apart from usual norms of family, labor, sexual practice, and material possessions to devote themselves to a life of prayer, teaching, and social service. They began appearing sometime prior to the mid-third century C.E. Some became known and sought out as spiritual guides and mentors. They became endeared to local people who sought their prayers and often supported them. Individually, these persons may have been the first to be called *monakos*, a monk. (At that time, monk referred to a person who was single-minded and single-hearted in pursuing a goal. It described, also, a person who lived a disciplined and celibate religious life.) As a group they were called *apotaktikoi* or those who stand out from the established order.[5] They chose to live an ascetic life, a life with specific spiritual disciplines, within or near local society and church in order to influence the values and behavior of society through faith and action. They remained in villages, towns and cities, although a few separated themselves a short walking distance away. They could own property and some remained involved in the daily activities of city or village life. There is an account in a papyrus of 340 C.E. from the village of Karanis of such a monachos who intervened in a dispute over a cow.[6] Aurelius Isidorus, a citizen of Karanis, was trying to remove a cow from his land when the owners of the cow assaulted him. Isidorus claimed that they would have killed him if "the deacon Antonius and the monk Isaac" had not come to his aid.

The apotaktikoi were not hermits living an austere life of prayer in solitude, nor were they members of a monastic community living under obedience to a rule or spiritual mentor. When these two later types of monastic life became well established the apotaktikoi were not always considered authentic monks. They were sometimes called "city monks" and held in low esteem in some monastic circles, especially by St. Jerome of Bethlehem who called them *remnuoth*, a word that could mean "solitary," inferring that they were on their own. It is likely that their independent life in the midst of urban settings away from specific monastic authority led to suspicion about them, rather than recognition of the integrity of their life of prayer. The integrity and humility of the apotaktikoi may be seen in an account of Eucharistus the Secular and his wife, Mary, who lived a monastic manner of life anonymously in an Egyptian village. According to *The Sayings of the Desert Fathers*, Eucharistus was a shepherd and he and his wife divided their household profits in thirds for personal needs, hospitality, and the poor.[7] They were celibate from their marriage day, lived in separate rooms and wore hair shirts at night and regular clothes by day. Their virtues and humility became an unintended example to priests and monks alike.

EREMITIC LIFE

The *hermit* was a different kind of monk from an apotaktikos. His or her life was lived entirely in solitude and isolation in the desert or another type of wilderness. While they sometimes offered spiritual guidance and teaching, their primary vocation was to be alone in prayer, study, and work. Early in the evolution of Egyptian monasticism, they were not part of a monastic community.

Antony of Egypt (ca. 251–356 C.E.) is revered as a primary example of eremitic life. His monastic life and teaching inspired the development of Egyptian desert monasticism that, in turn, became a major influence on the formation of monastic communities throughout the Christian church. Antony's influence and model for the ascetic life was established through the popularity of *A Life of Antony* written by the fourth-century bishop of Alexandria, Athanasius. Although the *Life* gives a largely idealized portrait of both Antony and the eremitic life, as well as some of the theological and political biases of St. Athanasius, it represents the priorities of monastic life in the third and fourth centuries from a source very close to the life it describes. The *Life* is one of the most influential examples of Christian hagiography, an idealized biography of a revered holy person. Hagiography usually integrates historical information with an exaggerated account of the saint's accomplishments and spiritual wisdom in order to inspire readers to seek the same virtues and maturity in their own lives. Themes in hagiographies are often related to the virtues and actions of Jesus, the Christ.

Other insights about Antony's eremitic life and learning come from *The Letters of St. Antony.* Although Antony came from a peasant family and led a simple monastic life, these personal letters portray a man well acquainted with the theological and philosophical issues of his day and represent the wisdom of both a practical and mature monastic mentor. Antony's innovation was, through his personal calling and need, to extend the already existing village monasticism further from society into the desert and to the deeper and more austere ascetic practices of the hermit. Even in his need for extreme solitude, he influenced other monks through their visits or decisions to live near his two places of refuge, the first in an abandoned fort near Pispir and later at his "Inner Mountain" cave deeper in the mountainous desert near the Red Sea. Hilarion, a monk of Palestine, spent three months with Antony, and returned to Gaza to live the life of a hermit and become a mentor to others who sought the eremitic life. In the same way that Antony had been inspired and mentored by his village apotaktikos, he and others influenced the spread of a desire for the eremitic manner of life.

It is clear that Antony, while a uniquely wise and ascetic model and teacher, did not originate monasticism or the eremitic life. Nor was this early monastic movement solely a male innovation. Antony's *Life* notes that when he began his monastic life, he left his younger sister in the care of a community of celibate women. Prompted by Roman persecution, belief in the immanent second coming of Christ, and a deep desire for personal and societal transformation, women throughout the empire embraced a new role outside traditional family structures. They left society for the deserts, became solitaries in their homes or formed small monastic communities in their homes. In the mid-third century, Macrina, the eldest daughter in a large Greek family in Cappadocia, became a celibate solitary in her own household. Her piety and learning were major influences on her brothers St. Gregory and St. Basil. Unfortunately, specific references to monastic women prior to the fourth century are rare. (For other detailed references to early monastic women see the bibliography.) In 295 C.E., only ten years after Antony went into seclusion in the desert, Abba Amoun and his new wife began eighteen years of celibate ascetic life together. Later, Amoun became the first monk to attract disciples in the large eremitic community at Nitria. The Egyptian hermit Paul of Thebes lived a separate life of solitude during the same period as Antony. According to tradition, the first monk in Palestine was Chariton, who arrived from Iconium in 275 C.E. and founded three monasteries.[8] During the lifetime of Antony, James of Nisibis also became a hermit in the mountains of Syria. He, like Antony, had a great influence on the development of monastic life and later became a bishop.

SEMI-EREMITIC LIFE

The fiber that formed the muscle of desert monasticism was experience of God. Like physical conditioning, each monk had to be mentored in a life of prayer, reflection on the Bible, and the difficult struggle to know one's self. These were fundamental exercises that opened the monk's heart for transformation and love of God and neighbor. The central role in guiding monks toward this type of transformation was played by older monks who were sought out as wise teachers. These abbas and ammas were indispensable in the desert tradition. They became spiritual parents to the novices. It was important for the new monks to be led into this way of life by persons who were able to live that life, themselves.

Abba Antony said:

Nine monks fell away after many labors and were obsessed with spiritual pride, for they put their trust in their own works and being deceived they did not give due heed to the commandment that says: "Ask your father and he will tell you." And he said this, "If he is able to, a monk ought to tell his elders confidently how many steps he takes and how many drops of water he drinks in his cell, in case he is in error about it."[9]

Imparting knowledge and the methods of spiritual discipline were not enough. This teaching was focused also on self-awakening and the moral and spiritual development of the whole person. The desert elders, following the example of Jesus, manifested their experience of God. Their words and actions were the fruit of what they heard with the ears of their hearts and what their openness to God's grace made possible in their lives.

Amma Syncletica said:

It is dangerous for someone not "formed" by experience of the ascetic life to try to teach; it is as if someone whose house is unsound were to receive guests and cause them injury by the collapse of the building. . . For the mere articulation of words is like the inscriptions painted in perishable colours which a very short period of time has destroyed with blasts of wind and splashes of rain. Teaching that is based on ascetic experience, on the other hand, not even all eternity could destroy. By chiseling away the rough edges of the soul, the spoken word bestows on the faithful Christ's everlasting image done in stone.[10]

The relationship between the abba or amma and their disciples had elements of both an *event* and a *conversation*.[11] Something would **happen** in the disciple's life because of this relationship. The teacher, also, experienced an offering of self through openness to the disciple and a sharing of his or her manner of life. Therefore persistence, trust, and obedience were essential if the novice was to make progress in the struggle toward transformation. But the relationship was not based simply on listening to the teacher and observing his or her life. There was intimate **dialog** that made demands on both teacher and disciple. The abba or amma had to be faithfully present to the disciple's inner life and mentor him or her through spiritual direction and discernment. The elder spoke primarily through her or his manner of life. The disciple had to expose his inner being to the abba in order to make this dialog possible. Through this conversation the novice learned that wisdom is being aware of one's own weakness and seeking the wholeness and strength that can come only through God's grace.

The wisdom of the abbas and ammas was the child of their patience in ascetic disciplines and their daily life experiences. They knew that true education is not the satisfaction of curiosity, but a process leading to a transformation of the whole person in which authentic human life is experienced and daily living becomes guided by purity of heart. The abba/amma and disciple relationship was about the "here and now" and it often lasted for years. The wisdom in this method of teaching is that the person seeking experience of God is mentored in that path by experiencing a committed personal relationship.

The need for novices to be near such a teacher led to the development of *semi-eremitic* life. Small communities were formed where one or up to a few novice monks lived in simple dwellings, cells, near the same ascetic teacher. These wise and experienced teachers were known as *hesychasts*. All monks desire hesychia, solitude and quiet, but the term hesychast referred to any hermit or anchorite who lived in extreme solitude and quiet, separate from other people. When a hesychast had disciples living nearby in separate cells, he or she was called a *geron,* the Greek word for elder or, as we have seen, abba or amma in Aramaic.

The hesychasts had learned that seeking a hermit's life was not simply a matter of calling. A person needed the mentoring in spiritual disciplines and the development of self-reflection described above before embracing the isolation of the hermit life. This mentoring usually took place in the context of an experienced elder and a small community. These very small groups of elders and disciples appeared throughout Egypt in both isolated and town settings. Groups of these small communities settled near each other until large areas were filled with abbas and their disciples as well as other hermits. Each area usually contained a central church, guest house, and small monastic dwellings scattered throughout the location. There was no organized link between each small community, except for the Eucharist on Sundays and holy days. The entire area was silent and each group was far enough from other groups to minimize distractions from their chanting of the psalms and prayers. There was usually no visiting between monks in their cells, except for talks between teachers and their disciples and visits from pilgrims. Some clusters of semi-eremitic groups spread out for miles in the desert.

> I also visited one of the fathers there (in Nitria) called Ammonius, who possessed beautifully constructed cells with a courtyard, a well, and other necessary things. Once a brother came to him, eager to attain salvation. He asked Ammonius to assign him a cell to live in, whereupon the father at once went out, ordering the brother not to leave the cells until he should find him suit-

able accommodation. Leaving him all he had, together with the cells themselves, Ammonius immured himself in a small cell some distance away.[12]

Hesychasts and their disciples lived in many areas of Egypt, including
villages. Several monks lived near Antony's hermitages at Pispir and his
cave in the mountains. Records and other archaeological evidence confirm
small semi-eremitic communities at the towns of Babylon, Memphis, Heracleopolis, and Oxyrhynchus.[13]

The three largest concentrations of these semi-eremitic communities
were in a region about a day's journey south of the city of Alexandria, west
of the lower Nile delta at Nitria, Cellia, and Scetis. Abba Amoun was the
first elder to settle in Nitria in 330 C.E. and soon disciples joined him. Abba
Macarius of Alexandria settled in Cellia, and soon other hesychasts and
disciples filled the area. After leaving Antony, Macarius the Great became a
hesychast in a small village and then settled in the forbidding desert of
Scetis where he became a revered elder. Over the years these three areas
were home to thousands of solitary monks, their disciples, hermits, and
monks from other lands drawn to their way of life. "They inhabit a desert
place and have their cells some distance from each other, so that no one
should be recognized from afar by another, or be seen easily, or hear another's voice. On the contrary, they live in profound silence, each monk
isolated on his own."[14]

COENOBITIC LIFE

Abba Pachomius (ca. 290–346 C.E.) is generally regarded as the person
who saw the need for persons living the eremitic life to have also the ad-
vantage and balance of living in community. In the monastic tradition this
is called *coenobitic* life. A person living in a coenobitic community is called
a *coenobite*. Just as Antony is seen as the inspiration for the eremitic vocation to prayer in isolation, and Amoun for the semi-eremitic life, Pachomius is considered the pioneer of this shared or coenobitic way of life.
He was converted to Christianity at the age of twenty during service as a
conscript in the Roman army. He spent seven years as a disciple of Abba
Palamon, a hesychast living just outside the village of Seneset (in Greek,
Chenoboskion), in Upper Egypt. Led by divine inspiration in a dream, he
built a monastery at the deserted village of Tabennesi. Eventually, other
men came to join him. At the urging of his sister, a monastery for women
was built across the river. Eventually nine male communities and two for
women were founded. These monasteries were called *koinonia*, from the
Greek word for community, and over time Pachomius developed a common Rule to order the life of the various communities.

As we have seen, semi-eremitic communities already existed in several forms throughout Egypt, and Pachomius' formation as a monk had taken place with the hesychast, Palamon. Yet Pachomius' innovation was to provide inspiration, organization, and ordering of common life for the growing number of smaller monastic communities being formed at this time. He gathered smaller semi-eremitic groups into larger communities under a common Rule. Pachomius' Rule provided a less austere and more flexible environment for monks to combine ascetic practice and communal life. Also, individuals joined his koinonia directly as novice monks. The koinonia provided a way for monks to share daily worship, more opportunities for learning, and regular labor together while still having time for personal solitude and spiritual discipline. Pachomius' model created another mentoring *conversation* in which the community helped form the monk and the monk contributed his or her unique wisdom and talents to the community. In contrast to Antony's eremitic pattern, Pachomius' coenobitic communities provided the most influential model for later monastic communities. As coenobitic communities evolved, the vocation to be a hermit or anchorite was usually discerned after being formed and gaining maturity in a monastic koinonia. It was essential for the practice of eremitic life to be predicated on formation in monastic disciplines and learning as well as mentoring by an elder with experience in eremitic life. In this context, a hermit or anchorite lived separate from his of her community, yet remained part of the community.

Notes

1. *The Lives of the Desert Fathers,* trans. Norman Russell and introduction Benedicta Ward, S.L.G. (Kalamazoo: Cistercian Publications, 1980) Prologue 5, 49–50.

2. *The Sayings of the Desert Fathers,* trans. Benedicta Ward, S.L.G. (Kalamazoo: Cistercian Publications, 1975) Theodora 2, 83.

3. Ward, *Sayings,* 82.

4. Mary Schaffer, *The Life of the Blessed and Holy Syncletica, Part Two: A Study of the Life* (Toronto: Peregrina, 2001) 90.

5. James E. Goehring, *Ascetics, Society and the Desert. Studies in Early Egyptian Monasticism* (Harrisburg: Trinity Press, 1999) 24.

6. Ibid., 44–45.

7. Ward, *Sayings,* Eucharistus the Secular, 1; 60.

8. Cyril of Scythopolis, *Lives of the Monks of Palestine,* trans. John Burns (Kalamazoo: Cistercian Publications, 1991) x.

9. Ward, *Sayings,* Antony, 37, 38; 8–9.

10. Pseudo-Athanasius, *The Life of Blessed Syncletica,* trans. Elizabeth Bryson Bongie (Toronto: Peregrina 1999) v. 79, 50.

11. See Douglas Burton-Christie, *The Word in the Desert. Scripture and the Quest for Holiness in Early Desert Monasticism* (New York: Oxford University Press, 1993) 18–23.

12. Russel and Ward, *Lives,* On the monks of Nitria, 9, 106.

13. Murad Kamil, *Coptic Egypt* (Cairo: Le Scribe Egyptien, 1968) 47–48.

14. Russell and Ward, *Lives,* 20:7 On the monks of Nitria, 106.

2 Oikoumene

The Inhabited Worlds Surrounding the Desert Fathers and Mothers

The Ethnic Coptic World

Origins and Religious Roots

The seven monks from Palestine who visited monks at eleven monastic sites in Egypt in 394 C.E. commented that "some of them were natives of that region, others were foreigners."[1]

The natives of the region were Egyptian Copts, a redundant description, for the word Copt is derived from the Greek "Aigyptos" a phonetic corruption of the ancient Egyptian word for Memphis, "ha-ka-ptah." Eventually the diphthong "ai" and the ending "os" of the Greek word were dropped and "gypt" remained, forming the modern words Egypt and Copt.

The native Copts at the time of the desert elders were an ethnic group of North African Mediterranean people descended from the ancient Egyptians. They formed the majority of the monks of Egypt during the period of the desert mothers and fathers. Religion was the formative element of ancient Coptic life long before Christianity arrived. Christian Copts believe that the evangelist St. Mark brought Christian faith to Egypt and Coptic Christians were and remain earnest in preserving what they believe is their "original faith." For this reason Christian Copts have always considered themselves orthodox in belief and liturgy, with a firm devotion to the Bible. They tend to be conservative by nature, yet are a "deeply spiritual and even mystical" people.[2] Their religious life has always been focused on stability, reflected in their ancient temples, the pyramids, and the constant tension between the arid and unforgiving desert and their dependence on the Nile as the source of fertility and life. Their traditional art is colorful and mystical, displaying interaction between humans, other living beings of the natural world and divine beings on whom their lives depended. Christian Coptic art retains this rich color and depth of spirit with a focus on the lives of the saints, the Bible, and the sovereignty of God manifest in the risen Christ.

If the native monks were Copts, who were the foreigners? Visitors and pilgrims came from all over the Roman Empire: laity, bishops, government officials, theological teachers, monks and pilgrims from Ireland and Wales, Syria, Palestine, Arabia, Asia Minor and what is now Europe. Some came to learn from the elders. Some came to pray or seek spiritual guidance. Others were simply curious or escaping military service or taxation. Some were fleeing personal problems, others came for healing. Many of the visitors stayed for the rest of their lives. The records are few, except in the writings of the more significant visitors and the *Sayings of the Desert Fathers*. Two more notable visitors stayed for a long time and left legacies through their writings about early desert monastic life that have influenced Christian monasticism throughout the world. Profiles of Evagrius of Ponticus and John Cassian appear toward the end of this chapter.

Language and Local Government

At the time of the desert elders, Egypt was still occupied and ruled by Rome. The Ptolemies had established Greek as the common language of government. Under Ptolemaic rule, local governments throughout Egypt were under the direct control of Roman occupation. During this period the older Demotic language of the Copts was gradually being phased out because it was far too complex and difficult for daily life. It was replaced by transliterating the older Egyptian language into Greek script, retaining seven characters from the Demotic to allow for indigenous sounds that could not be pronounced using the Greek alphabet. The new Coptic language retained the four local Egyptian dialects with two representing Lower Egypt (Boharic) and Upper Egypt (Saidic) along with Faiyumic and Akhmimic.[3]

Along with the Greek language, Roman culture continued to promote Hellenistic learning and philosophy in Egypt, focused in Alexandria, as well as the unique Roman forms of government and commerce, funded by heavy taxation. By the third century, Rome encouraged local government and Egyptian elite and middle class citizens were given responsibility for operation of infrastructures throughout Egypt. A sense of Egyptian identity seemed to be reviving after years of Roman domination. There was significant interaction between Egyptian and Greek communities. Along with local authority came *liturgies*, the actual work of governing and raising the money to support local life and commerce, including Rome's portion of the taxes. This placed heavy burdens on individuals and families. Many people withdrew to remote places and became monks or simply remained in hiding to escape either responsibility for the liturgies or to flee from burdensome taxation. This placed even more pressure on the Copts who remained at home, including peasant farmers. There were many poor Copts in cities, towns and villages without adequate food and clothing.[4]

The Coptic language became more essential, along with Greek, and it was not uncommon for Copts to be bilingual or to have partial access to Greek documents and speech. The practical need for both languages at local levels meant that more Copts, including monks, had access to Roman and Greek culture, learning, philosophy, and the mundane documents and conversations of daily life, in addition to their own Coptic oral and written traditions and conversations. Since Coptic monks came from all walks of life, it is reasonable to assume that they brought this varying background of language, learning, and experiences with them. This helps explain why many monks and monastic communities in Egypt had links with the local cultures that surrounded them. These links contributed to the life of the towns and influenced the monks and their communities. The monks at Nitria supported themselves by making cloth. Other monks and monastic communities traded with nearby towns and villages for supplies they needed and sold the produce from their own cultivated land. Monks obtained raw materials from towns for goods they made for their own use or for sale. Some monks became involved in the affairs of local towns. Hermits wove baskets and mats from palm fronds they gathered to buy bread and gave alms to the poor. Abba Serapion organized trade between monastic sites in middle Egypt and the city of Alexandria and sent boatloads of wheat and clothing for the poor because there were so few people living near his monastic community. Some smaller monastic communities were actually located in villages, towns, or abandoned communities.

> We also went to Oxyrhynchus, one of the cities of the Thebaid. It is impossible to do justice to the marvels we saw there. For the city is so full of monasteries that the very walls resound with the voices of monks. Other monasteries encircle it outside, so that the outer city forms another town alongside the inner.[5]

The access to and use of both Coptic and Greek had great implications for the desert elders' motives for leaving "the inhabited world." It affected their experiences as monks, their interactions with people around them, and their knowledge of Scripture. These influences helped form the life experiences that became sources of their wisdom.

Many Coptic monks were illiterate and were limited in their experience of culture beyond their town or village. But the stereotype of desert monks and elders all being simple and illiterate, yet wise, persons is no longer possible to accept. St. Athanasius seems to portray Antony in this way in *The Life of Antony*, as we have seen, yet the *Letters of Antony* make a strong case for Antony's familiarity with Greek language and philosophy.[6] His experience must have included conversations in Greek with theologians, philosophers, and secular leaders. Even Athanasius describes Antony visiting Alexandria on two occasions. He was, like other elders, able to use his experience of both cultures in spiritual guidance and to interpret Christian experience using images from Greek thought. We will explore the influence of Greek learning on the desert elders in more detail in the next two sections.

Education, Church Catechesis, and Suspicion of Greek Philosophy

The availability of the Coptic script and the bilingual skills of many Christians, including monks, enlarged the experience of the Coptic church during the period of the desert elders. It opened a wider door for the interaction of the Egyptian church with Greek philosophy and created a need to demonstrate the integrity and uniqueness of Christian faith in a world dominated by Greek thought.

"We also visited Abba Evagrius, a wise and learned man who was skilled in the discernment of thoughts, an ability he had acquired by experience. He often went down to Alexandria and refuted the pagan philosophers in disputations."[7]

Recent papyrus discoveries in or near monastic settings indicate that some literate monks were bilingual and that a bridge between Coptic Christian monastic study and writing and Greek learning was possible at this time.[8] This bridge made a dialog possible between the Christian faith and Greek thought that would expand the church's theological understanding of the significance of Jesus' life, death, and resurrection. Egyptian monastic life and prayer could not escape involvement in this dialog. At the same time, the dialog, itself, came under suspicion as a heretical and dangerous challenge to orthodox faith. Although separated spatially from some central venues of this dialog, the desert elders could not escape the consequences of this growing tension.

A major venue for this dialog and for Christian learning during this period was the influential Catechetical School in Alexandria, probably founded in the early to mid-second century. It was a focus for the formulation of Christian theology in the East at a time when the church at large was trying to articulate and embody its faith in worship, catechesis, evangelization and dialog with the dominant Greek worldview. Many church leaders were educated in the school's interdisciplinary curriculum that emphasized religion but included the humanities, science, and mathematics.

One of the first great leaders of the school from 190–254 C.E. was Clement of Alexandria. He was born in Greece, circa 160 C.E., and traveled throughout the Mediterranean world studying philosophy. After his conversion to Christianity he found a wise teacher in Alexandria, Pantaenus, who may have been the head of the Catechetical School. Clement was known for his efforts to seek a transition between biblical truth and Greek myth and philosophy. Yet he maintained that the Bible is central for Christian living, the firm foundation for living human lives, and an unparalleled source of truth in which God could be experienced in a personal way. Clement is one of the first early male theologians called "the Church Fathers." Although steeped in the scholarship of Greek and Latin philosophy and literature, these early Fathers were captivated by the simplicity and wisdom of the Bible. The Bible transcended the ideals and images of Greek thought, brought them down to earth and grounded them in human life. Clement used biblical language to interpret the goal of human life that had been articulated in more ideal terms in Platonic thought. He wrote that humans are created in the "image of God" (from *Genesis*) and our human vocation is to manifest "likeness to God" through our manner of life. For Christians, living according to the biblical example of Jesus Christ is the path from image to likeness, a transformation made possible by God's grace.[9]

Clement and later Church Fathers would have a significant influence on the lives of the desert fathers and mothers in three ways: (1) emphasizing the centrality of the Bible for Christian living, (2) articulating a vision of the end or goal of Christian life as a transformation, through grace, that makes embodiment of the likeness of God possible, and (3) exhorting openness to God's grace through baptism, the Eucharist and prayer. The Church Fathers were persons of prayer and their writing was rooted in both personal prayer and the Bible.

Perhaps the most influential leader of the Catechetical School was Origen of Alexandria who followed Clement in 254 C.E. He was a biblical scholar, theologian, and philosopher whose methods for reflecting on Scripture and using Greek thought for exploring and interpreting Christian faith in the third century world made him very controversial. He taught that reading and contemplation of Scripture initiates a dialog in which God is truly present to the reader and the reader is changed in his or her inner being. Reading at this time was vocalized, and silent reading was unknown in most places. Like his teacher, Clement, Origen emphasized the uniqueness of biblical wisdom for Christian life, yet he was more assertive in claiming the value of Greek philosophy and its language as a means of interpreting the Christian faith. He honored reason as a human faculty, but taught that the origin of Christian wisdom lies in God rather than human wisdom.[10] Origen's thought and the fruits of his contemplative life had an influence on many monks, including Antony and Evagrius.

The new Coptic script made it possible for the Bible, other religious and secular documents, and diverse literature to become available to Copts for study, reflection and worship in churches, catechetical schools and monastic settings. Most of the books of the Bible were available in Coptic by the early third century, and literate hermits and other monks in community would have had access to Coptic bibles. Illiterate Coptic monks were taught to read in order to study and reflect on the Bible. A papyrus codex of St. Paul's epistles in Coptic was available as early as ca. 200 C.E.[11] Recent discoveries of Coptic papyrus documents from this period indicate that a great variety of secular documents and religious literature, including gospels not included in the New Testament, were available to literate Copts. The most famous of these discoveries are the Nag Hammadi codices containing a wealth of Gnostic writings, including *The Gospel of Thomas*, other gospels, homilies, epistles, theological treatises, sayings, and prayers. They were found in the vicinity of Chenoboskion, the home village of Pachomius, near the site of one of his monasteries. No direct relationship has yet been made to the monastery, but it is clear that such literature was available to desert monks in Coptic.[12] The fear and tension created by this literature is demonstrated by an edict to monasteries from Athanasius, bishop of Alexandria, forbidding them to be read in monasteries.

Changes and Challenges in the Church's Theology

The first three centuries of desert monastic life witnessed a difficult and major challenge in the early church. Teaching about Jesus Christ became confused by the appearance of differing and often contradictory understandings of his relationship to God, human beings, and the world. At times the theological debate created a contentious storm whose clouds drifted over the deserts of Arabia, Egypt, Palestine, and Syria. It was a theological conflict in which ecclesiastical and political power was used by bishops, elite, influential lay persons, and emperors to prevent or enforce various theological positions. (One example concerned the theology of a priest in Alexandria named Arius. He taught that Jesus did not share the nature of God, but like all humans was created out of nothing. His teaching was declared false at the Council of Nicea in 325 C.E. in a statement affirming that Jesus proceeded directly from God.)

Some desert elders and groups of monks were involved in maintaining orthodox positions, while others were in favor of newer ideas. Some monasteries were persecuted and in some cases great numbers of monks who held the "wrong" position were killed. Theological positions and divisions were not always clear cut, but the fear of heresies and the defense of "truth" created stern and sometimes cruel conditions. Desert monasticism was born and learned to walk during this period of the church's disagreements and major councils, as well as the turmoil surrounding the decline and fall of the Roman Empire! It seems clear that the birth of desert monasticism was the work of God's spirit throughout the eastern region of the Empire to equip the church spiritually in a period of major transition, challenge and conflict.

Two major transitions had a direct effect on and were influenced by the desert elders:

- The first was *a transition from the primacy of the Biblical faith of the apostles as the sole revelation about Jesus Christ to permitting additional ways of articulating the* **regula fidei (the faith of the apostles)** *in the light of new intellectual knowledge and the relationship of the Church to a changing and more pluralistic world.* In other words, can the truth present in Christian belief and experience be found outside the biblical witness?

The biblical witness was based on the historical events surrounding the life, death, and resurrection of Jesus and the ways in which those events shaped the lives of the earliest Christians. This remained the foundation of the church's life and teaching for the first three centuries and continues to be the heart of Christian faith. But as the biblical witness, itself, demonstrates in Acts and the epistles, God's activity continues to be present in subsequent history and cultures. The lives of the desert elders witnessed the transition from biblical apostolic teaching as the only interpretation of God's revelation in Jesus Christ to an understanding that God's revelation is a continuous event present in the ongoing life of the church and history, itself. This transition was not an easy one and it continues to be an issue today!

• The second transition was *the development of a process for authenticating and governing the Church's articulation of its faith and life in the midst of a variety of cultures and Christian communities.*

There was a need to settle regional theological disputes that endangered apostolic faith through the promotion of unorthodox ideas. At the same time there was a desire to protect the freedom of the church's teachers and theologians to interpret the church's faith and life in the light of current thinking. This led to the great councils (synods) of the church in the fourth and fifth centuries that charted a course for Christian belief and life that still continues. These early councils especially at Nicea (325 C.E.), Ephesus (431 C.E.), and Chalcedon (451 C.E.) brought together bishops, secular leaders, and theologians who articulated statements and creeds that would guide the teaching and life of the church and provide authoritative statements about the nature of its faith. This new period in the life of the church honored the formative authority of the apostolic faith and at the same time acknowledged the church's authority to continue to discern and articulate the meaning of that faith in the light of the church's newer experiences and knowledge. This, too, was one of the worlds that surrounded and influenced the lives of the desert elders.

One clear example of the impact of this theological world on the desert tradition is the influence of Greek philosophical ideas present in St. Antony's letters of spiritual guidance.[13] His letters reflect ideas from the school in Alexandria that are influenced by the teaching of Origen.[14] Origen's work embodied the two transitions mentioned above. He attempted to integrate biblical faith and personal experience of Christ with an open intellectual quest for knowledge. He related Christian biblical faith to the intellectual and scientific issues of his time. He believed that orthodox faith is compatible with philosophical speculation and natural science.

Origen's genius and his life of prayer combined to form his theological response to Gnostic heresies. Gnosticism refers to many cults and religious perspectives present in the Mediterranean world in this period, yet there was no single Gnostic system. Gnostic thought was a response to the presence of evil in the world. It speculated that through *gnosis* (knowledge or revealed insight), human beings could be saved from the limitations of the material world and return to their original spiritual nature. From a Christian point of view some of the dangers of Gnostic thought were a denial of the goodness of creation and human life, a dualism that alienated matter from spirit, a denial of the need for responsible and ethical behavior in human life, and a denial of the operation of God's grace to transform human life on earth.

It is ironic that in Origen's efforts to deny aspects of Gnostic teaching, his own quest of knowledge through contemplation and philosophical and scientific inquiry placed his teaching under suspicion and eventual judgment. His teaching was the subject of a major controversy that became a threat to desert elders and monks who supported him. Although his teaching was firmly rooted in the Bible, his scholarship, language, and methods of interpreting Scripture became suspect. His intellectual skill was intimidating to some influential church leaders. In 231 C.E. he was banished from Alexandria and settled at Caesarea in Palestine where students from all over the world continued to seek his training. He was forty-three. He spent most of his remaining years there, but was severely tortured during the persecutions of the Emperor Decius. Although the persecutions ended after the death of Decius, Origen never regained health and died in Tyre, north of Caesarea, in 253 C.E. at the age of sixty-nine.

The philosophical and theological teaching of the Origenist school in Alexandria can be seen in the wisdom of Abba Evagrius, Abba Dorotheos of Gaza, and Abba Antony. In Antony's letters he refers to the importance of knowing one's self as essential in the path to seeking God because we are created in the image of God. Discovering the image of God in a person requires discernment between what is false and real in life. This, in turn, requires spiritual disciplines that help avoid the material and psychological pleasures and impulses that lead a person away from God and one's true self. In this way Antony shows that renunciation is not a negative attitude toward human behavior. Interior spiritual discipline does not put down the body, but restores its natural state of authentic goodness.[15] The object of spiritual discipline is not to escape the body, but to transform the whole person.

This same perspective may be seen in the teaching and wisdom of Evagrius and Dortheos of Gaza, both of whom would have had access to Antony's letters. Evagrius was a central figure in the Origenist party in Egypt.[16] There is evidence, also, in various sources from this early period that link Antony with monks in Nitria and Scetis who supported Origen's theology.[17] Antony, the renowned and wise hermit, was also an influential figure in the making of the Origenist tradition. His emphasis on discernment of Scripture, knowledge of self and relying on God's grace to transform lives is woven into his letters to fellow monks in a manner that mirrors Origenist teaching.[18] The world of theological and philosophical activity was not absent from the desert!

The desert monks were also very much aware and suspicious of the "worldly" values and behavior that became part of the church's life following Constantine's Edict of Milan in 313 C.E. Along with its new freedom, a process of acculturation entered the church's life from the dominant Roman society. Reactions against this secular and materialist influence led many men and women to the desert.

Evolving Christian Worship

Corporate worship was a fundamental part of desert monastic life, especially in the semi-eremitic and coenobitic communities. The Holy Eucharist, also known as Holy Communion and the liturgy, was celebrated on Sundays and holy days. The New Testament shows that the earliest forms of the Eucharist were deeply rooted in Jewish liturgies, especially the Passover. The Jews placed great emphasis on the religious dimension of every meal as a sharing of the gift of life. It was a foretaste of the kingdom of God at the end of time. Such meals were very important to Jesus, with the Last Supper being the most influential example. The Last Supper became the model for the Eucharist in the earliest Christian communities.

During the first three centuries C.E. the Eucharist was normally celebrated in the evening in the context of a meal, most often in homes. These celebrations followed a pattern from the New Testament epistles. It began with a blessing and sharing of bread, followed by the meal and ended with a blessing and sharing of wine. Following the accounts of St. Paul, the words of Jesus "This is my body . . . this is my blood" were added to the Jewish blessings of bread and wine. This was in response to Jesus exhortation "Do this in remembrance of me." Paul described the Eucharist as the sign of the unity in Christ of all Christians present at the meal.

As the Christian faith spread to a variety of places and cultures, the Eucharist began to change. By the third century it was not unusual for the meal to be omitted, and for a variety of readings from Scripture and prayers to be substituted in its place. The morning of the first day of the week, Sunday (in remembrance of the day of Jesus' resurrection), became the customary day for the Eucharist. Rather than being primarily an occasion for a fellowship meal, its demeanor became more formally liturgical. In some cases the meal was added after the Eucharist and called an agape, or love feast. The central feature continued to be the gathering of believers around a table for the sacred feast of unity with Christ and each other. When Christianity was endorsed by the Emperor Constantine and his son, it was possible to worship in public and churches were built throughout the Mediterranean world. The practice of gathering for Eucharist in homes gradually eclipsed.

These issues and transitions surrounding worship were also present in the world of the desert fathers and mothers. They would use patterns from the Jewish liturgies to form the rhythm and content of their corporate worship (called *synaxis*) from sunrise to sunrise. Their Eucharists were in Coptic and by the time of Antony reflected some of the changes taking place throughout the church. Indigenous Coptic prayers and chants were added to their liturgy.

Legacies of the Desert Elders

Two foreigners who lived with the Egyptian desert elders documented what they learned and experienced. Abba Evagrius and Abba John Cassian have given models to succeeding generations for learning from the desert monastic tradition. They can help us learn to know ourselves, find God's presence in our lives, and desire purity of heart and compassionate living in our own age.

Evagrius of Ponticus: Evagrius was born in Ibora, Asia Minor, in ca. 345 C.E. He was an intelligent student of two great Cappadocian Church Fathers, St. Basil and St. Gregory Nazianzen and became an articulate theologian. Evagrius accompanied St. Gregory to the Great Council of Constantinople in 381 C.E. An affair with an influential married woman resulted in his exile from Cappadocia to Jerusalem. In Jerusalem he was mentored by Amma Melania, the leader of a small monastic community where Evagrius embraced the monastic life. In 383 C.E. he left for Egypt and spent two years with the hesychasts in Nitria and then ten years as a disciple of Abba Macarius of Alexandria in Cellia. Evagrius became one of the most articulate voices for desert monasticism, synthesizing teaching and ascetic discipline into a path of spiritual formation. His writings provide a framework for monastic spirituality and its influence on Christian living. As noted above, Evagrius was a firm supporter of Origen's theology.

Evagrius summarized the monastic spiritual path in two complementary dimensions:

- *Praktikos.* Praktikos is the **practical life,** through which our thoughts, bodies, passions and actions are disciplined through ascetic praxis (a pattern of discipline) to be re-formed into their original and authentic nature, resulting in love of God and other people. This leads to *apatheia*, or non-attachment to unrestrained passions and desires, even the desire to be transformed, by grace, into our authentic selves.

- *Theoria.* Theoria refers to a two-fold **contemplative life.** It is experienced first through awareness of God's presence in the natural world as we come to know the essence of things and what God desires for them. Evagrius calls this *physike.* It is not an intellectual or scientific knowledge. Through experience of God in the world of creation we become aware of the spiritual meaning and divine purpose embodied in all things and of our mystical relationship to creation. This leads to *theologia,* a personal absorption in or experience of the reality of God that is beyond (not limited by) form or images. Evagrius describes the inner light of this experience as God sculpting the place of God in us.

Evagrius emphasized that this path requires total dependence on God. He discovered that the desert, itself, is both a metaphor and venue where one is stripped of personal control over material sustenance and possessions. Evagrius summarized this with a prayer from the psalms: "O God, come to my assistance, O Lord make haste to help me." For him, this attitude is the heart of desert asceticism. As we have seen, it was called apatheia *(dispassion),* or non-attachment (even to the quest for God) and leads to *purity of heart,* a person's most authentic state-of-being. This was a monk's goal: to have his or her will and attitude toward life open to and united with what God desires. This is union with God's will, not an annihilation of our own will. It is perfect freedom.[19]

John Cassian (360–435 C.E.). Cassian was born in what is now Romania and became a scholar in Greek and Latin. While still a young man he became a spiritual wanderer and found his way to Palestine and joined a monastery in Bethlehem. He left there with a friend, Germanus, to study monastic life in Syria and Egypt, spending fifteen years in Egyptian monasteries and hermitages. He recorded in great detail the practices and wisdom of desert monastic teachers and their methods of forming young monks to monastic life. Cassian left Egypt and spent a period of time in Constantinople studying with and assisting the great theologian, preacher and liturgist, Bishop John Chrysostom. From there he went to Rome where he was influenced by Pope Leo the Great, who ordained him priest. In 415 C.E. Cassian was called to the area of Provence, France, to promote the growing interest in monasticism. He founded two monasteries at Marseilles.

In 417 C.E. Cassian wrote his *Coenobitic Institutes,* a description of the monastic life he had seen and experienced in Egypt. Later he wrote the *Conferences,* which detail the wisdom of various abbas and abbots in the form of long conversations on a variety of topics.

Cassian's scholarship in Greek and Latin, his training in the theology of both Eastern and Western Christian faith communities, and his personal formation and experience in the ascetic life of Egyptian and Syrian

monastic communities equipped him well to become an articulate link between East and West. His writing about Egyptian monasticism became a
major resource for that tradition's influence on the development of monastic life in the West. It was a primary source in the formation of Benedictine
monasticism and continues to influence monastic spirituality to this day.

Notes

1. *The Lives of the Desert Fathers,* trans. Norman Russell, introduction by Benedicta
Ward, S.L.G. (Kalamazoo: Cistercian Publications, 1981) "On the Monks of Nitria,"
5; 105.

2. Murad Kamil, *Coptic Egypt* (Cairo: Le Scribe Egyptien, 1968) 27–29.

3. Kamil, *Coptic Egypt,* 23–25.

4. For details about this transitional period in Egypt and its influence on desert
monasticism, see Steven F. Driver, *John Cassian and the Reading of Egyptian Monasticism* (New York: Routledge, 2002) ch. 2; Philip Rousseau, *Pachomius. The
Making of a Community in Fourth Century Egypt* (Berkeley: University of California Press, 1985) ch. 1; Edward R. Hardy, *The Large Estates of Byzantine Egypt* (New
York: Columbia University Press, 1931); and Samuel Rubenson, *The Letters of St.
Antony* (Minneapolis: Fortress Press, 1995) ch. 2.

5. Russell and Ward, *Lives,* "On Oxyrhynchus," 1, 67.

6. See Rubenson, *The Letters of St. Antony,* 35–42.

7. Russell and Ward, *Lives,* "On the monks of Nitria," 15, 107.

8. Driver, *John Cassian,* 27–32.

9. My summary of Clement's thought is influenced by Robert Louis Wilken,
The Spirit of Early Christian Thought (New Haven: Yale University Press, 2003) 54–61
passim. I am grateful for his scholarship, but take responsibility for my conclusions.

10. See Wilken, *The Spirit,* 14–16 passim.

11. Kamil, *Coptic Egypt,* 24–25.

12. Rousseau, *Pachomius,* 26–28 passim.

13. See Rubenson, *The Letters of St. Antony,* 59–88 passim.

14. See Driver, *John Cassian,* 31–32.

15. See Rubenson, *The Letters of St. Antony,* Letters 1, 2, and 6 and 139. See also
Driver, *John Cassian,* 28–34 passim.

16. Russell and Ward, *Lives,* "On the monks of Nitria," 10, endnote 10.

17. See Rubenson, *The Letters of St. Antony,* 188–91 passim.

18. This assessment is influenced by the research of both Samuel Rubenson in
The Letters of St. Antony, 185–91 and James E. Goehring, *Ascetics, Society and the
Desert* (Harrisburg: Trinity Press) 126, 212–16.

19. For an excellent discussion of the Eastern Orthodox understanding of Eva-
grius's synthesis of desert monastic life, see Elisabeth Behr-Sigel, *The Place of the
Heart: An Introduction to Orthodox Spirituality,* trans. Fr. Stephen Bigham (Torrance:
Oakwood Publications, 1992) 64–70.

3   Sunrise to Sunrise

The Daily Lives of Early Egyptian Desert Elders and Monastic Communities

A Patterned Life

Although the lives of the monastic hermits, elders and monastic communities in Egypt did not follow a single pattern, all their lives were patterned. In earlier chapters we have seen that the initial development of monasticism, itself, followed simple, yet unintentional, patterns.

Skilled in Matters of Heart and Mind: An Internal Pattern

Hermits, hesychasts, and coenobites all shared a common monastic aim: union with God. Their desire was to become "citizens of heaven," both in this life and after death. This aim was manifested gradually into a pattern embedded in daily life, leading to conversion of the unrestrained ego and love of God and neighbor. It was a struggle that demanded dependence wholly on God in a binding of heart and mind, the whole person. In the same way that each human being requires an equilibrium and balance of body, mind, and spirit for a healthy life, the desert elders learned from their experience to develop a rhythm of ascetic praxis whose foundation was a balance of essential elements for love of God and neighbor. This balance had both **internal** and **external** dimensions. Abba Evagrius was one of the first elders to articulate the inner dimension.

A Transpersonal Psychology of the Self and Its Search for God

Abba Evagrius was a smart and articulate theologian who recorded the experience and wisdom of many desert elders. His sharp intellectual skills and gift of synthesis enabled him to articulate an **internal pattern** that was a foundation of monastic life. This pattern reflects the dynamics of the human psyche, intellect, heart and soul, and recognizes that it is the whole person who seeks God. It identifies essential components in this movement toward conversion as well as serious dangers that can deflect the monk from his or her path. Some of these components were described in the first two chapters, but will be summarized below to demonstrate their place in Evagrius's synthesis.

- *Politeia*: the elders recognized the need for "a way of virtue," an organized manner or rule of life that liberates the monk from a self-centered emphasis on bodily needs and integrates the will of the ego with the will of God.[1] Politeia is the regimen, the essential elements, of monastic life. It is the venue for the monk's daily conversion and transformation.

   For God brought us to Egypt and showed us great and wonderful things which are worthy of being remembered and recorded. He granted to us who desire to be saved both the foundation and the knowledge of salvation *(i.e., learning and contemplation)*. He provided us not only with a model of the good life, but also with an exposition sufficient to arouse the soul to devotion. He gave us a noble testimony to the way of virtue.[2]

- *Praktike*: is the threefold ascetic practice described in the last chapter that includes: (1) biblical knowledge and wisdom acquired through learning and meditation, (2) daily conversion through prayer and spiritual praxis, and (3) love of neighbor, manifested through labor and physical activity. This is the heart of ascetic discipline. The ascetic practices of praktike are not ends in themselves. They form a venue for experiencing the goodness in this life which leads a person to union with God.[3]

- *Passions*: The passions are distorted human awarenesses.[4] They are emotions or "movements of the soul" which become disordered through undisciplined mental or physical appetites.[5] This is not a denial of the goodness of human passions. It is awareness that the ego can distort natural human passions which, when unrestrained, can lead to sinful behavior.

   Another brother questioned Abba Poemen in these words: "What does 'See that none of you repays evil for evil' mean?" The old man said to him, "Passions work in four stages; first, in the heart; secondly, in the face; thirdly in words; and fourthly, it is essential not to render evil for evil in deeds. If you can purify your heart, passion will not come into your expression; but if it comes into your face, take care not to speak; but if you do speak, cut the conversation short in case you render evil for evil."[6]

Abba Poemen recognized that distorted and evil human behavior have their origin in the human heart. The aim of the monk, through ascetic practice, is to purify the heart, the seat of the will. When this happens the distorted passions are restored to their natural purpose. Amma Syncletica speaks, also, of the discipline necessary to control the passions. She sees three main sources of the passions and recognizes that the origin of evil behavior comes from within a human being:

> The main sources of the Enemy from which every evil springs are threefold: desire, pleasure, and sadness. These are connected one from another, and one follows another. It is possible to control pleasure to some extent, but impossible to control desire; for the end of pleasure is achieved through the body, but that (of desire) originates from the soul, while sadness is concocted from both. Well then, do not allow desire to become active, and you will dissipate the remaining two. But if you permit the first to emerge, it will develop into the second and they will form with one another "a vicious circle" and in no way will the soul be allowed to escape.[7]

The aim of praktike, the ascetic practice, is to overcome the influence of undisciplined passions and redirect them toward charity. This explains why spiritual discipline and personal prayer are essential in any person's life.

> • *Apatheia:* A monk can become attached to the passions and to the ascetic practice of overcoming the passions. Apatheia, which flows from praktike, ascetic practice, is "to be without passion." As we saw in chapter two, it is an abiding state of being unattached to both desires to sin and to the desire to overcome sinful behavior. Apatheia does not mean being sinless. It is a positive way of life that "relates to all things in a natural and appropriate way."[8] It is the source of a deep peace and joy, even though undisciplined passions may recur.[9] Apatheia may be compared to "mindfulness." It enables us to see what is present in our lives without trying to control the consequences of what we are experiencing.

> > The effects (i.e., apatheia) of keeping the commandments do not suffice to heal the powers of the soul completely. They must be complemented by a contemplative activity appropriate to these faculties

and this activity must penetrate the spirit. . . . The state of prayer can be aptly described as a habitual state of imperturbable calm *(ap-atheia)*. It snatches to the heights of intelligible reality the spirit which loves wisdom and which is truly spiritualized by the most intense love. . . . The man who strives after true prayer must learn to master not only anger and his lust, but must free himself from every thought that is colored by passion.[10]

• *Theoretike:* In chapter 2 we saw that apatheia paves the way for a more direct experience of God, theoretike. "For Evagrius it is unthinkable that a man should aspire to be united with God in pure prayer without first cleansing his heart fully. Only when he has attained apatheia, a state of abiding calm deriving from full harmony of the passions, can he speak of perfect charity. Only when he has perfect charity can he hope to know God."[11] Apatheia and contemplative prayer are complementary graces. As we have seen, Evagrius describes two ways the monk may experience God. The first is *theoria physike*, in which God is known indirectly through the physical world:

We seek virtues for the sake of attaining to the inner meaning of created things. We pursue these latter, that is to say the inner meaning of what is created, for the sake of attaining to the Lord who has created them. It is in the state of prayer that he [the Lord] is accustomed to manifest himself.[12]

The second way is *theoria theologike*, where God is experienced in contemplation, without words or images. This is direct experience of God.[13] The heart or aim of theoretike is the biblical sense of "knowledge," of being one with God, who is love:

When you are praying do not fancy the Divinity like some image formed within yourself. Avoid also allowing your spirit to be impressed with the seal of some particular shape, but rather, free from all matter, draw near the immaterial Being and you will attain to understanding.[14]

This complementary tension between praxis (or action) and contemplation is at the heart of Christian spirituality. Evagrius understood that the **whole** person, not just the soul, is involved in salvation. He honors the physical world, also, as a venue for experiencing God's presence. The wisdom of the desert elders is *incarnational,* while its aim is union with God. We experience God in all of life.

Praktike, apatheia and theoretike are not "stages" of progress or growth. They are integrated as each person persists in ascetic practice. At the same time Evagrius knew that they are difficult disciplines and that not all persons would commit themselves to the persistence necessary for theoria, direct experience of God. Evagrius was a realist and knew that there are distractions and dangers which can deflect any person from his or her chosen inner pattern to bind heart and mind in seeking God.

- *Logismois:* Logismois are images or thoughts within the human mind which distract and direct a person away from ascetic practice and, therefore, from God. They are "bad thoughts."

  > It happens at times that the demons suggest some bad thoughts to you and again stir you up to pray against them, as is only proper, or to contradict them. Then they depart of their own choosing so as to deceive you into believing that you have conquered your thoughts of yourself and have cast fear into the demons.[15]

John Cassian recorded sound advice from Abba Moses for overcoming these harmful thoughts:

> It is impossible for the mind not to be approached by thoughts, but it is the power of every earnest person either to admit them or to reject them. . . . But because we said it is impossible for the mind not to be approached by thoughts, you must not lay everything to the charge of the assault or to those spirits who strive to instill them in us. . . . For this purpose we employ frequent reading and continual meditation on the Scriptures to give us an opportunity for spiritual recollection. . . We also use earnest vigils and fasts and prayers, that the mind may be brought low and not mind earthly things but contemplate things celestial.[16]

- *Demons:* In the world of the desert elders demons were experienced as evil influences from within or outside the monk. There was a lingering belief in demons as malevolent spirits whose origins were in "fallen angels." Some monks believed in the existence of non-human, rational creatures whose purpose was to undermine human intimacy with God.[17]

The Greek words used for "devil," "demon" and "demonic" point to a fundamental danger in the ascetic life. All three words have their root in *"ballow,"* to throw or scatter. *"Dia-bollein"* refers to a traducer or Satan, the one who tires to scatter a person's resolve. *"Dia-bollein"* can mean a verbal assault or to throw through, i.e., to break into pieces. It is plain to see that a demonic or diabolical influence is one that scatters a person's focus and seeks to disrupt a person's center. If the monk's center lies in God, avoiding these demonic distractions is a matter of life and death. Athanasius, in *The Life of Antony,* describes such a battle early in Antony's life as a hermit:

> The assault and appearance of the evil ones, on the other hand, is something troubling, with crashing and noise and shouting—the sort of disturbance one might expect from tough youths and robbers. From this come immediately terror of the soul, confusion and disorder of thoughts, dejection, enmity toward ascetics, listlessness, grief, memory of relatives, and fear of death; and finally there is craving for evil, contempt for virtue, and instability of character.[18]

A man bringing Antony food found him exhausted and unable to stand upright after such an encounter. Confrontations with demons were often visualized and very real from the monk's point of view. Athanasius describes a visitation of demons to Antony that was witnessed by fellow monks:

> So he was alone in the inner mountain devoting himself to prayers and the discipline. And the brothers who served him asked him if when they came every month they might bring him olives and pulse (a type of flour made from roots that could be mixed with water) and oil, for he was at this point an old man. Furthermore, we know from those who visited him how many wrestlings he endured while dwelling there, *not against blood and flesh*, but against destructive demons. For there they heard tumults and many voices, and crashing noises like the sound of weapons; and at night they saw the mountain filled with beasts.[19]

Some desert elders experienced demons as external malign forces:

> The same Abba Theophilus said, "What fear, what trembling, what uneasiness will there be for us when our soul is separated from the body. Then indeed the force and strength of the adverse powers come against us, the rulers of darkness, those who command the world of evil, the principalities, the powers, the spirits of evil."[20]

The primary "weapons" against demons were calling on the name of Christ, the words of Scripture and the practice of humility. "Another time a demon approached Abba Macarius with a knife and wanted to cut his foot. But, because of his humility he could not do so, and he said to him, 'All that you have, we have also; you are distinguished from us only by humility; by that you get the better of us.'"[21] Antony describes his dependence on God during an encounter with a demon:

> Once a very tall demon appeared in an apparition and had the daring to say, "I am the power of God" and "I am Providence; what do you wish that I would give you?" But then, especially, I puffed at him, and speaking the

name of Christ I made an attempt to strike him. I seemed to have hit home, and at once, with the mention of the name of Christ, this giant figure vanished, along with all his demons.[22]

Demons were experienced, also, as an evil disposition **within** the monk, himself. Sometimes the words demons and logismois were used interchangeably. Evagrius listed eight distracting thoughts that were harmful to the spiritual path. He was influenced by Origen of Alexandria who places evil thoughts in a psychological rather than a moral context. Origen described demons as "specialists" in anger, lust and other emotions which can "shake our confidence in God through despair."[23] The elders learned from experience that evil thoughts lead to evil actions. They realized that their experience of demons matched the dispositions they found in their own hearts and that the demons had power only when the monk allowed them to have power. Evagrius believed that knowing the types of demons a monk experienced could, with spiritual discernment, lead to a transforming self-knowledge and openness that he called "purity of heart." The desert elders called this *kardio-gnosis*, knowledge of the heart. This type of discernment requires a great deal of personal honesty yet is essential in our path toward authentic transformation and compassionate living.

> If there is any monk who wishes to take the measure of some of the more fierce demons so as to gain experience in his monastic art, then let him keep careful watch over his thoughts. Let him observe their intensity, their periods of decline, and follow them as they rise and fall. Let him note well the complexity of his thoughts, their periodicity, the demons which cause them, with the order of successions and the nature of their associations. Then let him ask from Christ the explanations of these data he has observed.[24]

Yet the battle with demons, whether inner or exterior, was real and the outcome was crucial in the monk's desire for transformation. It is easy for modern readers to misunderstand these battles with demons as human aberration or superstition. Columba Stewart, O.S.B., reminds us that, however they were perceived by the desert elders, they manifest an ancient recognition of the deep psychological aspect of the spiritual journey:

> The troubles of the desert monks were not too different from those of today. However, the desert provided a stark backdrop for the actions of unhealed personality, and gave a dramatic edge to the work of recovering a sense of wholeness. The sharp awareness of sin and the dramatic vocabulary used to describe it should not mislead one into thinking that the desert monks were obsessed with evil and prone to superstition.[25]

• *Accidie:* Accidie has multiple meanings, but is best understood as lack of desire or initiative in ascetic practice. It can be described, also, as laziness or depression caused by illness, difficulties in the spiritual life, or the pressure of new challenges or personal failures. Amma Theodora describes accidie in this way:

> However, you should realize that as soon as you intend to live in peace, at once evil comes and weighs down your soul through accidie, faintheartedness, and evil thoughts. It also attacks your body through sickness, debility, weakening of the knees, and all the members. It dissipates the strength of soul and body, so that one believes that one is ill and no longer able to pray.[26]

Note that Amma Theodora recognizes that the malaise of a person's inner spirit can influence physical wellness. Abba Simon described his personal experience of accidie to John Cassian in vivid language:

> I am on fire with innumerable and various wanderings of soul and shiftiness of heart and cannot collect my scattered thoughts. I cannot even pour forth my prayer without interruption from useless images and memories of conversations and actions. I feel myself tied down by such dryness and barrenness that I cannot give birth to any spiritual ideas.[27]

Evagrius lists accidie as one of the eight primary evil thoughts. In the following passage he sets accedia in the context of a monastic day:

> The demon of accedia—also called the noonday demon—is the one that causes the most serious trouble of all. He presses his attack upon the monk about the fourth hour and besieges the soul until the eighth hour. First of all he makes it seem that the sun barely moves, if at all, and that the day is fifty hours long. . . . Then, too, he instills in the heart of the monk a hatred for the place, a hatred for his very life itself, a hatred for manual labor. . . . He depicts the monk's life stretching out for a long period of time, and brings before the mind's eye the toil of the ascetic struggle and, as the saying has it, leaves no leaf unturned to induce the monk to forsake his cell and drop out of the fight. No other demon follows close upon the heels of this one (when he is defeated), but only a state of deep peace and inexpressible joy arises out of this struggle (i.e., apatheia).[28]

Evagrius's words have a very familiar ring in the context of the frenzy, busyness and frustrations of twenty-first-century life and the fact that depression is one of the most common modern diseases. But note that the fruit of the struggle with accedia is the unattached state of peace and charity found in apatheia. The primary issue at stake in the demon of accidie is stewardship of the whole person. Each person is called to collaborate with God's grace in order to preserve and guard his or her life for union with God and love of neighbor. Evagrius refers to the wisdom of Abba Macarius the Great to emphasize stewardship of a person's whole being:

> Our holy and most ascetic master stated that the monk should always live as if he were to die on the morrow but at the same time he should treat his body as if he were to live on with it for many years to come. For, he said, by the first attitude he will be able to cut off every thought that comes from accedia and thus become more fervent in his monastic practices, by the second device he will preserve his body in good health and maintain its continence in tact.[29]

All these components or distractions influenced the **inner** pattern of the monks' ascetic practice. But what were the **outer** patterns of their lives? What was ascetic practice, itself? How did the monks spend their days and nights? Where did they live and how did they work? What did they eat? How did they worship? How did they care for themselves and each other? What was their monastic world like?

Sunrise to Sunrise: The External Patterns and Rhythms of Daily Life

As we have seen, there was no single rule of life or communal lifestyle shared by all the desert hermits and monastic communities. Yet there were fundamental similarities, born of the needs of desert living and climate, a common desire to seek God, and the individual and social psychologies of human life. In this section we will look at monastic life in the desert from a variety of perspectives, but with a focus on the monastic communities following a rule of common life begun by Abba Pachomius. In earlier chapters we have seen accounts of the lifestyles of several hermits. We turn now to observe the daily routines of small groups of monks and the larger monasteries, especially those in the Pachomian tradition. It is important to observe at the beginning of our exploration of desert coenbitic life that many of these communities were located in or near towns and smaller cities.

Fundamental Values of Pachomian Communities

Prior to looking at the daily routine of desert monasteries, it is important to see the process and values that formed these early coenobitic communities, as well as some details about monastic dwellings and diet. Pachomian monasteries were organized into "houses" of twenty cells each.

There is no evidence of a common theme constituting these early houses, but in later periods monks with specific tasks or responsibilities within the monastery had their cells in the same house.[30] Each house had a superior known as the *oikiakos*, who had the primary influence on monks in his house. The superior of the entire monastery was called the *oikonomos* and influenced all the monks primarily through his teaching at conferences every Saturday and Sunday and his authority over the leaders of the individual houses.[31]

The organization of monks into houses of twenty cells demonstrates Pachomius's intent for a balance between the individual's ascetic life and the interdependence of the monks in each house for material and spiritual needs. Pachomius, himself, does not seem to want to replace the existence of hermits or the small groups of disciples gathered around a revered teacher. In fact, the seeds for the formation of Pachomius's early monasteries probably lie in his relationship with his own teacher, Palamon. The Greek Life of Pachomius, known as the *Vita Prima* (translated from an earlier Coptic *Life*), and the *Boharic Life,* one of two Coptic *Lives* of Pachomius (translated from the same source used in the Greek *Life*), refer to (1) other ascetics joining Palamon and Pachomius at times, (2) their common labor for those in need, and (3) their proximity to a neighboring village and to other monks in nearby mountains.[32] When Pachomius receives a vision to form a monastic community near Palamon, they enter a provisional agreement ". . . that we shall visit each other in turn, you and I, so as not to be separated from each other from now on."[33] Pachomius was not rejecting the need for solitude in favor of communal life. Over the years he had experienced dimensions of ascetic life that would lead him to form new communities for the specific purpose of "mutual respect and mutual support."[34] This is described in the *Sahidic Life of Pachomius,* the first of the two Coptic *Lives,* using even earlier Sahidic sources:

> He established for them the following rule: "each should be self-supporting and manage his own affairs" and "bind themselves together in a perfect koinonia like that of the believers which *Acts* describes: 'They were of one heart and one soul.'"[35]

The need for solitude was preserved by a rule that the monks should not visit the cells of other monks or visit other monasteries.[36] This rule had the additional purpose of recognizing the charism present in the small "house," itself. Commitment to a specific community of monks and its common patterns of life would nurture the monk's ascetic praxis in a unique way.

Even the earliest monasteries of Pachomius benefited from the legacy of his years of experience after he left Palamon. During that period

Pachomius attracted other ascetics and villagers who shared resources, meals, and practiced ascetic disciplines together. Out of this varied transition the fundamental patterns and order of Pachomian coenobitic life evolved. "They lived a coenobitic life. So he established for them a rule in an irreproachable lifestyle and traditions profitable for their souls. These he took from the holy Scriptures: proper measure in clothing, equality in food, and decent sleeping arrangements."[37]

Commitment to the community was based on the values Pachomius had learned from his earlier experiences. "The peace and concord were the greatest value."[38]

The rules and patterns of common life supported a venue for the spiritual formation and growth of the individual monk. A common pattern of worship, labor, meals, and learning created a synthesis whereby an individual's commitment to others contributed to the formation of a community within which his own life with God would have health and stability. These early Pachomian monasteries de-emphasized differences between monks in order to share the richness of depending on each other.

The role of revered abba (known through experiences with hermits like Antony as well as the teachers with small groups of disciples, like Palamon) seems to have been passed on in a natural way to Pachomius's role of superior in his first two monasteries. This role was to guard the values of the monastery present in its pattern of life and to embody and teach the wisdom of ascetic life.

Monastic Cells and Dwellings

The limitations and resources of the desert determined the design and materials used for all monastic dwellings, from cells to refectories and churches. The only exceptions were communities or hermits that used existing buildings, such as Antony's first hermitage in a portion of an abandoned fort and monastic communities at Oxyrhnchus that lived in deserted dwellings and another community that used former temples in an abandoned village on a tributary of the Nile River. When it was necessary to build a cell or other monastic building the monks used the materials at hand, not simply from a commitment to poverty or austerity, but also from the practical needs imposed by desert resources and climate.

The primary resource was bricks, handmade from clay or mud, and dried in the sun. Local wood was used for support and furniture when available. Some dwellings were simple shelters, others were rooms connected to each other, surrounding a patio or garden. Local caves or tombs were used as rooms and were enlarged or connected to new rooms made of brick or stone. Some anchorites used caves high in rock cliffs accessible by rope or simple wooden ladders. Some free-standing cells were strong enough to permit monks to sleep on the roof. From the *Historia Monachorum* we learn that cells were often self-built from bricks and mortar and contained one or two rooms. These could be built in a day. John of Lycopolis had a two-roomed cell and built on another room to receive guests. One room had a window through which he talked with persons who came to see him daily. Some anchorites had cells with a courtyard so they could have complete privacy. Cells for hermits had inner and outer rooms, with the inner room for sleeping.[39]

When new persons asked to join an elder's group or a monastery the elders or coenobitic monks would join to build the newcomer a cell. Abba Or was a hermit and when monks came to live near him his response was typical of desert hospitality: "He called together everybody who lived near him and built cells for them in a single day, one delivering mortar, and another bricks, another drawing water, and another cutting wood. And when the cells had been completed, he himself saw to the needs of the newcomers."[40] There are accounts of abbas giving their own cells to new monks. It is clear that the value of community and interdependence flowed into the sharing of resources and labor necessary for shelter.

Will God Prepare a Table in the Desert? Space and the Spirit

Meals in the desert, like shelter, were congruent with what the land produced and the needs of ascetic life. Taken as a whole, monastic life in the desert, whether eremitic or coenobitic, linked the outer and inner environments of the monks through a spiritual awareness. Life in the desert was practical and demanded realism based on what was available and at the same time became the **venue** for the values that lead to love of God and neighbor. Food and shelter were taken from the basic and sustainable materials and natural growth of the desert and, **because** they were all that was available, became all that was necessary to sustain a life dedicated to God and neighbor. The world of the desert monks was a union of physical and spiritual realities that matched the natural patterns of human needs with the physical environment to support an ascetic path.

The desert monks were not indifferent to the beauty and productivity of the desert. Awareness of the spiritual and aesthetic power of the landscape may be seen in small gardens planted in courtyards surrounded by cells and near hermitages. The power of the austere, yet beautiful desert landscape was a sign of their dependence on God and what the desert could provide to support their lives. Just as they depended on the Bible as their primary source of spiritual nurture, they acknowledged the desert as the only source of food for the body. Both were signs of God's presence and love. Belden Lane points out that the desert was a perfect match for a life of austere ascetic discipline. "The desert fathers and mothers chose their barren locale because its values matched their own. They, too, opted to thrive on the boundary where life and death meet, living as simply as possible, with as few words as necessary, separated from the fragile anxieties of the world they had left behind."[41]

The desert elders experienced land as a gift and saw it as a venue for embodying their monastic virtues of stewardship, work, hospitality and charity. These virtues were expressed in very practical ways. Early in his life as a monk Abba Or saw the need for wood in the area he settled with other hermits. He replanted a marsh with trees to ensure a later supply of wood. "There was not a single green shoot here before the father came out of the (deeper) desert."[42] In the same way that Abba Or had reclaimed a marsh, Abba Copres, inspired by the faith and husbandry of local peasants, transformed his hermitage garden into a small grove of date palms and other fruit trees by adding fertile sand to the barren soil.[43] Abba Isidore's monastery in the Thebaid was surrounded by a high wall for protection and within the walls were wells and a garden supplying all their physical needs.[44] Hermits kept small gardens, not for themselves, but for the needs of visitors and pilgrims. We have seen that the isolated monastery of Serapion sent shiploads of wheat from their fertile gardens to the poor in Alexandria.

Benedicta Ward observes that the desert monks were responsible for substantial agricultural improvements in the desert that benefited the lives of their neighbors.[45] They made the desert come to life in more ways than one. The outer environment of their lives reflected and was influenced by the inner environment of their spirits. Their abilities to create sustainable environments in the desert, using resources at hand, supports similar efforts in today's society and should inspire us to become more aware of the spiritual dimensions of stewardship of the environment and sharing the earth's resources in a just and caring way.

Meals and Diet

Although the norm for hermits and semi-eremitic monks was one meal a day,[46] Pachomian monasteries ate a main meal during the work period and a lighter meal in the early evening.[47] Pachomian monks ate together in silence. Their usual diet was bread and vegetables and possibly dried fruit.[48] Other foods, mentioned in the *Historia Monachorum,* varied from place to place but included: a soup made from wheat and water, beans, lentils, dried bread, grapes, cheese, olives, dates and green herbs. Some hermits survived on a very austere diet of dried bread and water, with some vegetables on rare occasions, especially as hospitality for visitors. The *Lives* of Antony the Great and Mary of Egypt and the short reference to Amma Alexandra in the *Lausiac History* describe their diets as only dried bread and water for decades. Older monks and the ill were given a more complete diet as needed.

Bread was baked at some monasteries or purchased from nearby villages. Townspeople often brought bread and other foods to hermits as gifts or in trade for baskets, mats or rope woven by the hermits. Bread loaves were small, about twelve ounces, and when dried could be stored for long periods. They were moistened with water and eaten with light salt. The larger monastic communities and some *sketes* (areas containing a few or many clusters of hesychasts and their disciples) raised their own vegetables for meals and for sale and offerings to the poor. As we have seen, some anchorites and small communities of monks grew wheat for bread or soup and raised vegetables, usually to offer guests and the poor.

Habits of eating were controlled so that food would not interfere with ascetic discipline. The basic rule was to eat as little as possible. The *Historia Monachorum* describes the diet of Abba Or:

"When the father first came to live in the desert he ate herbs and certain sweet roots. He drank water whenever he found it, and spent all his time praying and singing hymns." And when Aba Or reached old age: "He built himself a small hut, and contented himself simply with picked vegetables, frequently eating only once a week."[49]

The monks acknowledged food as a gift to sustain the body in a way that would not be a distraction to the food of Scripture and the praxis of prayer. **Fasting** was a common practice and took many forms. Some monks fasted for two or four days at a time. Fasting was often linked to Sundays and holy days and as preparation for the Eucharist. The canonical (required) fasts on Wednesdays and Fridays were common and there are accounts of extreme fasting. But the common practice was moderation. Some of the desert elders warned against using disciplines such as fasting in prideful ways and insisted that abuse of the body was not an appropriate discipline.[50]

Abba Joseph asked Abba Poemen, "How should one fast?" Abba Poemen said to him, "For my part, I think it better that one should eat every day, but only a little, so as not to be satisfied." Abba Joseph said to him, "When you were younger, did you not fast two days at a time, abba?" The old man said, "Yes, even for three and four and the whole week. The Fathers tried all this out as they were able and found it preferable to eat every day, but just a small amount. They have left us this royal way, which is light."[51]

The fundamental virtue present in monastic use of material resources was and is an awareness of having and using only what is proper for the monastic manner of life. The desert elders did not reject material benefits *per se*. This is the reason for the monastic vow of poverty. It is interesting that in modern society poverty is seen as a problem rather than a virtue. It is true that millions of people today do not have basic needs. Yet this condition is, for the most part, the result of a hoarding of resources by others. What is proper for healthy and wholesome life today? What influence could the desert monastic understanding of poverty have on relieving the inequities and conflicts we face in our local and international communities? How does what we possess affect our spirit and behavior?

A Monastic Day in the Desert [52]

Early Morning

Daily life in the early monasteries of Pachomius had a simple pattern. The day began at sunrise. Each monk had spent the night in his or her cell asleep or in vigil. (Pachomius founded monasteries for both men and women. This profile is taken from data from a male community.) Since there was no formal night prayer, the night was spent in prayer, recitation of psalms or other portions of Scripture, and periods of sleep. Night was valued as a period of undistracted prayer and awareness of God's presence. As Abba Moses described to John Cassian:

> For this purpose we use the frequent singing of Psalms to provide constant feelings of compunction (sadness and regret for sin). We also use earnest vigils and fasts and prayers, that the mind may be brought low and not mind earthly things but contemplate things celestial. If these things are dropped and carelessness creeps on us, the mind, hardened with the foulness of sin, is sure to incline in a worldly direction and fall away.[53]

Some monks spent long periods standing or sitting on a chair without a back. It was common to alternate vigils with short periods of sleep.

At dawn the sound of a horn or gong called the whole community (all the "houses") to morning prayer called *synaxis*. This early community prayer was a combination of long readings of Scripture separated by recitation of the Lord's Prayer and intervals of silent reflection. The monks were expected to work quietly during the readings, presumably on simple tasks like weaving. On Sundays and days when the Eucharist was celebrated there was also recitation of psalms and singing. The reflection on Scripture at morning synaxis would form a pattern of meditation which extended throughout the monk's day, during a work period and into evening prayers. The focus on a portion of Scripture during the day's labor was called *meditatio*.

The monks returned to their cells after synaxis and waited for the leader of the house, the oikiakos, to assign work for the day. Work assignments were coordinated by consultation with the monastery superior, the oikonomos. In the earliest Pachomian monasteries work was very simple, consisting of gathering materials for weaving of baskets, mats, and rope and of work related to raising crops and delivering crops to villages for sale or offerings to the poor. There were also jobs related to baking, preparation of meals, and planning for liturgies. Pachomius had a strict rule that certain houses would be assigned specific tasks for only a week at a time. This ensured that all types of work were shared and to prevent houses or individuals from being identified consistently with a certain type of work. In the later and larger monasteries the work became more diversified with crafts such as tailoring, carpentry, copying manuscripts, baking, and gardening, etc. Pachomius taught that all work should be done in moderation.

Mid-morning to Late Afternoon

When work assignments were given, monks from each house were led in a line to their place of work for the day. Monks assigned to weaving remained in their cells. All this activity, especially in the later Pachomian monasteries, implies regular contact with neighboring villages and a significant impact on the local economies of the villages. These desert monasteries became an integral part of the culture of Egyptian village life.

All monks wore the same clothing or *habit* to eliminate differences which might cause pride or levels of importance. The basic desert monastic clothing consisted of (1) a simple undyed linen tunic with short sleeves or no sleeves, (2) a linen belt, and (3) a goatskin coat or cape with hood. Rough leather boots might be worn during the day for work, but were shared by the monks only when working. The short sleeved tunic was the ordinary dress for any laborer in that culture. Some monks in other small communities and hermits wore simpler clothes of sewn rags, woven palm leaves, or linen.

Late Afternoon and Early Evening

After the day's labor and a light meal, there was a period of teaching and common worship in the Pachomian monasteries. This part of the daily pattern of life was a major aspect in the formation of each monk and, at the same time, an opportunity for each monk to contribute to the formation of his confreres. From the Greek *Life* of Pachomius we learn that he gave conferences (teaching) only on Saturdays and Sundays. The head of each "house" of twenty cells gave conferences for his house on Wednesdays and Fridays. Following every conference each monk had a period for the recitation of Scripture verses from memory, and then the monks of each house recited prayers together. This common prayer was followed by open discussion of the evening's conference. This was a unique opportunity for the monks of each house to reflect in personal and intimate ways, and for each monk to relate the teaching and discussion to his personal needs and spiritual formation. This pastoral activity and openness is an example of the monastic community forming each member and each individual contributing to the needs and formation of other monks. Modern faith communities and congregations might benefit from such an intentional commitment to integrating the fruits of prayer with the workplace and enabling individuals to mentor each other while being formed by corporate worship and teaching.

Late Evening and the Night

The day ended with each monk in his cell resuming the rhythm of sleep and vigils until sunrise signaling the beginning of a new day.

A Pattern of Worship

As we have seen, worship in both personal and corporate venues was woven into the fabric of each day. It was a combination of synaxis with the whole community, shorter recited prayers within each house, and the private prayer of each monk in his cell. The Eucharist was usually celebrated in both monasteries and sketes on Sundays and holy days. In the sketes such as Nitria and Cellia the monks came together only on Saturdays and Sundays. In the *Historia Monachorum* there are many references to the constant chanting of the psalms and the centrality of the psalms in prayer. A common pattern for the welcoming of visitors, which usually included worship, is narrated in the following account by the seven monks from Palestine whose travels in Egypt formed the *Historia Monachorum*:

When the father [Abba Or] saw us, he was filled with joy, and embraced us, and offered a prayer for us. Then, after washing our feet with his own hands, he turned to spiritual teaching. For he was very well versed in the Scriptures, having received this charism from God. He expounded many key passages in the Scriptures for us, and having taught us the orthodox faith, invited us to participate in the Eucharist. For it is a custom among the great ascetics not to give food to the flesh before providing spiritual nourishment for the soul, that is, the Communion of Christ.[54]

This incident illustrates the crucial importance of worship in the lives of the desert monastic communities. Although there were monasteries where the Eucharist was celebrated daily, there were also monks who saw the Eucharist and regular synaxis as distractions to the monastic way of life. Most monastic communities lay in between these extremes.

The Spiritual Virtue of Order, Rhythm and Balance

An old man said, "Every evening and every morning a monk ought to render an account of himself and say to himself, 'What have we done of what God does not want, and what have we done of that which God wills?'" In this way he must live in repentance. This is what it means to be a monk, and this is how Abba Arsenius used to live.[55]

These internal and external patterns and rhythms of daily life among the monks of Egypt reflect the formation of a new society centered on dependence on God rather than personal or material sufficiencies. They did not choose poverty and simplicity as ends in themselves. In fact, the diet and work life of most desert monks was not that much different from the average working person in the surrounding Nile villages.

The key to this desert monastic society was that it made these ascetic men and women more accessible to God and other people. With the exception of the more austere hermits and smaller eremitic groups, the monks of Egypt did not live in total isolation from the society they left. They desired and formed a new world that valued a different sense of time and relationship to material possessions and the earth's resources. They rejected personal pride, embodied in the unrestrained ego, and saw themselves as imperfect sinners seeking transformation. They wanted to live in the realm of God. This quest was the foundation for the patterns of their daily lives that wove simplicity, silence, prayer, work, learning, humility, and love of neighbor into a tapestry of the power of the presence of Christ. These monastic values became their gift to the inhabited world that surrounded them.

Their lives, day by day, were both prayerful and practical. Although their eyes were directed toward heaven, they were realists and very much down to earth. This is why they were sought out by every kind of person as sources of equilibrium in a world dominated by materialism, secular power, and anxiety about the future.

Notes

1. *The Lives of the Desert Fathers,* trans. Norman Russell and intro. Benedicta Ward, S.L.G. (Kalamazoo: Cistercian Publications, 1981) Prologue, 49. See also n. 3, 123.

2. Ibid., Prologue, 1, 49.

3. Columba Stewart, O.S.B. From class notes in "Early Monastic Studies," a graduate course at Saint John's School of Theology, Collegeville, Minnesota, 2002.

4. Ibid.

5. Russell and Ward, *Lives,* 126, n. 122.

6. *The Sayings of the Desert Fathers,* trans. Benedicta Ward, S.L.G. (Kalamazoo: Cistercian Publications, 1984) Poemen 34, 172.

7. Pseudo-Athanasius, *The Life of Blessed Syncletica,* trans. with notes by Elizabeth Bryson Bongie (Toronto: Peregrina, 1999) 96, 60–61.

8. Stewart, *Early Monastic Studies,* class notes, 2002.

9. Evagrius Ponticus, *The Praktikos and Chapters on Prayer,* trans. and introduction by John Eudes Bamberger, O.C.S.O. (Kalamazoo: Cistercian Publications, 1972) 19, n. 5.

10. Ibid., 36, 53, 63.

11. Ibid., 49.

12. Ibid., 51, 63.

13. Stewart, *Early Monastic Studies,* class notes, 2002.

14. Evagrius, *The Praktikos,* 66, 66.

15. Ibid., 72. no. 134, 77.

16. *Making Life a Prayer: Selected Writings of John Cassian,* ed. Keith Beasley-Topliffe (Nashville: Upper Room Books, 1997) conference 1, ch. 15; 61.

17. Stewart, *Early Monastic Studies,* class notes, 2002.

18. Athanasius, *The Life of Antony and the Letter to Marcellinus,* trans. and introduction by Robert C. Gregg (Mahwah, N.J.: Paulist Press, 1980) 58.

19. Ibid., 68–69.

20. Ward, *Sayings,* Theophilus 4, 81.

21. Ibid., Macarius 35, 136.

22. Athanasius, *The Life of Antony,* 61.

23. Stewart, *Early Monastic Studies,* class notes, 2002.

24. Evagrius, *The Praktikos,* no. 50, 29–30.

25. Columba Stewart, O.S.B., *The World of the Desert Fathers* (Oxford: SLG Press, 1995) 25.

26. Ward, *Sayings,* Theodora 3, 83.

27. *Making Life a Prayer: Selected Writings of John Cassian,* conferences, 10, ch. 10; 57.

28. Evagrius, *The Praktikos,* 12, 18–19.

29. Ibid., 29, 24.

30. See Philip Rousseau, *Pachomius* (Berkeley: University of California Press, 1985) 79 and Derwas Chitty, *The Desert a City* (Crestwood, N.Y.: St. Vladimir's Seminary Press 1977) 40, n. 31.

31. Rousseau, *Pachomius,* 79, n. 10.

32. Ibid., 64–65.

33. Armand Veilleux, trans. and introduction, *Pachomian Koinonia, Vol. 1, The Life of Saint Pachomius* (Kalamzoo: Cistercian Publications, 1980) "The First Greek Life," 12, 305.

34. Rousseau, *Pachomius,* 66.

35. Ibid., 67.

36. Veilleux, *Pachomian Koinonia,* "The First Greek Life," 59, 338–39.

37. Ibid., 25, 312–13.

38. Rousseau, *Pachomius,* 88.

39. Russell and Ward, *Lives,* passim and 21 for details.

40. Ibid., Or, 11, 64.

41. Belden C. Lane, *The Solace of Fierce Landscapes: Exploring Desert and Mountain Spirituality* (New York: Oxford University Press, 1998) 162. I recommend this book as a profound commentary on the significance of landscape in the human spiritual journey, especially in our modern civilizations.

42. Russell and Ward, *Lives,* 63.

43. Ibid., 93.

44. Ibid., 101.

45. Ibid., 12–15 passim.

46. Ibid., 22.

47. Rousseau, *Pachomius,* 84.

48. Ibid., 84–85.

49. Russell and Ward, *Lives,* Or, 4, 5; 63.

50. Ibid., 24–25.

51. Ward, *Sayings,* Poemen 31, 171.

52. Data for this profile of daily life have been gathered from many sources, but primarily from Russell and Ward, *Lives,* passim; Ward, *Sayings,* passim; Rousseau, *Pachomius,* especially 76–86; and Chitty, *The Desert A City,* passim.

53. *Making Life a Prayer: Selected Writings of John Cassian,* conference 1, ch. 15; 61.

54. Ibid., Or 7, 8; 64.

55. *The Wisdom of the Desert Fathers, Apophthegmata Patrum,* trans. Benedicta Ward, S.L.G. (Oxford: SLG Press, 1981) 132, 39.

4   The Cell

Meeting God and Ourselves

The Path to the Desert

"A brother came to Scetis to visit Abba Moses and asked him for a word. The old man said to him, 'Go, sit in your cell, and your cell will teach you everything.'"[1]

As noted in the introduction, the roots of desert monasticism lay in distractions the desert elders experienced in the inhabited world. They withdrew to the desert where more intense dedication to God was possible. It is tempting to see this as a retreat from "the real world," and for some that was undoubtedly true. Yet the wisdom of the desert elders demonstrates that while their motives may have been mixed, their primary purpose was not to renounce life, but to embrace a more authentic human life. At the same time, they learned that the path to such authenticity required difficult renunciation. The ammas and abbas experienced this tension between the need to let go of the futility of their former lives and their desire for transformation as *spiritual warfare*. Warfare may seem like an inappropriate image for spiritual formation in our age of terrorism and world conflicts. Yet it was an honest image for the desert elders because it pointed to what they considered a difficult life and death struggle. Their spiritual warfare required letting go of all the self-imposed barriers, psychological wounds and misuse of human desires which deflect the grace of God and deny the image of God in a person. St. Paul described this tension between our natural desire for God and our human weakness with transparent honesty in his Letter to the Romans:

> So I find it to be a law that when I want to do what is good, evil lies close at hand. For I delight in the law of God in my inmost self, but I see in my members another law at war with the law of my mind, making me captive to the law

47

of sin that dwells in my members. Wretched man that I am! Who will rescue me from this body of death? (Rom 7:21-24, NRSV).

The uniqueness and mysterious lure of the desert is that a human being must learn to live within the limitations of its environment. Eventually it will strip us of the self-imposed defenses which deny our true nature, or "inmost self," as Paul described it. But it is no easy or casual task. The challenges of the desert dilute self-assertion and self-reliance. It will not tolerate impatience or "quick-fix" spiritual disciplines. The intense silence of the desert mentors a person to listen to someone besides one's self. It is God's auditorium of the Spirit. "Therefore, I will now allure her, and bring her into the wilderness, and speak tenderly to her" (Hos 2:14, NRSV). But we must let go of self in order to hear that tender voice. And that is not easy.

Amma Syncletica said, ". . . it is essential to be trained in austerities, I mean by fasting, by sleeping on the ground and by other austerities in turn. . . . For those who have not proceeded in this fashion, but who have suddenly rushed into rejecting their possessions are generally seized with regret."[2]

The teaching of Jesus exhorted a "dying to self" in order to gain one's self. In the world of the third and fourth centuries, the Christian ideal was entrance into the Kingdom of God through a life of penance and renunciation, largely in rejection of the worldliness and anxieties of life in the late Roman Empire.

> Amma Theodora said, "Let us strive to enter by the narrow gate. Just as the trees, if they have not stood before the winter's storms cannot bear fruit, so it is with us; this present age is a storm and it is only through many trials and temptations that we can obtain an inheritance in the kingdom of heaven."[3]

During the Roman imperial persecutions of Christianity martyrdom was esteemed as the highest offering of one's self to God. Martyrdom in blood, *red martyrdom*, was the most esteemed path toward sainthood. When the persecutions ended a new path to heaven led, for many, to the desert and a life of self-denial, *white martyrdom*. As we have seen, the first step was withdrawal, anachoresis. This was accompanied by *xeniteia*, or "indifference toward worldly values," through non-attachment and *amerimnesia*, or "freedom from the anxiety" produced from attachment to what is futile.[4] "The anchorite is not offended primarily by the world; he is offended by futility."[5] This distinction has great implications for twenty-first-century societies where so much of our efforts, resources, and time are spent pursuing the surface of life. We must give credence to the wisdom of these ancient elders, whose goal in spiritual formation was the *eschaton*, the eternal kingdom, the ultimately real, the completion or fulfillment of God's desires for creation. Their desert ascetic life would develop an **inner attitude** that would recognize the presence of the eschaton **in each person's spiritual practice and acts of charity.** In this context, renunciation is not denial of the goodness of creation, but taking offense at those aspects of society and personal behaviors that are not congruent with God's desires for creation. The purpose of anachoresis, then, is not turning our backs on the world or preferring anti-social behavior. It is *metanoia,* repentance, an intentional turning toward a new way of life. Jesus, himself, had proclaimed, "The time is fulfilled, and the kingdom of God has come near; repent [turn toward], and believe the gospel" (Mark 1:15).

In their spiritual warfare in the desert, the abbas and ammas learned that withdrawal gave them an opportunity to open themselves intentionally to a different world, the world of God's presence. By dying to self, as Jesus had exhorted, they experienced a death which led to a redeemed existence, an authentic self, which was not confined by the anxieties and limitations of chronological time.

The Desert Within

This wisdom was discovered in the desert, or more accurately, within each person engaged in spiritual warfare. The battle softened their hearts. The wisdom leading to transformation emerged from the motive to seek God in the desert and from an obscure longing that lured each person to anachoresis.

As we have seen, some were fleeing payment of taxes or military service. Others were fleeing a culture which they perceived as false for another world outside time and space. Some were criminals avoiding arrest or seeking penance and forgiveness. Most were led to the desert for a solitude they hoped would lead them to God. All had to learn that the treasure they desired already lay within. This was true, also, for those who sought a death to self as the means to white martyrdom and eternal life in heaven.

These motives, whether deep or shallow from a human perspective, opened the possibilities for experiencing the treasure within. They would be led, by grace, to experience God in a manner that earlier in their lives could only be glimpsed with longing. In the desert, separated from conventional necessities of life and voluntarily stripped from power to control their lives, these men and women were lured to depend totally on God. In their solitary ascetic life, which was extremely austere for some, the emptiness of the desert became filled with God and awareness of the communities of other seekers that surrounded them. In dying to self one could never escape others. Their spiritual warfare gave birth to the necessity of community and a passion for love of neighbor. They were indeed "separated from all and united to all," in the words of Evagrius. This confirms that they were called monks because they lived in solitude and were single-minded in their desire to search for God.

Since these ammas and abbas did not bring their wisdom with them to the desert, where did they find it?

The Cell

"The anchorite leaves the world and travels toward the desert. There he builds the cell of his repentance, the place of his rebirth, where he settles."[6]

The Physical Environment of the Cell

As we have seen, the cells of the desert monks, both male and female, were often caves or built onto caves, portions of abandoned forts or villages, tombs carved into rock cliffs, natural rock formations, simple hand-built dwellings within or attached to hand-hewn openings into cliffs, or free-standing hermitages. Building materials were a combination of rock, desert clay and local wood, when available.[7] In some cases, such as the apotaktikoi who lived in or near Egyptian villages, it may have been a separate room in a house. In the semi-eremitic communities where several disciples lived near their wise mentor, each disciple had a separate cell and all came to the abba or amma for instruction or worship. In the later coenobitic communities in the Pachomian tradition there were "houses," each comprised of twenty cells. Smaller coenobitic communities had individual cells or rooms for each monk, a common place to eat and a place for worship. Cells were simple and free of physical distractions. They were not intended as places of refuge from others or a locus for self-pity or indulgence.

There were always individual hermits called to the strict eremitic life who remained almost totally on their own. Some of the coenobitic communities would permit more mature monks to separate themselves from the koinonia for extended periods of solitude. Yet they, too, never severed their ties to the coenobium.[8]

The Significance of the Cell

"In the cell the human person comes face to face with God, and in this sense he becomes like a holy place."[9]

The cell is above all the place where the monk encounters God. It is a physical space, yet a space "in accordance with the image of one's inward nature."[10] The cell is the intentional environment where the monk is separated for personal prayer, meditation on Scripture, repentance, some manual labor, ascetic discipline, and transformation. It is the place where one comes face-to-face with what it means to be human and with one's self. The primary tools of the cell are solitude, silence, listening and the Spirit.[11]

Abba Antony said:

> Just as fish die if they stay too long out of water, so the monks who loiter outside their cells or pass their time with men of the world lose the intensity of inner peace. So like a fish going towards the sea, we must hurry to reach our cell, for fear that if we delay outside we will lose our interior watchfulness.[12]

The cell is a battleground where the monk is confronted with the desires and passions that deface his or her inmost self. It can be a terrifyingly vulnerable venue for naming the *ego* as the self-imposed ruler of the mind. The ego sets itself apart from God and the world in order to maintain its control over its self-created identity, desires, and needs. The ego knows it is limited by time and space, and this is the source of its anxiety and tyrannical need for control. Without its self-generated boundaries, it has no power. The ego is not, itself, evil, nor does it exist in isolation from the other aspects of a person's life. Yet, when unrestrained, the ego may create a false and self-serving self that is contrary to a person's natural state created to reflect the image of God. The ego can imprison the inner or true self, which then longs for transformation. Therefore, the cell is the place where the monk can be purged of the ego's unrestrained domination of his or her life and experience new birth. It is the place where the ego becomes open to God's grace.[13]

Abba John the Dwarf said:

> I am like a man sitting under a great tree, who sees wild beasts and snakes coming against him in great numbers. When he cannot withstand them any longer, he runs to climb the tree and is saved. It is just the same with me; I sit in my cell and I am aware of evil thoughts coming against me, and when I have no more strength against them, I take refuge in God by prayer and I am saved from the enemy.[14]

Stelios Ramfos points out that the cell exists in tension with the city.[15] The monastic understanding of cell is, according to the Greek word *topos,* a specific place or location. It is an environment where the monk can seek

God without distraction.[16] The place and the soul of the monk work together. This is in contrast with the Greek word *polis,* the city or plane. The
environment of the city causes distractions, busyness and scatteredness and
can deflect the monk from the soul's desire for God.[17] The cell, then, is a relationship between the soul and *a specific location.* It is a psychosomatic
harmony that nourishes the path to God and authentic human life. The cell,
also, is a state-of-being that can enrich and rebuild a person. It becomes a
battleground because the ego is not comfortable where it has no boundaries
and the cell is a place where **otherness** leads to transformation.[18] The cell, in
whatever form, is essential for any person because it is a place where the ego
can experience otherness and be led to the most real form of communion,
the presence of God and peace that passes human understanding.

> A brother asked Abba Rufus, "What is interior peace, and what use is it?"
> The old man said, "Interior peace means to remain sitting in one's cell with
> fear and knowledge of God, holding far off the remembrance of wrongs suf-
> fered and pride of spirit. Such interior peace brings forth all the virtues, pre-
> serves the monk from the burning darts of the enemy, and does not allow
> him to be wounded by them. Yes, brother, acquire it. Keep in mind your fu-
> ture death, remembering that you do not know at what hour the thief will
> come. Likewise be watchful over your soul."[19]

In the busyness, scatteredness, and expectations of modern Western
society there is a need for all of us to find a cell. It does not have to be in a
remote desert. Where is your cell? What happens there?

The Cell as a Place of Transformation and Salvation

The cell is a deeply personal place, a place to be solely with God. It is
a place where the monk can pray "before God's eyes alone" and not with
the added perspective of other people.[20] Jesus' life was filled with times for
personal prayer away from both the crowds and those who were closest to
him. He exhorted his followers to enter their own secret room and be present to their Abba.[21] As in Jesus' personal prayer and solitude, time in the
monk's cell was not anti-social. On the contrary, the cell, as an environment of grace, enables the monk to experience his or her true humanity
that authentically **embodies** the same presence of God experienced in the
cell. The monk **becomes** a cell, a place of God's presence. Stelios Ramfos
underlines the deep theological significance of what takes place within the
cell, for "the aim of human salvation clearly acquires a new meaning: it restores to the soul its **origin and true content** (author's emphasis)."[22]

St. Theodore of Pherme said, "The man who has learnt the sweetness of the cell flees from his neighbor but not as though he despised him." [23] Except for hermits, in the eremitic tradition of Antony, the cell is always related to the rest of the monastic community. As mentioned earlier, in the Pachomian model a monk was required to live in community and gain experience and maturity there before gaining permission to be in a cell that was separated from the community. The desert monks realized the essential rhythm between solitude and community.[24] Solitude and community were seen as complimentary, not competitive. This rhythm has atrophied in modern life. Our responsibilities and needs for productivity have pushed solitude and personal prayer to the margins of personal and public life. Solitude is seen as a benign option for the few, rather than an integral aspect of each person's health and wholeness. The lack of civility, genuine conversation, and desire for collegial approaches to the challenges in our world reflect the absence of solitude in our lives. The outside of our lives reflects the inside of our lives.

The Cell as a Place of Discipline

In addition to its solitude and silence, the cell is an environment for an ascetic discipline that makes space in a person's heart and mind for God's presence. It should not be neglected if one is serious about depending on God for assistance. The discipline of the cell is an attitude of openness, a continual willingness to abide in its environment and to persist in ascetic practice.[25]

"Abba Sisoes was sitting in his cell one day. His disciple knocked on the door and the old man shouted out to him saying, 'Go away, Abraham, do not come in. From now on I have no time for things of this world.'"[26]

"Someone said to Abba Arsenius, 'My thoughts trouble me, saying, "You can neither fast nor work; at least go and visit the sick, for that is also charity."' But the old man, recognizing the suggestions of the demons, said to him, 'Go, eat, drink, sleep, do no work, only do not leave your cell.' For he knew that steadfastness in the cell keeps a monk in the right way."[27]

The "work" of the cell must have its own integrity in relation to the monk's life outside the cell, yet persistence in the cell required **trust**. The fruits of that trust would lead to wisdom, transformation of self, and an inner healing of the monk and, through the monk, to the world.[28] Fidelity to and regularity in the cell would help the monk look into every person and action outside the cell in a new way.

The cell is an environment for salvation because in that specific place the monk turns to God as the **source** of his or her true self. Salvation is the restoration of the soul to its **true content** rather than a purification of "the pollution of the body."[29] This desert understanding of salvation is in contrast to both the contemporary Greek Gnostic thought of that period which valued the spirit over the body and to the later medieval Christian theology of salvation. The desert elders, and through them the Eastern Orthodox churches, deny any metaphysical dualism separating body and soul. At the same time they acknowledge the immense power of the body, when dominated by the unrestrained ego, to influence and dominate the soul, distracting a person away from his or her natural and sacred state. Therefore, emphasis is given to discipline the body and to place its influence under control of the soul. While this may appear as a dualistic relationship it is in reality a very street-wise recognition of the struggle every human being experiences. It reflects an "ethical dualism" or dilemma of **behavior,** rather that a dualism of **being.**[30] In this context, salvation is the union of the desires and behaviors of the body with the soul, the completion of the whole person. Salvation is congruency between the image of God in each person and the manifestation of the likeness of God in his or her manner of life. Salvation is the birth of the true self, made possible by God's grace.

A glimpse of this awareness of salvation may be seen in two comments by Pachomius relating to what he calls spiritual miracles:

> After the manifest healings of the body, there are also spiritual healings. For if a man intellectually blind, in that he does not see the light of God because of idolatry, afterwards is guided by faith in the Lord and gains his sight, in coming to know the only true God, is not this a great healing and salvation? . . .
> One of the brethren asked me [Pachomius], "Tell us one of the visions you see." And I said to him, A sinner like me does not ask God that he may see visions: for that is against His will, and is error. . .Hear all the same about a great vision. If you see a man pure and humble, it is a great vision. For what is greater than such a vision, to see the Invisible God in a visible man, His temple?[31]

The desert elders' experience of salvation clearly has roots in the Jewish heritage of Jesus. The Hebrew Scriptures, especially the Psalms, were an essential focus for meditation in the cell. The comments by Pachomius reflect an earlier understanding of transformation expressed by the prophet Ezekiel, speaking as God's messenger: "Have I any pleasure in the death of the wicked, says the Lord God, and not rather that they should turn from their ways and live?" (Ezek 18:23, NRSV). At the same time, the wisdom of

Pachomius, as well as Evagrius, would have a significant influence on the thinking of the great hesychast and Archbishop of Thessalonica, Gregory Palamas (1296–1358): "What connection should we have with Christ, if he had made a temple in the first fruits taken from men, without making us temples of his divinity?"[32]

The monk's experience of God in the cell occurred in a variety of ways, but the role of meditation on the Scriptures, the Word of God, was central. The Bible was central, but not as an end in itself. It provided a monk, through meditation, with opportunities to encounter the Spirit in prayer for personal guidance and discernment, not simply as "knowledge," but as encounter. "For interpretation of the Bible, the imperative is to probe beyond the letter and history to the spiritual mysteries (sacramenta) within, to get under the skin of the text and live inside it so that the biblical words become one's own spiritual bones, sinews, and flesh."[33] This understanding of Scripture as "personal encounter" reflects the thought and experience of Origen of Alexandria. As we have seen, he taught that within a person's recitation of and meditation on Scripture a grace is present through which that person is led beyond the meanings of the words to experience the divine Presence unique to that person's experience.[34]

The monks in Egypt had access to the Bible in their own Coptic language and would have heard Scripture in the liturgy and in the teaching of their mentors. They were able to memorize great portions of Scripture and many of those who were illiterate were taught to read. In the same way that the Bible was not an end in itself for prayer and meditation, it was never divorced from the pastoral and practical activities of daily life:

> The silence and solitude of the desert, for instance, which so clearly revealed the hidden motivations of the heart, focused the attention of the desert fathers upon moral, ascetical, and psychological questions in a particularly acute way. The practical orientation of the desert fathers means that interpretation of Scripture in the Sayings almost never occurs for its own sake but is imbedded in the life and concerns of the desert.[35]

In this way, the Bible was an integral part of the personal transformation that took place in the cell. One could say that the Bible was part of the mystical "topos" of the cell and led the monk to contemplate his or her true "content" as a human being.

"His divine power has given us everything needed for life and godliness, through the knowledge of him who called us by his own glory and goodness. Thus he has given us, through these things, his precious and very great promises, so that through them you may escape from the corruption that is in the world because of lust, and may become participants of the divine nature" (2 Pet 1:3-4, NRSV). "Do you not know that you are God's temple and that God's Spirit dwells in you?" (1 Cor 3:16, NRSV).

In summary, the cell restores a monk, or any person, to true humanity that **embodies** God's presence. By turning to God as our true Source and content (by receiving the Other), we are disposed, by choice, to be compassionate to all others. The practicalities of daily life must be interwoven with the resurrected life we seek. Thus, the cell, whose integrity and environmental influence must be guarded, does not reject either the body or society. Rather, the cell is the place where each person learns to embody truth and the presence of God. By turning away from the self-serving control of the ego, we become open to grace, which lies beyond our control, yet teaches us who we really are. The cell is the place where one experiences authentic humanity and learns of God's desires.

The Cell as Sacred Space

As we have seen, the cell is the reason for anachoresis. The monk withdraws to find a **place** for solitude, silence, and transformation. The cell is different from the rest of the inhabited world because of what happens in the cell and in the interior life of the monk. For this reason the monk must **guard the cell** both by being a good steward of what takes place within the cell as "topos" and by a manner of life that manifests God presence in that place.

> The place does not hold the monk; the monk guards the place, because by his life he brings God to it. This is how the inward character of the guarding of the place is to be explained, its direct correlation with spiritual rebirth, which is a matter completely different from any external guarding.[36]

The cell is **guarded** by not allowing anything to profane the integrity of its purpose or to misuse it. This "guarding" does not infer militaristic protection. It is a fundamental aspect of the monk's ascetic practice and applies both to the cell, itself, and to the "cell" of the monk's interior and exterior life.

> Amma Syncletica said, "There are many who live in the mountains and behave as if they were in the town, and they are wasting their time. It is possible to be a solitary in one's mind while living in a crowd, and it is possible for one who is a solitary to live in the crowd of personal thoughts."[37]

Guarding the cell acknowledges that what a person thinks, does, sees, takes into his or her life or habitually experiences will facilitate a positive openness to grace and movement toward transformation. At the same time it can negatively direct the "content" of a person's life away from his or true self. This tension between what happens in solitude and in relation to the rest of the world was sometimes uneasy.

> Monastic life is often described as consisting in the renunciation of the world. Properly understood, the statement may stand, but its starkness may lead to misconceptions. The caricature of the monk as a world-hater, unfortunately supported by evidence from monastic literature itself, misses the point. The separation from ordinary society effected by withdrawal to the desert, or by the cloister, or by vows, is ideally less a quarantine than an opportunity. Nonetheless, the break with conventional human society is genuine, and these stories depict the tensions which can arise from the decision to choose the monastic alternative.[38]

This is true, also, for persons who are not monks. It is not easy for us to integrate the movements of our spiritual lives and values into our families, our workplaces and the rest of our "inhabited world." At the same time we must avoid letting the values and behaviors of a materialistic and often profane society deflect us from the "cell" of our personal relationship with God. By guarding this cell we learn to manifest what happens there in the way we live. It is stewardship of the sacredness of our lives.

The Cell and Love of Neighbor

The external environment of a society, family or religious community reflects the internal environment of the human beings who form it. Jesus said, "By their fruit you shall know them" (Matt 7:16, NRSV). In the cell the monk's interior life is formed in such a way that he or she becomes what the cell makes possible. The physical enclosure of the cell houses the activities of God's transforming Spirit. In the same way, the monk's flesh and whole being become a cell, a place of transformation wherever he or she is living. The monk's anachoresis makes an ascetic praxis possible, which in turn transforms the monk and his manner of life. The external life of the monk has the possibility to transform other people and society. This **sacrifice,** the offering of one's self to God that restores a monk's original nature, is what can establish a moral climate in society.

Amma Syncletica said:

> Their attitude is characterized by brotherly love rather than self love, for they regard those who sin as houses on fire; giving no thought to their own interests, they apply their efforts to save what belongs to others and is being

destroyed. . . . This is the sign of genuine love; these people are custodians of pure love.[39]

The cell can become the womb that gives birth to morality. At the same time moral decadence can pollute any place, whether it is the cell, society or the natural world. Abba John the Eunuch said, "My sons, let us not make this place dirty, since our Fathers cleansed it from demons."[40]

This brings to mind Jesus' cleansing of the Temple. The "cell" of his faith community had been morally compromised by the money changers and the Temple authorities. The monks of the desert realized the wisdom of Jesus' action. The moral integrity of a faith community (a corporate "cell") is where authentic human living is formed. The sacrifice of time and commitment to the life of that community is necessary to "guard" the sacredness of all life.

In the cell a person's soul is open. This vulnerability to the movement of God is necessary for the control of the ego's self-centeredness to be overcome. In the solitude of the cell we learn, also, how to live in community. The aim of our "inwardness" and ascetical practice is **not to abolish** the unrestrained ego, the false self, but to open the ego to grace. When a person experiences a new birth, as Jesus explained to Nicodemus in John 3:1-10, that person's new "first breath" is communion with God. This is the source of personal self-giving to the world and of a truly creative and authentic civilization. This self-giving requires an awareness which dispels divisions and produces ethical living.

> The same amma [Theodora] said that a teacher ought to be a stranger to the desire for domination, vain-glory, and pride; one should not be able to fool him by flattery, nor blind him by gifts, nor conquer him by the stomach, nor dominate him by anger; but he should be patient, gentle and humble as far as possible; he must be tested and without partisanship, full of concern, and a lover of souls.[41]

The Cell and the World

Is anachoresis a rejection of the inhabited world? Is the solitude and inwardness of the cell a selfish endeavor? The desert abbas and ammas helped form a wider Christian monastic tradition that combines seeking God with **conversion of life.** In the cell the monk risks all in the battle between the ego (subjectivity) and openness to the Other. Through ascetic praxis the boundaries of the self are extended beyond itself and the opportunity for transformation is made possible.[42]

One purpose of the cell is to make a new reality of time present to the "open soul."[43] This new experience of time fills the soul with a life of prayer that absorbs the love of God and **expands** the cell to include the monk's daily living beyond the cell.

> One day Abba Daniel and Abba Ammoes went on a journey together. Abba Ammoes said, "When shall we, too, settle down, in a cell, Father?" Abba Daniel replied, "Who shall separate us henceforth from God? God is in the cell, and, on the other hand, he is outside also."[44]

The goal of the monk's openness in the cell is to allow the realm of God to fit itself within the monk's soul. **The cell and the world can then occupy the same space.** "Abba Poemen said, 'Teach your mouth to say what is in your heart.'"[45] The spiritual praxis of the cell becomes integrated with all other aspects of the monk's life.

> A brother questioned Abba Poemen saying, "I have found a place where peace is not disturbed by the brethren; do you advise me to live there?" The old man said to him, "The place for you is where you will not harm your brother."[46]

In the cell, where ascetical practice occupies the monk's chronological time, eschatological time breaks in so that the monk can see all time in the context of the eternal purposes of God. The values of God's realm become embodied in chronological time and the monk experiences eternal life within time and space![47]

In summary, the grace of a cell is that through openness we can see ourselves as **more** than our ego. We learn that we are not fully human until we become aware of our completeness in a Reality beyond ourselves. The cell, then, is a home where we are guided to that complete humanity whose boundaries are congruent with the realm of God. Therefore, the cell **extends** our experience rather than limiting it. Union with God initiates a simultaneous communion with our historical and chronological community, but with eyes to see its eternal purpose and sanctity. The cell is necessary to overcome **insensitivity** to the world, which is sin. It does not imprison us from life. It extends us further into life. It brings us home.

The influence of a cell extends far beyond the deserts of Egypt and the lives of the desert fathers and mothers. We must find ways to withdraw from our twenty-first-century "inhabited world" and balance our busy and responsible lives with disciplined prayer in a cell appropriate for each of our lives. Without this intentional withdrawal for solitude, we risk closing our hearts and minds to the flow of God's Spirit in our lives. Personal prayer in our cells, whenever they are, is opening our souls to the energies of God.

Notes

1. *The Sayings of the Desert Fathers: The Alphabetical Collection.*, trans. Benedicta Ward, S.L.G. (Kalamazoo: Cistercian Publications, 1984) Moses 6, 139.

2. Pseudo-Athanasius, *The Life of Blessed Syncletica*, trans. Elizabeth Bryson Bongie (Toronto: Peregrina, 1999) v. 31, 26.

3. Ward, *Sayings*, Theodora 5, 83–84.

4. Stelios Ramfos, *Like a Pelican in the Wilderness*, trans. Norman Russell (Brookline: Holy Cross Orthodox Press, 2000) 11.

5. Ibid., 11.

6. Ibid., 25.

7. For photographs, see *Coptic Orthodox Monastery of St. Antony the Great-Red Sea Egypt.* Prepared by Bishop Dioscorous for the Coptic Patriarchate. Anba Reuis Press. Photographs by Nabil Selim Atalla.

8. Philip Rousseau, *Pachomius:The Making of a Community in Fourth Century Egypt* (Berkeley: University of California Press, 1999) 78–79. For a detailed description of daily life in a Pachomian community, see chs. 4 and 5.

9. Ramfos, *Pelican*, 29.

10. Ramfos, *Pelican*, 26. The remainder of this section is indebted to the research of Ramfos in ch. 5 of *Pelican* entitled "The Cell." I take responsibility for my own conclusions.

11. Charles Cummings, O.C.S.O., *Monastic Practices* (Kalamazoo: Cistercian Publications, 1986) 154.

12. Ward, *Sayings*, Antony 10, 3.

13. See Ramfos, *Pelican*, 36ff.

14. Ward, *Sayings*, John the Dwarf 12, 87.

15. Ibid., see 32–33.

16. Ibid., see 31–34.

17. Ibid.

18. Ibid., see 33.

19. Ward, *Sayings*, Rufus 1, 210.

20. Cummings, *Monastic Practices*, 155.

21. Luke 9:18; Mark 1:35; and Matt 6:5-6, for example.

22. Ramfos, *Pelican*, 34.

23. Ward, *Sayings*, Theodore of Pherme 14, 76.

24. For a detailed study of the relationship between monastic solitude and community, see A. M. Allchin, ed., *Solitude and Communion* (Oxford: SLG Press, 1983).

25. Cummings, *Monastic Practices*, 156–57.

26. Ward, *Sayings*, Sisoes 27, 218.

27. Ibid., Arsenius, 6, 10.

28. Cummings, *Monastic Practices*, 159.

29. Stelios Ramos, *Pelican*, 34.

30. See Nicholas Arseniew, *Mysticism and the Eastern Church*, trans. Arthur Chambers (London: Student Christian Movement, 1926) Chapter 3 "Asceticism and Transformation," 45–54.

31. *S. Pachomii Vita graecae*, ed. Halkin, Subsidia hagiographica 19, Brussels, 1932, cc. 47–48, quoted in Derwas J. Chitty, *The Desert a City* (Crestwood, N.Y.: St. Vladimir's Seminary Press, 1995) 28.

32. *Against Akindynos, III, fol. 74v.* trans. John Meyendorff in *A Study of Gregory Palamas* (Crestwood, N.Y.: St. Vladimir's Seminary Press, 1998) 182.

33. Columba Stewart, O.S.B., *Cassian the Monk* (Oxford: Oxford University Press, 1998) 85.

34. See Joseph Milne, *The Ground of Being: Foundations of Christian Mysticism* (London: Temenos Academy, 2004) 29.

35. Douglas Burton-Christie, *The Word in the Desert* (Oxford: Oxford University Press, 1993) 61.

36. Ramfos, *Pelican*, 30.

37. Ward, *Sayings*, Syncletica, 19, 234.

38. Columba Stewart, O.S.B., *The World of the Desert Fathers* (Fairacres: SLG Press, 1995) 6.

39. Pseudo-Athanasius, *The Life*, v. 71, 46.

40. Ward, *Sayings*, John the Eunuch, 5, 105.

41. Ward, *Sayings*, Theodora 5, 83–84.

42. See Ramfos, *Pelican*, 34.

43. Ibid., see 35–36 for a discussion of the movement of God in an open soul.

44. Ward, *Sayings*, Daniel 5, 52.

45. Ibid., Poemen 164, 189.

46. Ibid., Poemen 159, 189.

47. This section on the monk and the world is indebted to Stelios Ramos in *Pelican*, 37–39, but I take responsibility for my own research and conclusions.

5   Patience

Learning Not to Run from God or Ourselves

Abba Antony said "Whatever you find in your heart to do in following God, that do, and remain within yourself in Him."[1]

Partners in the Cell

"Go, sit in your cell, and your cell will teach you everything."[2] Abba Moses knew the cell was essential for the ascetic life of the monk. There must be a specific place for encountering God and one's self. But the "place" was not an end in itself. Abba Ammonas said, "A man may remain for a hundred years in his cell without learning how to live in the cell."[3] There was also the **"sitting."** The **enclosure** of the cell and **remaining in the company of God** within the cell are partners that make ascetic life possible.

"Abba Andrew said, 'These three things are fitting for the monk: exile, poverty and endurance in silence.'"[4] The place for anachoresis is the cell, but as Abba Antony exhorted, patience makes remaining ". . . . within yourself in Him" possible. It is the **"time"** of the ascetic life.[5]

A brother asked an old man, "What shall I do, father, for I am not acting at all like a monk, but I eat, drink, and sleep carelessly; and I have evil thoughts and I am in great trouble, passing from one work to another and from one thought to an other?" The old man said, "Sit in your cell and do the little you can untroubled. For I think the little you can do now is of equal value to the great deeds which Abba Antony accomplished on the mountain, and I believe that by remaining sitting in your cell for the name of God, and guarding your conscience, you also will find the place where Antony is."[6]

The time in the cell was always related to the reason for being in the cell. The monk's path was a way directed toward seeking God and it was a **lifelong** journey. Although all monks were walking this same path there was no single method or body of teaching leading to the destination. Walking the path was always a personal journey, even though it was in the company of others. The ammas and abbas could share their wisdom gained from life experience, but each monk must persist in his or her personal spiritual work. When a brother asked Abba Antony to pray for him, the abba replied, "I will have no mercy on you and neither will God have any, if you yourself do not make an effort and if you do not pray to God."[7]

To modern ears this may sound harsh. But Antony reminds his brother that he must rely not on the merits or experience of others. The Christian's path to transformation requires personal collaboration with the Spirit. Abba Agathon said: "Prayer is hard work and a great struggle to one's last breath."[8]

Yet "the great struggle," like the cell, was not an end in itself. The movement was always toward God and love of neighbor. The "hard work" developed single-minded intent, rather than self-effacing inflexibility. A monk was not only to be patient, but **patient with his- or herself.**

It was said of Antony that one day he was relaxing with the brothers outside the cell when a hunter came by and rebuked him. Antony said, "Bend your bow and shoot an arrow," and he did so. "Bend it again and shoot another," and he did—and again and again. The hunter said, "Father, if I keep my bow always stretched it will break." "And so it is with the monk," replied Antony; "if we push ourselves beyond measure we will break; it is right for us from time to time to relax our efforts."[9]

The turning of one's heart and will to God did not take place in one sector of life; it was and is **a way of life.** It was not an enhancement of life; it was the gradual movement toward authentic human life, itself. Although many people came to visit the ammas and abbas out of curiosity, their monastic life was not a "fad." The desert was not a spiritual "theme park." These men and women were not offering a "quick fix" or a prescription to be applied by others.

They did not have a systematic **way;** they had the hard work and experience of a lifetime of striving to re-direct every aspect of body, mind, and soul to God, and that is what they talked about. That, also, is what they meant by prayer: prayer was not an activity undertaken for a few hours each day, it was a life continually turned toward God.[10]

The patience and persistence of desert ascetic life was hard work, but not gloomy. It was empowered by God's love and vision for each person. The dedication and guarding of time in the cell produced a new vision of life, God's vision. Roberta Bondi, in a beautifully pastoral reflection on the desert tradition, writes:

> The love of the monastics was also extravagantly patient and extravagantly hopeful, based as it was on the patience and hope of God. . . . Whatever happened, (they) knew that (they), and all people, live out of and in the love of God.[11]

And, as the Syrian monk Pseudo-Macarius knew from his years of patient experience in the desert:

> As near as the body is to the soul . . . . so much nearer is God present, to come and open the locked doors of our heart and to fill us with heavenly riches . . . . (God's) promises cannot deceive, provided we only persevere to the end . . . . Glory be to the compassionate mercies of (God) forever! Amen.[12]

There is encouragement here for our busy lives and those parts of our society that seem hopelessly polarized. If we can develop patience in our relationship with God then we will learn to value patience in our relationships with other people. It will affect how we listen to each other and how we resolve conflicts. Persistence in our personal prayer helps us to be present to God and await God's movement in our lives. This same stature of waiting will help us become more present to the persons we encounter each day, especially in times of pain and misunderstanding. Patience is the virtue that makes civility and mutual love possible.

The Biblical Roots of Patience in Desert Asceticism

The sources of desert wisdom are the sayings of the abbas and ammas and written accounts of incidents from their lives. The wisdom embodied in their actions and teaching was formed through years of meditation and teaching about the Bible and the life of Jesus of Nazareth. The Greek words used for patience in these sources can help us understand the role of patience in the lives of the desert monks.

The Greek verb *"hypomeno"* can have many meanings in English depending on its context: stay behind, remain alive, await attack from another, abide patiently, stand one's ground, wait to do a thing, endure patiently and await something.[13] As a noun, hypomeno can mean endurance (of a condition), a negative obstinacy, or sojourn in a specific place. In the Greek translation of the Hebrew Scriptures, the *Septuagint,* patience is associated primarily with endurance of consequences from an external influence. The sufferings of Job are the clearest example. In the New Testament and early Christian patristic writings patience refers to not only a sense of enduring **exterior** challenges or hardships, but also an interior virtue of the soul or a personal characteristic. St. Paul speaks of an exterior context in 2 Corinthians 1:6 (NRSV): "If we are being afflicted, it is for your consolation and salvation; if we are being consoled, it is for your consolation, which you experience when you **patiently endure** the same sufferings that we are suffering." In interior contexts patience takes on a demeanor of waiting, expectation and trust. St. Paul speaks, also, of these latter meanings:

". . . but we also boast in our sufferings, knowing that suffering produces **endurance,** and **endurance** produces character, and character produces hope, and hope does not disappoint us because God's love has been poured into our hearts through the Holy Spirit that has been given to us" (Rom 5:3-5, NRSV), and "For whatever was written in former days was written for our instruction, that by **steadfastness** and by encouragement of the scriptures we might have hope" (Rom 15:4, NRSV).

Thus, patience can mean resisting an exterior force or challenge as well as a demeanor of trust. The monk (the monk's ego) realizes that he or she does not possess all that is necessary for life and is willing to extend the boundaries of his or her sufficiency to include God. Jesus spoke of this kind of patience often and added the challenge that patience is a form of "dying" to one's control of life in order to find life in its fullness. "Very truly I tell you, unless a grain of wheat falls into the earth and dies, it remains just a single grain; but if it dies, it bears much fruit. Those who love their life lose it, and those who hate their life in this world will keep it for eternal life" (John 12:24-25, NRSV).

Patience as a Characteristic of Prayerful Living

Patience Is a Fundamental Human Virtue

One of the natural consequences of ascetic life in the desert was the manifestation of God in the abbas and ammas. People around them recognized an authority and authenticity that did not depend on external knowledge or credentials. Like Jesus, they "glorified God's name" by the way they lived. Although they would never have described themselves in this way or taken credit for such a role, the wisdom of the ammas and abbas was the child of their patience and persistence in ascetic practice in the context of their experience of daily life.

What was their patience like? Is it possible for us to understand what they meant by "patience" or "persistence"? How did they manifest patience?[14] Patience was, simultaneously, both a means and an end. It helped **form** the monk and, in time, became a **characteristic** of monastic life. There is no doubt that "staying with the program" and "showing up" in the presence of the hard work of ascetic praxis was a necessary part of seeking God. Abba Esias said, "Nothing is so profitable to the beginner as being insulted; for the beginner who bears insults with patience is like a tree which is watered every day."[15] In this context, insults were directed to the wearing down of both self-sufficiency and personal credit for proficiency. It takes time to develop a willingness to depend on God and the example of others.

Patience Is Practical

Patience is practical in that it is necessary, within chronological time, to overcome obstacles to seeking God and barriers which prevent openness to God's grace. It is a **factor** that contributes to transformation. Patience is also a **manifestation** of an open and God-filled life. It is a **characteristic** of a manner of life which embodies God's presence.

Patience was seen as an alternative to the mind's and the ego's need for "immediate action." A perceived need for progress in sanctification or responding to a physical need or challenge could easily deflect the monk from the necessary balance between body and soul in ascetic life.

> Abba Ammonas once went to cross the river and found the ferry untended and seated himself nearby it. Just then another boat arrived at that place and embarked the people waiting there in order to take them across. And they said to him, "You come too, Abba, and cross over with us." But he said, "I will only board the public ferry." He had a bundle of palm leaves and sat plaiting a rope and then undoing it until the ferry was made ready. And so he went across. Then the brothers bowed low before him and said, "Why did you do this?" And the elder said to them, "That I may not always be dwelling on my thought." And this is also an example that we may walk the path of God in tranquility.[16]

From the monk's mind's or ego's point of view, life's challenges, opportunities, and hardships often demand a rapid response or solution. This impatience can overlook a deep spiritual perspective on the situation. It can mask the "real situation" and lead to choosing inappropriate actions or resources to meet the need. It can lure the monk away from his or her cell and from communion with God.

> An affliction befell some brothers in the place where they were living, and wishing to abandon it they went to find Abba Ammonas. And it happened

that the elder was coming by boat down the river. And when he saw them walking along the bank of the river, he said to the boatman, "Put me ashore." And calling to the brothers he said to them, "I am Ammonas, whom you wish to visit." And having encouraged them, he made them return to the place from which they had come. For the matter was connected not with spiritual damage, but with human affliction.[17]

Various calamities and hardships may lead a person to become discouraged, fearful, or hopeless. But unless such thoughts are allowed to harm a person's soul, he or she can, with patient asceticism, gain the strength to live through such hardships. Patience helps a person avoid letting such physical hardships become harmful to the soul.

Twenty-first-century cultures have become increasingly impatient. Fast food, fast credit, ever faster traffic and quick and efficient solutions to conflict, including war, are hallmarks of our era. It is difficult to be a leader in today's society. The pressures for results are intense. With communications and events taking place with greater speed, the public demands quicker responses and solutions. Leaders in all sectors of modern life have little time to ponder decisions. Patience is no longer a virtue in this age of "rapid response teams." Politicians and leaders in business are often considered weak or "flip-floppers" if they take time to weigh options or balance their public responsibilities with scholarly, literary or even technical reflection. Leaders who have learned from experience and who change their minds, in time, are considered dishonest. This modern impatience places a higher value on the moment and short-term results than on longer-term vision and development.

There are dangers in such a fast-moving society. The soul of society as well as individual souls are at stake. What are we becoming and who are we becoming in our "results rule" frenzy? How is the speed of modern life affecting the sacredness and quality of human lives and the earth's resources. Is it possible to change this momentum? What will happen if our impatience continues indefinitely?

Patience Supports Commitment to Personal Prayer

The work of ascetic life was not easy. Its pattern could never be taken for granted. There was no room for simply "going through the motions." "It was said of Abba Agathon that for three years he lived with a stone in his mouth, until he had learnt to keep silence."[18] There were temptations to "give up" or leave and there was always the possibility of "greener pastures."

The fathers used to say, "If a temptation comes to you in the place where you live, do not leave the place at the time of temptation, for wherever you go you will find that which you fled from there before you. But stay until the temptation is past, that your departure may not cause offence and may be done in peace, and then you will not cause any distress amongst those who dwell in the place."[19]

An old man said, "Just as a tree cannot bring forth good fruit if it is always being transplanted, so the monk who is always going from one place to another is not able to bring forth virtue."[20]

A monk could become easily discouraged from ascetic praxis by the presence of lingering thoughts, especially those related to the life they had left behind in "the inhabited world." Unless these passions were redirected toward God's desires for the monk, spiritual transformation would not be possible. In this intense aspect of spiritual warfare, the ammas and abbas learned that wicked thoughts or opportunities can be neutralized by delaying the time from the thought to its being put into action. According to Abba Poemen this delay takes place through patient endurance.

It is like having a chest full of clothes, if one leaves them in disorder they are spoiled in the course of time. It is the same with thoughts. If we do not do anything about them, in time they are spoiled, that is to say, they disintegrate. . . . If someone shuts a snake and a scorpion up in a bottle, in time they will be completely destroyed. So it is with evil thoughts: they are suggested by the demons; they disappear through patience.[21]

Patience Manifests a New Awareness of Time

Another old man came to see one of the Fathers, who cooked a few lentils and said to him, "Let us say a few prayers," and the first completed the whole psalter, and the brother recited the two great prophets by heart. When morning came, the visitor went away, and they forgot the food.[22]

Sanctification of the monk is a state of being in which the life of the person manifests the likeness of God. Sanctification is a living in the **now**, rather than a goal to be achieved at some later time. The cell is a place where the challenges and hardships of life, inside and outside the cell, may be seen from a wider point of view. This wider perspective is essential to developing openness to God's grace.

Patience, therefore, was not seen as the simple passing of time. It was a different **understanding** of time, itself. It was a willingness to place one's self in "God's time" (in Greek, the *eschaton,* or *eschatological time*). In eschatological time each moment is filled with both "what needs to be done" and the inner awareness that God is present in that need and desires its fulfillment. Once again, I am indebted to insights of Stelios Ramfos for understanding the relationship between monastic patience and time from the Eastern Orthodox point of view.[23] While this wisdom is present in Western churches, especially in monasticism and liturgy, it has remained a hallmark of Eastern Orthodox spirituality since the formation of the desert tradition.

Time was **experienced** differently by the desert elders. Chronological time depends on duration. It can impose limitations on the ego when it is associated with completing a goal. It establishes a boundary for expectations and the ego strains to accomplish what it desires. Time accentuates the need for control of what happens within time. This is a major source of anxiety and can lead to despair.[24]

> An old man said, "For nine years a brother was tempted in thought to the point of despairing of his salvation, and being scrupulous he condemned himself, saying, 'I have lost my soul, and since I am lost I shall go back to the world.' But while he was on the way, a voice came to him on the road, which said, 'These nine years which you have been tempted have been crowns for you; go back to your place, and I will allay these thoughts.' Understand that it is not good for someone to despair of himself because of his temptations; rather, temptations procure crowns for us if we use them well."[25]

Patience is the resistance to duration. We resist the duration of time, not its passing—time does not demand resistance, seeing that it passes anyway. We resist that which endows time with duration: affliction, waiting, anxiety, and it is precisely in this resistance that the soul is shaped.[26]

In the case of the monk mentioned above who despaired of his temptations, the duration of time was filled with traces of pain, anxiety, endless wicked thoughts and fear for his salvation. The old man was saying that patience resists these traces which give the duration, the seemingly endlessness, of time its power. The patient enduring of the temptations in the context of ascetic praxis is an opportunity for the soul to be formed and grow. The power of enduring patience (in this case nine years!) is its awareness that in the midst of the temptations the "crown" or fulfillment of the monk's seeking God is also present. The old man had learned from his own temptations that patience is not merely the "passing of time," but the faithful awareness that **God's time is present in our waiting.** By being open to the presence of God in the duration of what the monk is experiencing, with its anxieties, the monk is also open to release from the temptations and inner healing.

The young monk despaired for his salvation because his ego-controlled mind assumed his progress was too slow. The old man was aware that lack of patience can lead to despair because what the young monk wanted to accomplish was linked to the passage of time. When this happens we panic and lose vision because it seems we do not have "enough time." A patient person links his or her hope to the new life which is possible, not to the passage of time. Time is no longer the master. Patience makes the boundary of chronological time transparent. Without patience, time is a despot (managed by our ego) in which we succumb to ". . . . the illusion that we hold in our hands all the potentialities of existence."[27]

Patience Provides Space for Daily Repentance and Transformation

Abba Antony said:

Having therefore made a beginning, and set out already on the way to virtue, let us press forward to what lies ahead. And let none turn back as Lot's wife did, especially since the Lord said, "No one who puts his hand to the plow and turns back is fit for the Kingdom of heaven." Now "turning back" is nothing except feeling regret and once more thinking about things of the world. But do not be afraid to hear about virtue, and do not be a stranger to the term. For it is not distant from us, nor does it stand external to us, but its realization lies within us, and the task is easy if only we shall will it.[28]

Repentance is a turning toward God with a desire for newness of life. Although initially it may have a specific beginning in time, it is a continuous movement toward God. Repentance creates a daily environment for transformation. It is not a moment etched in stone that lasts forever. Abba Antony speaks of this daily environment as "the way of virtue" and reminds monks and lay persons, alike, that if one is serious about this path one must keep looking forward. Although the destination lies within us, the journey away from attachment to "the things of the world" allows no looking back. This illustrates the intersection of chronological time and the eschaton, God's time. Each monk's transformation already lies within and yet the manifestation of that virtue is a struggle within chronological time. This is the struggle, the spiritual warfare of the desert: the tension between the monk's desire for what already lies within and the distractions and disturbances of the world which he allows to deflect him from what he desires.[29]

The abbas and ammas realized there are many things which can deflect and scatter the monk's desire for God. The ego would rather not have us discover our true self and the virtue within us. The list of distractions and temptations includes "good" things as well as "wicked" things. Listen again to Arsenius:

> Someone said to Abba Arsenius, "My thoughts trouble me, saying, 'You can neither fast nor work; at least go and visit the sick, for that also is charity.'" But the old man, recognizing the suggestions of the demons, said to him, "Go, eat, drink, sleep, do no work, only do not leave your cell." For he knew that steadfastness in the cell keeps a monk in the right way.[30]

Arsenius, echoing Antony's wisdom, is aware of the danger of being scattered. The frustration of not being able to follow the rule within the cell leads the monk, through the demons in his thoughts, to "try something else." Arsenius remembers the importance of "patient endurance" in the cell. If the work is discouraging, relaxation is possible and appropriate. But the monk should not leave the environment where, through the rule, he turns toward and experiences God's presence.

Patience Withstands Demonic Influences

When the desert monks left the inhabited world, every monk brought parts of his or her former life with them. Memories, thoughts, fantasies, regrets, old lusts, pride, unfulfilled desires, anger, fear, unresolved conflict and a host of other remnants of the "world" were present in their cells. At the same time they found a new "world" in the desert in the lives of other monks, visitors, local towns and villages and the rich, yet austere ascetic life they had chosen.

Any of these influences could become disturbances along the monk's path toward virtue and **scatter** the monk's focus to stay centered on the path. As we saw in chapter 3, this danger was personified in the presence of demons and the chief of demons, diabolos, the "devil." Sometimes it was difficult to discern the influence of the demons and only the wisdom of the more experienced "warriors" could identify a demonic presence for what it was. Abba Antony offered advice for recognizing the presence of demons and patiently withstanding their influences:

> Let us likewise understand and take it to heart that while the Lord is with us, the enemies will do nothing to us. For when they come, their actions correspond to the condition in which they find us; they pattern their phantasms after our thoughts. Should they find us frightened and distressed, immediately they attack like robbers, having found the place unprotected. Whatever we are turning over in our minds, this—and more—is what they do. For if

they see that we are fearful and terrified, they increase even more what is dreadful in the apparitions and threats, and the suffering soul is punished with these. However, should they discover us rejoicing in the Lord, thinking about the good things to come, contemplating things that have to do with the Lord, reflecting that all things are in the hand of the Lord, and that a demon has no strength against a Christian, nor has he any authority over anyone—then seeing the soul safeguarded by such thoughts, they are put to shame and turned away.[31]

Abba Antony had experienced everything he describes in this passage. He learned that evil is the scattering of mind and spirit away from God's presence. When the monk's focus is deflected away from God he or she becomes subject to the demons. The demonic influences do not drive out God; they mask the awareness of God's presence and transformative power. Patient endurance in prayer, contemplation, and "things that have to do with the Lord" is required. Antony knew that a new moment of repentance will restore a turning toward God, **who has never abandoned the monk.** He also said, "For the joy and the stability of the soul attest to the one who is in your presence."[32] Patience is not inactivity. It is a courageous act of detachment from thoughts, temptations or acts that try to shatter the monk's heart and drive it away from the Spirit within. Patience and trust in God's presence gives birth to a **purity** or wholeness of heart which can re-harmonize the monk's whole being in God.

A brother questioned an old man, saying, "My thoughts wander and I am troubled by this." The old man said to him, "Remain sitting in your cell and your thoughts will come to rest. For truly, just as when the she-ass is tied her colt runs here and there but always comes back to his mother wherever she is, so it is with the thoughts of him who for God's sake remains steadfast in the cell: even if they wander a little they will always come back to him."[33]

Daily Awareness of One's Death

Abba Antony said:

Therefore, my children, let us hold to the discipline, and not be careless. For we have the Lord for our co-worker in this, as it is written, God works for good with everyone who chooses the good. And in order that we not become negligent, it is good to carefully consider the Apostle's statement: I die daily.[34]

Abba Antony taught that a monk must live in such a way that the presence of God is always before him and, likewise, that God's presence should become a reality in his manner of life. This manner of life is made possible by an open heart, an inner place that is always watchful and receptive to the presence of God. But how does one practice this essential aspect of monastic life?

Abba Evagrius said:

> Sit in your cell, collecting your thoughts. Remember the day of your death. See then what the death of your body will be; let your spirit be heavy, take pains, condemn the vanity of the world, so as to be able always to live in the peace you have in view without weakening. . . . Always keep your death in mind and do not forget the eternal judgment, then there will be no fault in your soul"[35]

A brother asked Abba Cronius, "How can a man become humble?" The old man said to him, "Through the fear of God." The brother said, "And by what work does he come to the fear of God?" The old man said, "In my opinion, he should withdraw from all business and give himself to bodily affliction and with all his might remember that he will leave his body at the judgment of God."[36]

These passages may sound morbid to modern ears and could be interpreted as a renunciation of earthly life. Yet abbas Cronius and Evagrius recommend consciousness of one's death as a way of becoming more aware of the sanctity of life. When we are able to see life as a gift and acknowledge our dependence on God, we are released from the anxiety of being in control of our lives. The body and its mortality take on a new value. Being aware of one's mortality and conscious of one's death takes a person beyond the ego's concept of time as an endless resource. It releases us from the ego's desire for time to keep going and the accompanying anxiety of knowing that it **will** end. It opens the heart to value existence in a new way. Accepting one's "end" reminds each person to remain present to Christ's new life each day and await daily conversion. Acknowledging one's mortality creates a new vision of the **body** by linking a person's limited physical life to a **timeless** value. This inspires each person to shape his or her life in a way that is congruent with Christ, whose life is not dependent on time. It keeps us from taking ourselves too seriously. Abba Antony's words are worth repeating:

> Therefore, my children, let us hold to the discipline, and not be careless. For we have the Lord for our co-worker in this, as it is written, God works for good with everyone who chooses the good. And in order that we not become negligent, it is good to carefully consider the Apostle's statement: I die daily.[37]

Patience Is a Trustworthy Guide for Living with Other People

There were two monks living in one place, and a great old man came to visit them with the intention of testing them. He took a stick and began to bang about the vegetables of one of them. Seeing it, the brother hid himself, and when only one shoot was left, he said to the old man, "Abba, if you will, leave it so that I can cook it that we may eat together." Then the old man bowed in penitence to the brother, saying, "Because of your long-suffering, the Holy Spirit rests on you, brother."[38]

Patience is also manifested in **long-suffering,** a commitment to being present. In this way a person can live with another in personally troubling times. It makes "spiritual solidarity"[39] possible in the midst of conflict.

Abba Paul the Barber and his brother Timothy lived in Scetis. They often used to argue. Abba Paul said, "How long shall we go on like this?" Abba Timothy said to him, "I suggest you take my side of the argument and in my turn I will take your side when you oppose me." They spent the rest of their days in this practice.[40]

Patience is not an aspect of moral action. It is "a moral power which creates time."[41] In the absence of time that could be filled with impulsive activity we are able to see the challenge or decision before us in the light of our communion with God. In this way any subsequent actions have the opportunity to manifest the actual life of God. Patience makes both simplicity and humility possible by creating a **holy waiting,** regardless of its duration in chronological time. In this holy waiting we are guided to discern or act not only from personal desire or need, but also from the perspective of God's time and life in the situation. This is not a simplistic "resting between the rounds" in a boxing match. It is not some **thing** that is applied to a situation. It is a characteristic and pattern of holy living. It is difficult to practice and it does not always "work." But even when we fail, **God's unconditional presence** (long-suffering), often in the life of another person, accepts and inspires us:

It was said of Abba Isidore, priest of Scetis, that when anyone had a brother who was sick, or careless or irritable, and wanted to send him away, he said, "Bring him here to me." Then he took charge of him and by his long-suffering he cured him.[42]

Abba Isidore became a living expression of the patience of God. He never lost sight of the sanctity of the quarrelsome and abusive brothers he took in. There are few details about what he did with them. It could not have been easy. It must have been hard work, the fruit of a lifetime of prayer. Love, itself, is not efficient. It is the motivation that gives meaning and integrity to our actions, regardless of how long they take.[43]

> A brother asked (Isidore), "Why are the demons so frightened of you?" The old man said to him, "Because I have practiced asceticism since the day I became a monk, and not allowed anger to reach my lips."[44]

Isidore made Christ tangible. This is the most profound achievement in any person's life. By patient prayer and love of neighbor, a person is shaped into a manifestation of Christ and shares that presence with others as a legacy so that, in turn, they too may have life. Isidore's awareness of the value of the troublesome brothers' lives was shaped by his experience of God.

> The same Abba Isidore said, "It is the wisdom of the saints to recognize the will of God. Indeed, in obeying the truth, man surpasses everything else, for he is the image and likeness of God. Of all evil suggestions, the most terrible is that of following one's own heart, that is to say, one's own thought, and not the law of God. A man who does this will be afflicted later on, because he has not recognized the mystery, and has not found the way of the saints in order to work in it. For now is the time to labor for the Lord, for salvation is found in the day of affliction: for it is written, 'By your endurance you will gain your lives'" (Luke 21:19).[45]

Patience is not passivity. We can be sure that Isidore did not just sit around, in prayer, and wait for the irritable brothers to "shape up." We do not know the details, but the way he held them accountable for their actions must have been informed and empowered by his patience. He must have lured them beyond what currently brought them satisfaction. Patience is filled with energy that leads to moral behavior. It conserves and guards the fundamental spiritual values of the world and forms each person into someone whose life is congruent with those same values. Patience helps incarnate the mind of Christ, and this requires the self-awareness learned in the monk's or lay person's cell in prayer. In this way, our practice of patience creates a **culture** in which every human being becomes valued as a sacred being. This transforms the motivation for moral behavior from external obligations to an internal desire to manifest God's love in all aspects of one's life.

The following excerpt from the additions of Rufinus to the *Historia Monachorum* gives a moving picture of a culture where, through patient endurance, the sacredness of life was manifested in the lives of the monks.

We saw a certain venerable father there, called Ammonius, a man in whom God had gathered together all his graces. When you saw how much charity he had, you would think you had never seen anything like it. If you considered his humility, you would think him more powerful in this than in anything else. But if you thought about his patience, or his gentleness or his kindness, you would think he excelled in each of these virtues and you would not know which came first. The gift of wisdom and learning was given him by God so abundantly that you would suppose none of the fathers to have gone so far into all the ways of knowledge. All that saw him said that no-one else had ever been so deeply drawn into the inner courts of the wisdom of God.

Also there were his two brothers, Eusebius and Euthymius, while Dioscorus, who was senior to him, had already been raised to the episcopate. These were brothers not only according to the flesh but were kin in their way of life, their practices and in all the virtues of their souls. As for all those brethren who lived in that place, they nourished them as a nurse with her children, strengthening them with teaching, and by their words leading them to shine at the height of perfection.[46]

Notes

1. *The Wisdom of the Desert Fathers,* trans. Benedicta Ward, S.L.G. (Fairacres: SLG Press, 1975) xviii.

2. *The Sayings of the Desert Fathers,* trans. Benedicta Ward, S.L.G. (Kalamazoo: Cistercian Publications, 1984) Moses 6, 139.

3. Ibid., Ammonas, 96, 180.

4. Ibid., Andrew 1, 37.

5. Stelios Ramfos, *Like a Pelican in the Wilderness* (Brookline: Holy Cross Orthodox Monastery Press, 2000). See discussion on 42.

6. Ward, *Wisdom,* 23.

7. Ward. *Sayings,* Antony 16, 4.

8. Ward. *Wisdom,* xii.

9. Ibid., xv.

10. Ibid., xii.

11. Roberta C. Bondi, *To Love as God Loves* (Philadelphia: Fortress Press, 1987) 108–9.

12. *Intoxicated with God: The Fifty Spiritual Sermons of Marcarius,* trans. George C. Maloney, S.J. (Denville: Dimension Books, 1978) homily 11, 82.

13. A more detailed study of the uses of patience in the Bible and the desert tradition is found in Stelios Ramfos, *Pelican,* 45–49. The definitions used in this paragraph are taken from Liddell and Scott's *Greek-English Lexicon.*

14. I am indebted to Stelios Ramfos for his emphasis on the fundamental role of patience in desert asceticism, particularly ch. 4 in *Like Pelican in the Wilderness.*

I am grateful also to Fr. Columba Stewart, O.S.B., professor of monastic studies at St. John's School of Theology, Collegeville, Minnesota, whose course on monastic history has given me many insights.

15. *Gerontikon,* P. B. Paschos, ed. (Athens: 1961) Esias, 180D-181-A. Quoted in Ramfos, *Pelican,* 40.

16. Ibid., Ammonas 6, 120D-121A. Quoted in Ramfos, *Pelican,* 43.

17. Ibid., Ammonas 5, 120CD. Quoted in Ramfos, *Pelican,* 41.

18. Ward, *Sayings,* Agathon 15, 22.

19. Ward, *Wisdom,* 23.

20. Ibid., 24.

21. Ward, *Sayings,* Poemen 20, 21, 169–70.

22. Ward, *Wisdom,* 5.

23. See Ramfos, *Pelican,* 46–49.

24. Ibid., see 47.

25. Ibid., 25.

26. Ibid., 47.

27. Ibid., 47.

28. Athanasius, *The Life of Antony and the Letter to Marcellinus,* trans. Robert C. Gregg (Mahwah, N.J.: Paulist Press, 1980) 46.

29. This struggle is recognized in the monastic vow of *conversatio.* It is a commitment to daily growth and transformation, recognizing that mystery of our life with God is not a goal we attain, but an evolving manner of life that draws us ever deeper into the heart of God and is manifested in the way we live.

30. Ward, *Sayings,* Arsenius 11, 10.

31. Anthanasius, *Life of Antony,* 63.

32. Ibid., 46.

33. Ward, *Wisdom,* 22.

34. Athanasius, *The Life of Antony,* 45.

35. Ward, *Sayings,* Evagrius 1, 63–64.

36. Ibid., Cronius 3, 115.

37. Athanasius, *Life of Antony,* 45.

38. Ward, *Wisdom,* 57–58.

39. This is a valuable insight and phrase used by Stelios Ramfos in *Pelican* in a discussion of the active nature of patience. See 44–45.

40. Ward, *Sayings,* Paul the Barber 1, 204.

41. Stelios Ramfos, *Pelican,* 44.

42. Ward, *Sayings,* Isidore 1, 96.

43. See Gerald May, *The Awakened Heart* (New York: HarperSanFrancisco, 1991) 3–5.

44. Ward, *Sayings,* Isidore 2, 96–97.

45. Ibid., Isidore 9, 97–98.

46. Ward, *Lives,* 149.

6   Stillness and Silence

Being Present to God, Ourselves, and the World

While still living in the palace, Abba Arsenius prayed to God in these words, "Lord, lead me in the way of salvation." And a voice came saying to him, "Arsenius, flee from men and you will be saved."[1]

Having withdrawn to the solitary life he made the same prayer again and he heard a voice saying to him, "Arsenius, flee, be silent, pray always, for these are the sources of sinlessness."[2]

The call of Abba Arsenius in 394 C.E. from the luxury and influence of the imperial palace in Constantinople to fifty-two years in the deserts of Egypt emphasizes two of the most fundamental virtues of desert monasticism: **stillness**, the withdrawal from conventional activities and **silence**, withdrawal from commonly practiced patterns of speech. These two monastic virtues seem uniquely appropriate for the life Arsenius chose and in short supply both in his world and in modern Western society. Do these virtues constitute antisocial behavior? Did Arsenius and the other desert elders flee the inhabited world because they did not like human relationships and conversations? Is it necessary to withdraw from society in order to pray and be open to God's grace? To modern ears many of the sayings of the elders seem to be saying "Yes!" But a closer look at the context of the elders' lives will reveal the sources of the wisdom embedded in these sayings. Ironically, stillness and silence have much to say about the integrity of human activities and conversations. Human behavior and speech manifest great power and, therefore, can promote both good and evil. This is why stillness and silence were necessary virtues in the lives of the desert elders that guided their path to transformation.

"Abba Antony said, 'He who stays in the desert and practices stillness is delivered from three temptations, that of hearing, that of speaking, and that of seeing. He has only one temptation, that of the heart.'"[3]

Amma Syncletica said, "We who have chosen this way of life must obtain perfect temperance. It is true that among seculars, also, temperance has the freedom of the city, but intemperance cohabits with it, because they sin with all the other senses. Their gaze is shameless and they laugh immoderately."[4]

Abba Aio questioned Macarius (the Great), "Give me a word." Abba Macarius said to him, "Flee from men, stay in your cell, weep for your sins, do not take pleasure in the conversation of men, and you will be saved."[5]

Why would anyone want to be "delivered" from hearing other people, speaking to them, or laughing with them? What is to be gained from withdrawing from involvement in society? What is the benefit of "enduring in silence"? How does "fleeing from people" and not taking "pleasure in the conversations of people" result in a person's salvation? Answers to these legitimate questions will emerge as we review aspects of life in the inhabited world that the desert elders called "futile" and observe the manner of life that led to the abbas' and ammas' commitment to love of God and neighbor.

To be open to the wisdom of the elders we must always keep in mind that they **chose** their austere life voluntarily as a vocation. Although their life stood in stark contrast to the society they left, it became a source of freedom and peace to them. While they preferred their manner of life as a path to salvation, they did not condemn those who continued to seek God within conventional society. While most readers, and the author, are not called to this type of monastic life, our lives can be edified and enriched by the wisdom of the desert elders. Our manner of life is different, but we walk the same path as Christians. "It was revealed to Abba Antony in his desert that there was one who was his equal in the city. He was a doctor by profession and whatever he had beyond his needs he gave to the poor, and every day he sang the Sanctus with the angels."[6]

Stillness

A brother asked Abba Poemen, "How should I live in the cell?" He said to him, "Living in your cell clearly means manual work, eating only once a day, silence, meditation; but really making progress in the cell, means to experience contempt for yourself, not to neglect the hours of prayer and to pray secretly. If you happen to have time without manual work, take up prayer and do it without disquiet. The perfection of these things is to live in good company and be free from bad."[7]

Abba Evagrius said, "Sit in your cell, collecting your thoughts. Remember the day of your death. See then what the death of your body will be; let your spirit be heavy, take pains, condemn the vanity of the world, so as to be able to live always in the peace you have in view without weakening."[8]

Abbas Poemen and Evagrius give a vivid summary of the life of stillness (hesychia). They echo Antony, Syncletica, and Macarius. Stillness is a withdrawal from customary activity that enables a concentration on attentiveness and openness to God in prayer. This is not a rejection of life's activities or of life itself. It is a "fleeing" from influences that are futile and that can distract or prevent a person from pursuing his or her path **toward** experience of God and authentic human living. The outer stillness in the cell becomes a venue for an inner stillness that makes prayer possible and becomes a pathway for the action of the Holy Spirit. As Antony points out, physical stillness removes the layers of noise, words, and attention that can hide and constrict the heart—the center of human will and experience of God. Evagrius reminds a brother monk that "the vanity of the world" can weaken the monk from "the peace you have in view." And Syncletica warns how vulnerable a person's senses are to the temptations present in city life.

These desert elders are saying that every person must be attentive to what is most important in human life and that conventionally accepted human activity should be avoided or limited when it distracts anyone from a path to holiness and charity. They are insisting that authentic human life is not compatible with a society that values materialism and unrestrained pleasure. The desert elders are not condemning basic human interaction, relationships and conversations. By being attentive to God in prayer and aware of one's own limitations a person can live and work "in good company" and find peace. This interaction of outer and inner stillness is present in an incident in the lives of Abba Paul and Abba Timothy reported by Abba Sisoes the Theban:

> The same Abba Paul and Abba Timothy were sweepers at Scetis and they used to be disturbed by the brothers. And Timothy said to his brother, "What do we want with this job? We are not allowed to be still the whole day long." And Abba Paul said to him, "The stillness of the night is sufficient for us, if our minds are vigilant."[9]

Stillness is not an end in itself, neither does it exclude a person from the responsibility of labor in the community. At the same time, Abba Paul is aware that the stillness he and his brother have in the night provides the "vigilance" for prayer and mindfulness. The primary virtue of inner stillness is to direct the monk to the transformation of his or her heart. Although stillness is the intentional limitation of external pursuits to devote focus and energy on internal transformation, it is not an avoidance of or indifference to activity. Stillness, for the self-centered sake of stillness, can produce an unhealthy insensitivity toward other people and an inwardness that imprisons a person in their own self-created world. This is not the intent of the abbas and ammas, as Abba John Cassian comments so clearly:

> Self-reform and peace are not achieved through the patience which others show us, but through our own long-suffering towards our neighbor. When we try to escape the struggle for long-suffering by retreating into solitude, those unhealed passions we take there with us are merely hidden, not erased; for unless our passions are first purged, solitude and withdrawal from the world not only foster them but also keep them concealed, no longer allowing us to perceive what passion it is that enslaves us. On the contrary, they impose on us an illusion of virtue and persuade us to believe that we have achieved long-suffering and humility, because there is no one present to provoke and test us.[10]

The interior object of stillness is the life and health of each person's soul. The wisdom of the sayings quoted above summarize the grace made possible in stillness: mindfulness of one's sins; avoidance of the futility of material pleasures and concerns that mask a person from his or her soul's health; prayer and meditation; and inner peace leading to a heart that wills what God desires. Abba Peomen goes on to illustrate that the fruits of stillness are manifested in a variety of ways. The venues of stillness may differ, but they all **redirect** a person's activity to the heart. "Abba Poemen said, 'If three people are living in the same place, and one of them is practicing stillness successfully, the second is ill but gives thanks, and the third serves with a pure mind, all three are performing the same work.'"[11]

The wisdom of the elders points toward aspects of stillness that contribute to the "opening of the soul" of the monk:[12]

- withdrawal from activity and conversation
- awareness of God and one's self
- an inner stillness centered in prayer
- a vigilance of mind (both thought and intuition)
- an attitude of the heart, leading away from self-interest and toward self-giving and gratitude
- a freedom born of desiring what God desires
- easily satisfied needs
- a refinement of the whole person in God

When these aspects of stillness influence the life of the monk they bear fruit in his life with God and his neighbor.

In summary, the **vocation** of the one who desires stillness, the hesychast, is manifested in an external way by the enclosure of the cell, limited contact with other people, and avoidance of noise, conversations and relationships (i.e., limitation of stimuli to the senses). This exterior vocation makes an interior stillness possible with a focus in the cell on an inner life of prayer. Stelios Ramfos comments that this enclosing of the monk from the stimuli of exterior senses is **not a loss of the monk's humanity.**[13] On the contrary, it is an opening of doors to a more complete humanity through an inner tranquility. This is the fruit of prayer that Abba Evagrius called "the peace which you have in view."

Hesychios of Sinai said:

> Snow can never emit flame. Water can never issue fire. A thorn bush can never produce a fig. Just so, your heart can never be free from oppressive thoughts, words, and actions until it has been purified internally. Be eager to walk this path. Watch your heart always. Constantly say the prayer "Lord Jesus Christ have mercy on me." Be humble. Set your soul in quietness.[14]

Stillness Is the Colleague of Prayer

The tranquility born of stillness is the grace of God present in a person's life. This leads us away from the vanity and futility of material pleasures, unhealthy relationships and the struggle of our egos to control our lives. How does this happen?

> Abba Moses said to Abba Poemen, "If a man's deeds are not in harmony with his prayer, he labours in vain." The brother said, "What is this harmony between practice and prayer?" The old man said, "We should no longer do those things against which we pray. For when a man gives up his own will, then God is reconciled with him and accepts his prayers." The brother asked, "In all the affliction which the monk gives himself, what helps him?" The old man said, "It is written, 'God is our refuge and strength, a very present help in trouble'" (Ps 46:1).[15]

Stillness is the venue for the attentiveness that leads a person to union with God in prayer. As we offer our hearts to God, our prayers are "accepted" because reconciliation has taken place in which our wills become congruent with what God desires. In this way our prayer and daily life become united. Stillness leads to simplicity of needs and cares. We are no longer distracted by the demons of the unrestrained ego's desires for pleasures, unnecessary possessions, honor, revenge or impure relationships. Abba John Klimakos said, "Let your prayer be completely simple."[16] Abba Moses reminded Abba Poemen that "God is our hope and strength." When we are freed from the multiplicity of cares that can dominate our lives, we experience a freedom that opens our hearts to love God and our neighbor. Rather than isolating us from others, stillness leads to a union with all beings.

> Abba Isidore of Pelusia said, "To live without speaking is better than to speak without living. For the former who lives rightly does good even by his silence but the latter does no good even when he speaks. When words and life correspond to one another they are together the whole of philosophy."[17]

Prayer, born in stillness, unites every person with what is most fundamental in life rather than what is peripheral and futile. Like the continuum of space/time in cosmology, stillness and prayer weave a seamless garment that wraps us in an awareness of the unity of all things in God, rather than the loose and unconnected threads of the "many." Stillness slows the treadmill of events and desires that distracts us from the One who is essential. Prayer turns a person's mind away from all that distracts and scatters it from its home in God. Life's periphery dissipates and isolates, while prayer bonds and unites. The stillness/prayer continuum removes both stillness and prayer from becoming ends in themselves. Stillness for personal gain rejects the world. Prayer as an end in itself rejects the body and mind for an otherworldly experience. In union, stillness and prayer guide the **whole person** to a new understanding of both the world and human behavior in it. "Abba Poemen said, 'If Nabuzardan, the head-cook, had not come, the temple of the Lord would not have been burned: (2 Kgs 24:8f.) that is to say: if slackness and greed did not come into the soul, the spirit would not be overcome in combat with the enemy.'"[18]

Stillness/prayer reconnects a person to her or his authentic center by freeing her or him from the centrifugal force of attachment to material things. God responds to this prayerful desire by filling the world with a new meaning and delight, free from the limitations of unrestrained desire and the need to control what a person acquires. Abba Moses said, "The monk must die to everything before leaving the body, in order not to harm anyone."[19] When a person is no longer imprisoned by attachment to anything he or she becomes free to enjoy them for what they truly are. **This is interior stillness.**

> One day Abba John the Dwarf was sitting down in Scetis, and the brethren came to him to ask him about their thoughts. One of the elders said, "John,

you are like a courtesan who shows her beauty to increase the number of her lovers." Abba John kissed him and said, "You are quite right Father." One of his disciples said to him, "Do you not mind that in your heart?" But he said, "No, I am the same inside as I am outside."[20]

Wonder, Gratitude and Generosity Flow from the Well of Stillness

One day Abba Arsenius consulted an old Egyptian monk about his own thoughts. Someone noticed this and said to him, "Abba Arsenius, how is it that you, with such a good Latin and Greek education, ask this peasant about your thoughts?" He replied, "I have indeed been taught Latin and Greek, but I do not know even the alphabet of this peasant."[21]

Stillness opens the heart of the monk to a sense of wonder. When the monk is free from attachment, he or she is able to see the world apart from self-interest and self-importance. There is a willingness to look for God's presence everywhere, even in unexpected places and people. The vulnerability of stillness becomes an environment for incarnation. The monk's soul and body are filled with experience of God. "Abba Daniel used to tell how when Abba Arsenius learned that all the varieties of fruit were ripe he would say, 'Bring me some.' He would taste a very little of each, just once, giving thanks to God."[22] Wonder creates a mutual seeing in which the monk acknowledges the world as a gift. Because the monk's world has expanded beyond his own accomplishments his heart is filled with gratitude, even for a small taste of life's fruits. It was Arsenius's grateful heart that united him with both the gift and the Giver. This spiritual union becomes a person's wellspring of self-offering and charity.

"Abba Agathon said, 'I have never offered **agapés** (love feasts, a sharing of food, in the context of a Eucharist); but the fact of giving and receiving has been for me an agapé, for I consider the good of my brother to be a sacrificial offering.'"[23] A person's availability to the Spirit in stillness becomes a spring of generosity. This transforms our actions and use of material things into acts of communion with God. This holy communion also connects us with the world in a new way, as authentic human beings. Our hearts are turned toward the life of the world because our interior prayer is united with our exterior actions. This purity (authenticity) of heart is the goal of all monastic praxis. Monastic life, when it is not abused or romanticized, manifests authentic human life. Its wisdom should not be limited to monastic communities.

"Amma Syncletica also said, 'It is written, "Be wise as serpents and innocent as doves." (Matt 10:16). Being like serpents means not ignoring attacks and wiles of the devil. Like is quickly known to like. The simplicity of the dove denotes purity of action.'"[24] By withdrawing in stillness/prayer the monk releases herself to God and God responds by embracing her with her true self, in time/space. This is God's refinement of the whole person in God, the true Good, the One Who Is. The monk responds by manifesting this image of God in a eucharistic offering of self in every relationship and activity of daily life. "Abba Antony said, 'Our life and our death is with our neighbor. If we gain our brother, we have gained God, but if we scandalize our brother, we have sinned against Christ.'"[25]

Making spaces for stillness in our lives is neither selfish nor self-serving. It helps us retreat from our usual responsibilities and patterns of activity in order to become better listeners. Today we are bombarded by the one-way and aggressive communication of the media and are losing our ability to listen. Conversation is threatened by increased polarity. Stillness guards our souls from over-activity and over-stimulation of mind and body that scatter our openness to God and our neighbor. Stillness helps our actions keep pace with our hearts, even in a few moments of a busy day. Rather than escaping from life, stillness **reacquaints** us with life and the Giver of life. Being in a place apart reminds us of the sacredness of life. Stillness is a fresh spring quenching our inner thirst for love of others, even our enemies.

Silence

Speaking of Silence

Abba Poemen said, "In Abba Pambo we see three bodily activities; abstinence from food until the evening every day, silence, and much manual work."[26]

A brother asked Abba Poemen, "Is it better to speak or to be silent?" The old man said to him, "The man who speaks for God's sake does well; but he who is silent for God's sake also does well."[27]

Stillness provides an environment for **silence**. Abba Poemen understands silence as one of the **bodily** disciplines, recognizing that the body, itself, is involved in the monk's path to transformation. This is important because the "emptiness" of silence could be seen as a way to transcend bodily existence. The desert elders are clear that the **whole being of the monk** is a sacred gift involved in his or her path to holiness. This is both a sacramental and incarnational understanding of the body's place in the path toward sanctification. "The body is not left behind or ignored in the pursuit of purity of heart but becomes an essential and even sacramental element of God's transformation of the whole person."[28] Abba Poemen declares that silence takes place, also, in the context of other bodily virtues such as fasting and labor. Its practice should not exclude other activities that become opportunities for prayer and love of neighbor that lead to humility. In the second saying, Poemen stresses that silence is not an end in itself. Its purpose is not to eliminate speech because silence is a higher virtue. Silence is not fleeing from words. It makes words of integrity and charity possible. When balanced, silence and speech are colleagues rather than competitors. The absence of spoken words makes hearing the Word of God (the **Logos**) possible. When a person is able to hear God's voice in the silence of the cell or in meditation, he or she is able, also, to hear God's voice in the other activities of daily life and to speak in a charitable and helpful manner. In this way both silence and speech are used "for God's sake."

What is monastic silence? The desert elders experienced silence as a withdrawal from exterior speech, conversations and the noises of daily human activities. They limited their hearing to engage in a more intentional dialog with God, and themselves, as they progressed toward other virtues of holiness.

Why did the abbas and ammas want to avoid speech and noise? They were acutely aware of four dimensions of human speech that could produce both positive and negative consequences.[29]

> • Abba Poemen said, "If man remembered that it is written: 'By your words you will be justified and by your words you will be condemned' (Matt 12:37), he would choose to remain silent."[30]

Obviously, Poemen is not advocating a boycott on speech. He used words in teaching, prayer, and necessary conversations. He quoted words of Jesus in this saying. He is reminding other monks of the tremendous **freedom** speech gives a human being. We are free to say anything we desire. At the same time, what we say will have consequences that can either justify or condemn us. **This freedom of speech carries such an awesome responsibility that we should consider remaining silent rather than speaking words that will harm others and bring judgment on us.** Abba Poemen is using hyperbole to challenge his disciples to be good stewards of their freedom of speech.

> • Abba Agathon said, "Freedom of speech, or familiarity, is like a period of intense heat. When it comes, everyone takes shelter from it, and it shrivels up the fruit of the trees."[31] And "It was said of Abba Ammoes that when he went to church, he did not allow his disciple to walk beside him but only at a certain distance; and if the latter

came to ask him about his thoughts, he would move away from him as soon as he had replied, saying to him, 'It is for fear that, after edifying words, irrelevant conversation should slip in, that I do not keep you with me.'"[32]

The elders knew that **words have great power to harm and distract or to give life and edify.** Since human speech affects the lives of others in such profound ways the abbas and ammas valued silence as a steward of both hearing and speech. They took the power of words very seriously and, as illustrated in the incident about Abba Ammoes and his disciple, guided the patterns of their relationships to ensure appropriate use of speech. Ammoes did not want idle speech to distract him or his disciple from the power of God's truth present in their conversations and silence. Some of the elders' behaviors to avoid the negative power of words seem very austere, but embody a desire to let words be a source of life rather than harm.

• Abba Psenthaisius, Abba Surus and Abba Psoius used to agree in saying this, "Whenever we listened to the words of our father, Abba Pachomius, we were greatly helped and spurred on with zeal for good works; we saw how, even when he kept silence, he taught us by his actions. . . . We thought that sinners could not live devoutly, because they had been so created. But now we see the goodness of God manifested in our father, for see he is of pagan origin and has become devout; he has put on all the commandments of God. Thus even we can follow him and become equal to the saints whom he himself has followed."[33]

Words have powerful spiritual influence. They can lead a person away from or toward the spiritual dimension of life. They can deceive as well as reveal with integrity. The disciples of Abba Pachomius were "greatly helped and spurred on with zeal for good works" through the teaching of their abba. His words had even more power, because even in his silence, he taught his disciples "by his actions." The power of Pachomius's words and silence changed the **consciousness** of his disciples. They heard and saw "the goodness of God manifested in our father." This transformed their theology of human nature and helped them see that God desires to be present in all people, sinner and saint alike.

• Abba Theodore of Pherme asked Abba Pambo, "Give me a word." With much difficulty he said to him, "Theodore, go and have pity on all, for through pity, one finds freedom of speech before God."[34]

He also said, "A man may seem to be silent, but if his heart is condemning others he is babbling ceaselessly. But there may be another who talks from morning to night and yet he is truly silent; that is, he says nothing that is profitable."[35]

Abba Theodore reminds us of the power of the spoken word in the desert: "Give me a **word**." **The power of words had great social influence. The teaching of the elders and the words of the Bible helped form the monastic culture of the desert.** But that culture was, itself, formed in response to a negative social power of words in the inhabited world. In response to Abba Theodore's request for "a word," Abba Pambo reminds him of the direct relationship between words and action. "Freedom of speech before God" is manifested in having "pity on all." The fruit of conversation with God is love of neighbor. Abba Pambo, has learned from experience (probably his own faults) that there is also a direct relationship between one's heart and one's speech. He warns about the social consequences of having judgmental thoughts about brother monks during periods of silence and about the futility of speech that does not benefit its hearers.

These four aspects of speech provide insights to the motivation for and value of monastic silence. The motivation for anachoresis was avoidance of what was futile and worldly. The elders realized that without periods of **silence**, life becomes hidden in a constant flow of activity, noise and words, which may have little or no reference to truth. In the midst of life's frenzy they sought places and moments of peace where they could become aware of God's presence. Abba Poemen also said, "If you are silent, you will have peace wherever you live."[36] **The abbas and ammas desired silence because it was an environment that extended the boundaries of their experience of God and knowledge of themselves.** Their desire for silence, an interior form of anachoresis, enabled them to know in the most personal way that "The word is near you, on your lips **and in your heart**" (Rom 10:8, NRSV).

The guarding of the tongue and avoidance of the noises of activity through silence became a pathway to prayer. The spoken word could describe God and various forms of praxis. Silence brought experience of God to a **personal dimension in the present moment.** It gave the soul "equal time." Stelios Ramfos points out that a handicap of the ancient written Greek language was that it had no punctuation marks. It became much easier to read when the grammarians of Alexandria invented punctuation marks and allowed space between words.[37] Human speech, theater and music would lose their meaning without pauses and silence. The monastic periods of separation from contact and conversations with others allowed space for conversation with God. It was this conversation, especially **listening to the Word,** that gave meaning to the monk's material life and opened his or her heart to the movement of the Spirit.

Silence and Purity of Heart

The disciples of Abba Pachomius learned that silence is not simply the absence of sound. It is a unique form of human consciousness. In the silence of their teacher they were drawn beyond themselves into a transpersonal form of listening, seeing and learning. They witnessed the presence of God in Pachomius in such a way that the judgments of their egos were released. They were lured beyond the boundaries of seeing him as "pagan" and "sinner." As they let go of the limits imposed by the duality of self/other they saw Pachomius as a person whose heart was pure. In that moment they knew that the transformation that had taken place in Pachomius's life could also be their own. This gave them joy and hope, **without a word being spoken.**

The Silent Power of the Heart

"Abba Poemen also said, 'Teach your heart to guard that which your tongue teaches.'"[38] The desert elders valued silence because they knew the power of words. They did not want to let words and careless speech have unnecessary control over their attention, thoughts and actions. Their attitude was: guard your use of words so that their use or absence will enable you to live a pure life. The abbas and ammas learned from experience that **the heart is the source of both words and actions.** A person must listen with the "ear of the heart" if his or her words and behavior are to bring salvation. A pure life begins with a pure heart. What did the desert elders mean by the word "heart"?

Pseudo-Marcarius said:

> For the heart directs and governs all the other organs of the body. And when grace pastures the heart, it rules over all the members and the thoughts. For there, in the heart, the mind abides as well as all of the thoughts of the soul and all its hopes. This is how grace penetrates throughout all parts of the body.[39]

These words were written in the fourth century. Greek Orthodox Bishop Kallistos Ware is one of the twenty-first century's finest Eastern Orthodox scholars of the desert and hesychast traditions. He points out that at the time of the desert elders people did not think of the heart as the muscular pump of the cardio-vascular system, "but they viewed it as a container or empty vessel, full of space and air."[40] They perceived the heart as a bodily organ that dominates all the other organs and is the physical center of the body that relies on it for life to continue. The heart is also the psychic and spiritual center of the human being. When it is open to God's grace it "pastures" (shepherds) body, mind and hope (expectations and intuition). Bishop Kallistos concludes that people at the time of the desert elders considered the heart to be the "axial" organ that centers the physical, psychic and spiritual dimensions of human life. It is the seat of "reasoning," "intuitive insight and mystical vision," as well as "the place of wisdom and spiritual knowledge" and "the meeting place between the Divine and the human."[41]

In the silence of Abba Pachomius' activities his three disciples could see the presence of God in his life with "the eyes of their hearts." In the silence of their cells the desert elders could listen to God with "the ears of their hearts." By limiting their activities through **stillness** and their conversations through **silence,** the desert monks made space within their hearts for the grace (the creative energy) of God to "pasture" their lives. By extending the boundaries imposed by their unrestrained egos, the abbas and ammas became open to **an expansion of the heart** that made space for God's grace to unite their physical, psychic and spiritual faculties into a transformed and authentic human being. Their speech, behavior, thoughts, intuition and desires were united with God's desires for them and their neighbor. They could see and love the world in a different way. They were not perfect and still considered themselves to be sinners and "beginners," but their hearts were authentic. This is what John Cassian called "purity of heart," birthed by grace in the praxis of stillness and silence. It is what Evagrius meant by apatheia.

The Practical Dimensions of Silence

Abba Gregory Nazianzus, the theologian, said, "These three things God requires of all the baptized: right faith in the heart, truth on the tongue, temperance in the body."[42] The desert elders taught that there must be a direct flow from purity of heart to speech and action. When words have their origin in the silence of purity of heart they will be congruent with the monk's behavior. The common vocation of all Christians is to have the heart, the tongue and use of the body in equilibrium in order to "speak" God's presence from the silence of the heart. The elders insisted that there is no other "spirituality" than **applied spirituality.** Abba Gregory of Nyssa said, "Silence is the beginning of salvation."

"A brother asked Abba Sisoes, 'What am I to do?' He said to him, 'What you need is a great deal of silence and humility. For it is written: "Blessed are those who wait for him" (Isa 30:18) for this they are able to stand.'"[43] A litany of the voices of the younger monks echoed throughout the desert: **"Give me a word"** and **"What should I do?"** The response was always the same, **"Your words and actions must come out of silence."** In this case Abba Sisoes recommends a "great deal" of silence for what was probably a "type A" monk who, in his great desire to seek God, wanted fast results from praxis. The abba chastises the monk for not being willing "to wait for him." It is possible to search for God with such outward activity and conversation that a person cannot see or hear the patient God who waits in the silence of his or her heart. Silence teaches patience and patience enables us "to stand" in the presence of the One who is already present.

Sometimes being able to "stand in the presence" takes a long time. "It was said of Abba Agathon that for three years he lived with a stone in his mouth, until he had learnt to keep silence."[44] Here is a man who loved to talk! One can see the traces of both a smile and agony on his face as he lived among his brothers dying to speak, but knowing the wisdom of learning to keep silent. How big was the stone? What were the practical results of his three-year apprenticeship in the art of being silent?

> Abba Agathon was wise in spirit and active in body. He provided everything he needed for himself, in manual work, food, and clothing . . . . Whenever his thoughts urged him to pass judgment on something which he saw, he would say to himself, "Agathon, it is not your business to do that." Thus his spirit was always recollected . . . . Abba Agathon said, "If I could meet a leper, give him my body and take his, I should be very happy." This indeed is perfect charity.[45]

There seems no doubt that the desert elders had had experiences of putting their feet in their mouths. Pride, vainglory, insensitivity, and the need to be in control are often motives for giving advice, speaking in judgment, and wanting to fix things. At the same time, motives for speaking without thinking can be genuine desires to help others. But in both cases the elders knew the dangers of not speaking from a heart that is sensitive to God and one's neighbors. A brother said to Abba Poemen, "If I see something do you want me to tell you about it?" The old man said to him, "It is written: 'If one gives answer before he hears, it is his folly and shame.' (Prov 18:3). If you are questioned, speak; if not, remain silent."[46] Silence is a powerful way to learn and discern because it makes listening, self-restraint and patience possible. It opens a person to wisdom and the possibility of wise behavior. "A brother who shared a lodging with other brothers asked Abba Bessarion, 'What should I do?' The old man replied, 'Keep silence and do not compare yourself with others.'"[47]

> Another day when a council was being held in Scetis, the Fathers treated Moses with contempt in order to test him saying, "Why does this black man come among us?" When he heard this he kept silent. When the council was dismissed, they said to him, "Abba, did that not grieve you at all?" He said to them, "I was grieved, but I kept silence."[48]

With the exception of extreme hermits, the monks of the desert did not live in isolation. Over the years different forms of community life evolved, and the monks were not always polite or patient with each other. They faced the same challenges and turf wars as people in any other type of community. Pride, anger, jealousy, fear, and selfishness lurked in their shadows, too. Yet in their silence they learned not to take themselves too seriously and became aware of the dangers of using each other as benchmarks for measuring progress along the spiritual path. Silence requires time, and in that "timeless space" they often received grace to control emotions and learn how to respond to conflict without perpetuating conflict. Unless we have the courage to enter our hearts and be pastured by God's grace and wisdom we will never learn the restraint and respect necessary for living in peace with each other and our neighbors. Silence is the womb of civility and compassion.

A Last Word About Silence

Amma Syncletica said:

> It is dangerous for anyone to teach who has not first been trained in the "practical life." For if someone who owns a ruined house receives guests there, he does them harm because of the dilapidation of his dwelling. It is the same in the case of someone who has not first built an interior dwelling; he causes loss to those who come. By words one may convert them to salvation, but by evil behavior, one injures them.[49]

Notes

1. *The Sayings of the Desert Fathers*, trans. Benedicta Ward, S.L.G. (Kalamazoo: Cistercian Publications, 1984) Arsenius 1, 9.
2. Ibid., Arsenius 2, 9.

3. P. B. Paschos, ed., *Gerontikon*, 1961. Antony 4, 128A.

4. Ward, *Sayings*, Syncletica 2, 231.

5. Ibid., Macarius the Great 41, 138.

6. Ibid., Antony 24, 6.

7. Ibid., Poemen 168, 190.

8. Ibid., Evagrius 1, 63.

9. *Gerontikon*, Sisoes the Theban 2, 381B.

10. G.E.H. Palmer, P. Sherrard, and K. Ware, trans. and eds., *The Philokalia* (London: Faber and Faber, 1979) vol. 1, John Cassian, "On the Eight Vices," 85.

11. Ward, *Sayings*, Poemen 29, 171.

12. The phrase "opening of the soul" is taken from Stelios Ramfos, *Like a Pelican in the Wilderness* (Brookline: Holy Cross Orthodox Press, 2000) 164. In his chapter on monastic stillness, Dr. Ramfos describes the fruits of stillness. My identification of these specific aspects is influenced by his commentary as well as my own research.

13. Ramfos, *Pelican*, 67.

14. Palmer, et al., *The Philokalia*, vol. 1, Hesychios of Sinai, "On Watchfulness and Holiness," 122, 183.

15. Ward, *Sayings*, Moses 4, 141–42.

16. John Climacus, *The Ladder of Divine Ascent*, trans. Lazarus Moore (London: Mobrays, 1959) 28, 5.

17. Ward, *Sayings*, Isidore of Pelusia 1, 98.

18. Ibid., Poemen 17, 169.

19. Ibid., Moses 2, 141.

20. Ibid., John the Dwarf 46, 95–96.

21. Ibid., Arsenius 6, 10.

22. Ibid., Arsenius 19, 11.

23. Ibid., Agathon 17, 23.

24. Ibid., Syncletica 18, 234.

25. Ibid., Antony 9, 3.

26. Ibid., Poemen 150, 188.

27. Ibid., Poemen 147, 188.

28. Harriet A. Luckman and Linda Kulzer, eds. *Purity of Heart in Early Ascetic and Monastic Literature* (Collegeville: Liturgical Press, 1999) 14.

29. My descriptions of these four dimensions are influenced by a similar discussion in Ramfos, *Pelican*, 74–78.

30. Ward, *Sayings*, Poemen 42, 173.

31. *Gerontikon*, Agathon 1, 109A.

32. Ward, *Sayings*, Ammoes 1, 30.

33. Ibid., Psenthaisius 1, 245.

34. Ibid., Pambo 14, 198.

35. Ibid., Poemen 27, 171.

36. Ibid., Poemen 84, 178.

37. Ramfos, *Pelican*, 179.

38. Ward, *Sayings*, Poemen 188, 193.

39. Pseudo-Macarius, *The Fifty Spiritual Homlies and the Great Letter,* trans. George A. Maloney (New York: Paulist Press, 1992) 116.

40. James S. Cutsinger, ed., *Paths to the Heart. Sufism and the Christian East* (Bloomington: World Wisdom, 2002) Kallistos Ware, "How Do We Enter The Heart," 12–13.

41. Ibid., 12–14.

42. Ward, *Sayings,* Gregory the Theologian 1, 45.

43. Ibid., Sisoes 42, 220.

44. Ibid., Agathon 15, 22.

45. Ibid., Agathon 10, 18, 26, 22–24.

46. Ibid., Poemen 45, 173.

47. Ibid., Bessarion 10, 42.

48. Ibid., Moses 3, 139.

49. Ibid., Syncletica 12, 233.

7 Praxis

An Ascetic Vocation That Forms, Nourishes and Guards the Soul

Abba John the Dwarf said:

Renounce everything material and that which is of the flesh. Live by the cross, in warfare, in poverty of spirit, in voluntary spiritual asceticism, in fasting, penitence and tears, in discernment, in purity of soul, taking hold of that which is good. Do your work in peace. Persevere in keeping vigil, in hunger and thirst, in cold and nakedness, and in sufferings. Shut yourself in a tomb as though you were already dead, so that at all times you will think death is near.[1]

Amma Sycletica said:

In the beginning there are a great many battles and a good bit of suffering for those who are advancing towards God and afterwards, ineffable joy. It is like those who wish to light a fire; at first they are choked by the smoke and cry, and by this means obtain what they seek (as it is said: "Our God is a consuming fire" [Hebrews 12:24]) so we must also kindle the divine fire in ourselves through tears and hard work.[2]

Praxis: The Habits of Spiritual Formation

Listening to a Different Language and Way of Life

The words of Abba John and Amma Syncletica may sound austere or uninviting to modern ears. Some readers may ask, "How are they related to experiencing 'ineffable joy'? Who would choose what seems to be an 'abnormal' human life? Are the elders suggesting inhumane behaviors? Does spiritual 'warfare' suggest punishing one's self to warrant God's acceptance and love? Do these two sayings mirror a dualism that denigrates the body in favor of the spirit? Is it necessary to 'reject' the body in order to find salvation"? On the surface, such questions raise legitimate concerns. Creation and human life are, indeed, gifts of God. But patience is warranted, so that we do not take the words of Abba John and Amma Syncletica out of context. It is tempting to look at the lives of the abbas and ammas through the lenses of modern conventional values about what is "normal" and make judgments about their penitential disciplines based upon spiritual paths and theological perspectives we have chosen today. Unless we make an effort to understand their language, motives, and worldview, we risk missing their wisdom.

The Meaning of Praxis

The ammas and abbas identified two essential aspects of living as *kopos* and *praxis*.[3] Kopos, the Greek word for "labor that expends physical energy," contributes to God's continuing creation of the world and helps create a physical venue in which the monk's spiritual labor can take place. Praxis, the Greek word for "action that is habitually repeated," is labor and vigilance directed toward inner spiritual formation, leading to love of God and neighbor. An additional aspect of praxis, emphasized by Gregory of Nyssa, is that it is always "in progress" and never completed. This is a fundamental truth of desert monasticism. In the next chapter we will explore the influence of praxis on physical labor, time, and the responsibilities of daily life.

The focus of praxis is spiritual formation through the disciplines of *ascetic life*. As we have seen, ascetic refers to the Greek word *askesis*, training and exercise. In classical Greek usage it could refer not only to athletic training (St. Paul uses it in this context as a metaphor for the spiritual life), but also to repetition of skills in the arts, training in the virtues or vices, or a specific mode of life, such as philosophy or religion. In early Christian usage it became associated with a monakos, a person who lives a solitary, celibate, and ascetic life, a monk.[4]

The Bi-Axial Experience of Praxis

What life experiences and desires are embedded in the sayings of Abba John and Amma Syncletica? Both sayings give a picture of the purpose and content of praxis. **Praxis is a discipline that includes the whole person.** Praxis may include both **mental** and **physical** disciplines, such as meditation on Scripture or standing with the arms raised in prayer, as well as an

inner movement of character that influences the monk's whole being. Both John the Dwarf and Syncletica are aware that this "voluntary spiritual asceticism" is a **psychosomatic experience** whose goal is not to suppress the body and the mind in favor of the spirit. The fasting, vigils, hunger, thirst, cold, nakedness, tears, and sufferings are integrated with poverty of spirit, penitence, discernment, and purity of soul in the "hard work" of "advancing toward God." To "Live by the cross. . . ." is to recognize that both the horizontal and vertical aspects of life must be included if the monks are to "obtain what they seek." And what are they seeking? What is luring them to "Renounce everything material and that which is of the flesh"? Does "advancing toward God" deny the goodness of the flesh and the material world?

Abba John sees praxis as a path toward "taking hold of what is good" and being able to "work in peace." The virtues which make these behaviors possible are "purity of soul" and "discernment." The desert elders did not leave the materialism, hedonism and power struggles of the inhabited world because they rejected the goodness of creation. They renounced a way of life that had become **futile** through attachment to material security and fleshly pleasures as ends in themselves. They desired a path that advanced toward union with God (a vertical dimension) and discovered that the venue for that movement was the expansion and transformation of their whole being (a horizontal dimension). The path toward this authentic human life was praxis. Although it varied in its degrees of austerity and its specific patterns, it must always be understood in this wider context. And, as Amma Syncletica learned, the ineffable joys of being truly human do not come easily. "In the beginning there are a great many battles and a good bit of suffering. . . ."

Praxis Is Chosen Freely, in the Company of Others

Abba Evagrius said:

You know very well, my brother, that someone who wants to set out on a long journey will first of all examine himself, and then he will attach himself to other travelers with whom he is able and willing to keep up; otherwise he may get left behind by his companions on the journey and come to harm. It is exactly the same with the person who wants to travel on the road to righteousness. First of all let him look into himself and see how strong he is, then let him **choose a way of life that is appropriate to himself** (author's emphasis).[5]

Praxis is not an imposed discipline. It is chosen freely as a path of transformation. Its ascetic practices are chosen for a spiritual aim: "to travel on the road to righteousness," the embodiment of the true self desired by God for the monk. Yet for all monks, even the hermit, there are companions and mentors on the path. Praxis is never intended to isolate the monk totally from other people or from society, even when that may be an initial personal motive for some who sought anachoresis.

Abba Dorotheos of Gaza said, "I have told you all this so that you may know how much rest and tranquility a man may have—and that with all security—by not settling anything by himself, but by casting everything that concerns himself upon God and on those who, after God, have the power to guide him. Learn then, brothers, to enquire; be convinced that not to set one's own path is a great thing. This is humility, this is peace of soul, this is joy!"[6]

Choosing a path of praxis becomes the source of a true joy and happiness for the monk because the austerity of the path was not chosen as an end in itself. The praxis becomes an exercise of personal sacrifice, resulting in freedom and joy. This freedom of choice embraces a path that harmonizes the desires of the body and the soul with the will of God. By making a choice to submit to an ascetic discipline the monk experiences true freedom. The renunciations and boundaries which the praxis imposes do not limit the monk's life. They extend his or her capacity to live according to the image of God that lies within.

Praxis is directly related to the monk's desire to seek God. This is the underlying purpose of the austerity described by Abba John the Dwarf and Amma Syncletica. The limits on the body's desires make the monk's spirit more open and receptive. If the praxis is imposed on the monk or chosen to satisfy personally perceived moral or spiritual obligations, the exterior benefits are meaningless. Without interior transformation, praxis may become a source of pride and self-interest.

> Abba Gerontius of Petra said that many, tempted by the pleasures of the body, commit fornication, not in their body but in their spirit, and while preserving their bodily virginity, commit prostitution in their soul. "Thus it is good, my well-beloved, to do that which is written, and for each one to guard his heart with all possible care."[7]

Praxis is not a generic spiritual tool to be applied at random. It is not simply saying prayers, doing vigils, and being silent. It requires the personal and unique desire and cooperation of each monk. Abba John the Solitary said, "Let your outward actions testify to your inward ones: not in a pretence before other people, but in truth before the Lord of all."[8] Once chosen, praxis is a constant path of being present to God's grace and transforming power as a new way of life is being formed and lived. The grace in praxis is uniquely manifested in each monk's life.

The Exterior Disciplines of Praxis

The Context for Praxis

Praxis forms each monk's active life in the same way that politeia creates an environment in which that life may take place. Politeia is the blueprint for a heavenly city in the desert. Praxis is the manner of life that makes the heavenly city a reality in time and space. It embodies God's presence in the lives of the monks. At the same time praxis is the **specific** means that forms each life of purity of heart and charity.

Praxis has many exterior faces. Yet the heart of praxis beats with a rhythm of activity that integrates prayer, learning (words of the elders), Scripture (the Word of God), silence, stillness, labor, and love of neighbor. The next chapter will describe the **fruits** of the integration of labor and various forms of prayer. We will see that work is sanctified by filling it with the vertical axis of human life. Labor sanctifies basic and mundane human tasks as the venue for humility and love of neighbor. In chapter 3 we discovered the rhythms of the corporate monastic day in coenobitic and hesychast communities. The faithful presence of God is found (1) when monks assemble for daily prayers and the weekly celebration of the Eucharist, (2) when they are formed by the words of their elders and holy Scripture, and (3) when their shared labor is the mortar bonding individuals into a community and the food sustaining body and soul. The exterior praxis of individual monks took place in this **larger context.**

What were the personal exterior disciplines of praxis? The list is long, but no single monk practiced them all. Some of the most common were: renunciation of material pleasures and desires of the flesh that lead to sinful behavior; limitations on daily food consumption; limitations on sleep; wearing of a monastic habit; poverty of possessions; celibacy; obedience to abbot, superior or teacher; participation in daily monastic offices, unless a hermit or hesychast; participation in the Eucharist on Saturday and Sunday, unless a hermit; commitment to learning about the ascetic life and Scripture from an abbot, superior or personal teacher; discussion of teaching with other monks (in Pachomian monasteries); regular work to support one's self or to assist in the support of a monastic community; acts of charity toward other monks and persons from the surrounding society; recitation of Scripture, especially the Psalms; *meditatio (meletē),* i.e., the

recitation of Scripture during work; meditation on Scripture; contemplation (imageless experience of union with God); remaining in one's cell, except for common assembly and worship, work and learning in a monastic
community; remaining in the same monastery, scete (if semi-eremitic) or
hermitage (if a hermit); fasting; vigils; penitential prayer; tears; battles with
demons; endurance of heat, cold, tiredness, pain; personal prayer, including body prayer with hands uplifted, genuflections, prostrations; hospitality to other monks and guests; singing of hymns; silence, except when
speech is necessary in a monastery or in assisting guests, pilgrims, the poor
and in buying and selling goods; solitude, except during worship, work,
conferences with a teacher, or works of charity; not visiting other monasteries or monks in their cells.

It is time to look in more detail at some of the most common personal and external ascetic disciplines practiced by each monk, usually alone,
in his or her cell.

Renunciation: The Fundamental Psycho-Spiritual Dimension of Praxis

It is essential to understand renunciation in the desert monastic context because all the other ascetic disciplines flow from and, at the same
time, manifest the praxis of renunciation. It is one of the most misunder-
stood aspects of monastic vocation because it may appear to be a denial of
the goodness of creation and the human body. Abba Dorotheos of Gaza in
his *Discourse on Renunciation* uses the narrative of Adam and Eve in the
Garden of Eden to set the biblical foundation for renunciation. The dis-
obedience of Adam (humankind) caused him to fall ". . . from a state in
accord with his nature to a state contrary to nature, i.e. a prey to sin, to am-
bition, to a love of the pleasures of this life and the other passions: and he
was mastered by them, and became a slave to them through his transgres-
sion."[9] Abba Dorotheos is saying that sin is the state of living in a nature or
"self" (created by a person's unrestrained ego) which is not a person's true
nature. Healing and transformation of the false self begin, says Dorotheos,
with a desire for reorientation (repentance) and renewal of the heart and
its desires through the power of Christ (redemption to our true self). "For
he renewed man in his nature, restored the depraved senses and sensibility
of human nature to **what it had been in the beginning**" (author's emphasis).[10] This understanding of God's desire to restore the true self of every
person is the wider context for the monk's pursuit of renunciation of material pleasures and fleshly desires. But renunciation must be accompanied
by a humble heart. Abba Dorotheos continues:

He, (Christ), shows us that pretensions to superiority (pride) cast us down and that it is impossible to obtain mercy except by the contrary, that is to say, by humility.[11]

Among the seniors it used to be told how a brother asked one of the elders, "What is humility?" And the elder replied, "Humility is a great and divine work and the road to humility is labor, bodily labor, while seeking to know one's self and to put one's self below everyone else and praying to God about everything: this is the road to humility, but humility itself is something divine and incomprehensible."[12]

Without humility it is impossible to obey the Commandments or at any time to go towards anything good. . . . The holy men of old thoroughly understood this and through all their training and guidance in humility (praxis) were zealous in uniting themselves to God. Thereby, in becoming friends of God, they were able, after Holy Baptism, not only to cut out sins arising from evil passions, but to conquer the passions themselves and to acquire complete control of their passions (i.e., reorient them to God's will for humankind). Such were Saint Antony, Saint Pachomius and the rest of the God-bearing Fathers. . . . Their aim was to purify themselves, as the Apostle says, "from every blemish of the flesh and the spirit." They knew that by the keeping of the Commandments the soul is purified and the mind too is enlightened, and they perceived that it starts functioning **as nature intended it to** (author's emphasis).[13]

The aim of renunciation is purity of heart, soul and mind. It is not a denial of the goodness of God's creation, but a rejection of the use of that same creation in ways that profane the original goodness of creation and humankind. In this context purity is not defined as "moral correctness" but "being in our natural state" as God intended. (Morality will flow, voluntarily, from our natural state.)

Abba Dorotheos describes the monk's **habit** as an ever-present symbol of each monk's vocation to live in her or his natural state.[14] A tunic with short sleeves symbolizes that the monk will not use his or her hands for sinful behavior. A purple mark on the tunic is a sign that the monk "fights" for Christ, the King, not some earthly monarch. A belt symbolizes that the monk is ready for work and is also a sign of bodily mortification of fleshly desires. A cape or scapular is placed across the shoulders as a sign that the monk has taken up the cross of Christ through renunciation. A hood or cowl is a symbol of abasement, "that we may be the little ones in malice, having no desire for revenge or claim to glory." The hood also symbolizes the presence of God's grace covering the monk's mind, as a hood warms the head of a child.

Vigils: The Stature of Attentive Waiting

Abba Evagrius said, "Let us make provision for protecting this power of our soul by praying to Christ in our nightly vigils . . . ."[15] *The Historia Monachorum* describes the process:

> Then, after having eaten, they sit and listen to the father's teaching on all the commandments until the first watch of the night. At this point some of them go out into the desert and recite the Scriptures by heart throughout the night. The rest remain where they are and worship God with ceaseless hymnody until daybreak. I saw them myself with my own eyes begin their hymns in the evening and not stop singing until the morning.[16]

A vigil is an attitude of inner wakefulness "aimed at awakening and opening our heart for the experience of God."[17] The desert elders placed great importance on being open and vulnerable to God's grace. Therefore each monk took both time for watchfulness and used methods to assist him or her to remain in readiness for God's presence. These methods disciplined both body and mind to avoid distractions which interfere with experience of God. Biblical inspiration for vigils came from St. Paul's exhortation, "We belong neither to darkness nor to light. Therefore let us not be asleep like the rest, but awake and sober" (1 Thess 5:6, NRSV).

"Abba Arsenius used to say that one hour's sleep is enough for a monk if he is a good fighter."[18] Obviously, Abba Arsenius's comment speaks of an extreme practice. (But he practiced what he preached!) Yet, why does he place such emphasis on the vigil? A vigil has three purposes that were valid for the desert monks and are valid for most of us as well. The first is to discipline the body, through voluntary limitation of sleep, so more effort can be directed to the work of God. Misdirected bodily activity and desires create disharmony between body and soul and deplete the energy needed for an awakened heart. **How a person fills his or her life influences what he or she is becoming.** The second purpose is to help a person be intentionally awake and open to the movement of God in one's life. **Giving attention to unnecessary distractions or desires can blind a person to God's presence.** The third is to remind a person that his or her spiritual transformation can not be pushed, rushed or grasped. **Being awake and watching for the movement of God is the only way to learn to live with the slow and deliberate pace of being transformed.** The awakened heart and its watchfulness during the night vigil also helps a person learn to recognize God's presence in the activities of daily life.

Monks who lived in hermitages at Nitria, Cellia and Scetis (in the Lower Nile region, south of Alexandria), rose in the middle of the night for their personal vigils called the "little synaxis." Often they created a little niche in the east wall of their cell where a cross was sometimes painted on the bricks or plaster. They remained in their cell, with arms raised in prayer, until dawn.[19]

Abba Evagrius gives a vivid description of personal night vigil in his *Admonition on Prayer* to other monks. It is worth quoting at length to convey the integrity, difficulty and psychological depth of a vigil:

> And when you want to get up to pray during the night and your body is feeling sluggish, ponder all these things and recall how many others are standing in prayer on their feet, or are bowed, or kneeling; how many are weeping and gasping amid groans, how many are lamenting at the body's sluggishness, how many are drunk with love and have forgotten their own natures, how many are singing in their hearts to the Lord.
>
> If you think about all this, then you will find relief from all your sluggishness and weariness, and you will offer up your prayer eagerly and with many tears. Then recollect how many are awake and at their work, how many are traveling on journeys, are ploughing, or carrying out various crafts; remember the shepherds, the night watchmen, those guarding their treasures. If all these take trouble over things that are transient, how much more should I take trouble over my Lord.
>
> When you stand up for prayer, do not begin in a slovenly way, lest you perform all your prayer in a slack or slovenly and wearied way. Rather, when you stand up, sign yourself with the sign of the cross, gather together your thoughts, be in a state of recollection and readiness, gaze upon him to whom you are praying, and then commence. Force yourself, so that right at the beginning of your prayer tears may flow and you feel suffering in yourself, so that your whole prayer may prove beneficial.
>
> When you do not have thoughts which hinder you, it is not necessary to make space between one group of psalms and the next. But if your thoughts are in turmoil, you should spend more time in prayers and tears, than in the recitation of psalms. Drive the thoughts away by whatever means you have tested out, whether by varying the words or by some other means. Take in what I am telling you. If you should then have some beneficial thought, let it take the place of the psalms for you: do not push away from yourself what is the gift of God just in order to fulfill your prescribed portion of psalms.
>
> Prayer that does not have mingled into it the thought of God and interior vision is a weariness of the flesh.[20]

It is clear that Evagrius is speaking from his own experience and the wisdom of other desert elders. This passage demonstrates the **realism** of praxis: the difficulty in getting up in the middle of the night, the tension between "nothing happening" and patient watchfulness, the need for physical activity and posture in prayer, the presence of psychological turmoil, the struggle with distracting thoughts, the vulnerability to suffering and tears, the danger of letting proper form stand in the way experience of God, and the necessity for inner participation in prayer rather than "just getting it done."

Abba John Cassian emphasized the importance of vigils as a direct response to the long, dark hours of the night when the monk was more vulnerable to scattering and corrupting thoughts, fantasies and temptations, whether awake or asleep. This heightened time of solitude and silence in the cell could easily be filled with demons of the monk's weaknesses or opportunities for inner spiritual growth. This was a time when the monk's natural sexual energy or unrestrained desires could fill his mind and body with urges, memories or fantasies resulting in guilt, regret or behavior that could deflect him from his chosen path of chastity. One of the virtues of the vocation to chastity was to give the monk more time and energy for care of the soul and the heart.[21] This was a struggle for both male and female monks. Both had left a hedonistic society where sexual impurity was common and one's sexual partners were valued primarily for the fulfillment of personal urges and desires. Amma Syncletica addressed her monks about this difficult part of the life they had freely chosen:

> When, moreover, we do confine ourselves to our houses, not even there should we be careless, but should maintain our vigilance, for it has been written: "Stay awake!" The more we secure ourselves in chastity, the more we are plied with galling thoughts. . . .Were you victorious over actual physical sexual impurity? Then the Enemy will inflict it upon you through the senses. And when you protect yourself from this, too, he continues to lurk in the crannies of the mind, stirring up a battle of the spirit for you. Even for women who live as solitaries he conjures up handsome faces and old relationships. . . . Giving your assent to these fantasies, moreover, is equivalent to sexual impurity in the world. . . .[22]

Vigils integrated the inner praxis of the soul with very specific praxes of the body. The purpose of training the body to remain awake as long as possible gave opportunities to drive away unrestrained or self-destructive passions of the ego. It extended, also, the boundaries of the monk's experience of God at one of the most sensitive and personal times of his or her daily life. Abba John was well aware that the vigilance of the night, also, became a powerful influence on the monk's life in community during the day:

> This, I say, is the end of all perfection—that the mind purged of every carnal desire may daily be elevated to spiritual things, until one's whole way of life and all the yearnings of one's heart become a single and continuous prayer.[23]

These desert monastic experiences of vigils reflect an awareness of the depth and complexities of personal prayer. They mirror prayer as an interaction of body, mind and spirit that illumines the desires, anxieties and barriers that are scattering or blocking our openness to God's grace. They teach us that prayer is a demeanor of wakefulness and expectation that enlarges our experience of God. The desert elders teach us that prayer is an honest awareness, often through sadness, tears and regret, of how our personal control of life has brought harm to others and ourselves. Such transparency of self leads to a psycho-spiritual desire for change. Vigilance in prayer is the soil in which our desires and the desires of God become one. The experiences of the abbas and ammas show us that prayer is a trans-personal experience wherein we are lured beyond our self-sufficiency to a freely chosen dependence on the energies of God's Spirit. Very few of us today are able to practice all-night vigils, but all of us can discern places in our daily lives where a commitment to vigilant prayer can open us to constant growth and transformation. What we experience and become in prayer will help us listen to and manifest God's presence in the words, decisions, and actions of our daily lives.

Praxis of Scripture

The words of the Bible and the words of elders, in whose lives the words of Scripture were embodied, formed one half of an essential and dynamic polarity in early Egyptian monasticism. The power of the word was in constant and generative tension with action. Douglas Burton-Christie emphasizes this life-giving complementarity by calling attention to the two things monks often asked their elders: "Abba, give me a word," and "Abba, what should I do?"[24] These questions summarize the awareness that words must lead to action and action must embody the wisdom of Scripture. This reflects a very **practical asceticism.** Words are meaningless when they do not lead to a very specific new way of life. Scripture and the teaching of the elders were never meant to be learned only for the sake of intellectual knowledge. Oral teaching was directed toward an integration of heart and mind and then manifested in action. Often, the words of Scripture and the teaching of elders were put into action and their meanings discovered much later through experience. How did this transformation of words into action take place?

Meletē

Abba Lot went to see Abba Joseph (of Panephysis) and said to him, "Abba, as far as I can I say my little office, I fast a little, I pray and meditate, I live in peace as far as I can, I purify my thoughts. What else can I do?" Then the old man stood up and stretched out his hands towards heaven. His fingers became as ten lamps of fire and he said to him, "If you will, you can become all flame."[25]

A brother asked Abba Poemen, "How should I live in the cell?" He said to him, "Living in your cell clearly means manual work, eating only once a day, silence, meditation; but really making progress in the cell, means to experience contempt for yourself wherever you go, not to neglect the hours of prayer and to pray secretly."[26]

Both abbas Joseph and Poemen include *meditation* as a fundamental part of exterior praxis. Meditation refers to several practices, but is not equivalent to the modern practices of *lectio divina* or centering prayer. Rather than involving discursive thought or rational analysis, meditation was a way of **memorizing** Scripture, **reciting** Scripture and **repeating** Scripture for long periods of time. It was primarily a prelude to personal prayer during vigils and led, ultimately, to an inner assimilation of the wisdom of Scripture that influenced the active life of the monk.

Meletē was a disciplined praxis of keeping the Bible present throughout the monk's day and night. Its roots lay in Greek and Roman culture where repetition and memorization were combined to learn and ponder philosophical rules. The purpose was an intentional mindfulness, leading to awareness of what lies beyond the human realm.[27] The desert elders used meletē as a means of reciting memorized texts aloud and as a way of letting go of distractions and turning their thoughts to God's presence (silent reading or recitation were unknown at that time). This environment of recited biblical texts created by meletē was a pathway leading to personal *prayers*, especially prayers of *supplication* (contrition for specific sins and desire for forgiveness) and prayerful *vows* to seek God with earnestness of heart and remain faithful to the monastic life.

In Abba John Cassian's *Ninth Conference: On Prayer*, Abba Isaac describes two other basic types of prayers. "In the third place there are *intercessions*, which we are also accustomed to make for others when our spirits are fervent, beseeching on behalf of our dear ones and for the peace of the whole world. . . ." and "Finally, in the fourth place there are *thanksgivings*, which the mind, recalling God's past benefits, contemplating his present ones, or foreseeing what great things God has prepared for those who love him, offers the Lord in unspeakable ecstasies."[28]

Meletē and recitation of the Psalms were complementary, yet basic, parts of praxis for each monk. During vigils, meletē, and personal prayers became an antiphonal pattern of praxis throughout the night. In this context meletē was also called *meditatio*. In chapter 3 we saw that meditatio was a required and essential personal praxis in Pachomian monasteries. It was like a thread, weaving the monk's daily activities into a tapestry of awareness of God's presence through recitation and reflection on texts of the Bible. They were recited in procession to work and worship, during the day's labor, following teaching by the abbot or leader of each house, and in the solitude of each monk's cell.

The most revered form of meletē/meditatio is recommended by Abba Isaac to Abba John Cassian:

> The formula for this discipline that you are seeking, then, shall be presented to you. Every monk who longs for the continual awareness of God should be in the habit of meditating on it ceaselessly in his heart, after having driven out every kind of thought, because he will be unable to hold fast to it in any other way than by being freed from all bodily cares and concerns. Just as this was handed down to us by a few of the oldest fathers who were left, so also we pass it on to none but the most exceptional, who truly desire it. This, then, is the devotional formula proposed to you as absolutely necessary for possessing the perpetual awareness of God: "O God, incline unto my aid; O Lord, make haste to help me" (Ps 70:1).
> . . . . Not without reason has this verse been selected from out of the whole body of Scripture. For it takes up all the emotions that can be applied to human nature and with great correctness and accuracy it adjusts itself to every condition and every attack.[29]

Lectio and Memorization

Abba John Cassian emphasized the essential relationship between meletē/meditatio and two related forms of exterior praxis. The first is *lectio,* the simple oral reading of a biblical text. This involved the body in praxis and the sound of the text was an effective antidote to distracting thoughts or attention given to evil desires and activities. The second is *memorization.* Memorization, while important in itself, also facilitated the practice of lectio and meletē/meditatio. Abba Nesteros speaks clearly about the grace present in memorization:

> Hence, the successive books of Holy Scripture must be diligently committed to memory and ceaselessly reviewed. This continual meditation will bestow on us double fruit. First, inasmuch as the mind's attention is occupied with reading and with preparing to read, it cannot be taken captive in the entrapments of harmful thoughts. Then, the things that we have not been able to understand because our mind was busy at the time, things that we have gone through repeatedly and are laboring to memorize, we shall see more clearly

afterward when we are free from every seductive deed and sight, and especially when we are silently meditating at night. **Thus, while we are at rest
and as it were immersed in the stupor of sleep, there will be revealed an
understanding of hidden meanings that we did not grasp even slightly
when we were awake.**[30] (author's emphasis)

Thus, lectio and memorization can work together to bring a text to
the attention of the monk and in the praxis of meletē/meditatio the constant repetition of what is being heard produces an "inner knowing." The
body, mind and spirit are blended in an inner dialog with the Word of God.
Meletē/meditatio led to a "spiritual knowing" of what was being recited.
The constant repetition of what was being memorized and recited transformed the words of Scripture from an exterior experience into two interior languages of prayer. The trio of lectio, memorization, and
meletē/meditatio enabled the Bible, itself, to become an active prayer of
the monk as well as leading the monk to his or her own personal interior
prayers. These three forms of external praxis illustrate the fundamental
role of the Bible in desert monastic life and the link between God's Word in
Scripture and the interior dialog taking place within the monk. The fruit of
this rich praxis would be seen in the monk's daily life; in humility, love of
neighbor, and love of God.[31] "Thus the contemplation of Scripture became
for Christianity the birth of contemplative life and the foundation of monasticism, beginning with the early desert fathers."[32]

Fasting

"Abba Theodore said, 'Privation of food mortifies the body of the
monk.' Another old man said, 'Vigils mortify it more.'"[33] Even though the
other old man gave preference to the power of vigils, fasting was an integral part of external ascetic practice. Like all praxis, fasting was more austere for some, and there was no single rule for all monks. Amma Syncletica
gets to the heart of the virtue of fasting. She tells her sister monks:

> Let not the delights of those who are wealthy by worldly standards entice
> you as being something useful. For the sake of pleasure they honour the culi-
> nary art; by fasting and through frugality surpass their superabundance of
> foodstuffs. For Scripture says: "A soul, when satisfied, scorns honey." Do not
> fill up with bread and you will not crave wine.[34]

Notice that Amma Syncletica points to the **futility** of the world's stand-
ards about wealth. The limiting of food, through fasting, enables the monk

to avoid using the gift of foodstuffs primarily as a means for the satisfaction of pleasure. The art of cooking was also practiced in the monastery, but the preparation of food was not an end in itself. The limitation of food through "frugality" does not negate its value or taste. It enables the monk to go beyond the "superabundance of foodstuffs" and be fed, not only by the food, but by the discipline of **being satisfied with only what is needed for the day.** Amma Syncletica reminds her monks that when pleasure becomes its own virtue, human beings "scorn" the grace and wisdom of God's natural gifts. Fasting enables the monk to surpass the abundance of self-induced pleasures in order to experience the superabundance of a more authentic human wealth, the "honey" of dependence on God's gifts for body and soul.

Fasting is not simply a pattern of denial for its own sake. It is not a negative judgment about food or the body's need for sustenance. The desert elders valued fasting for many reasons. It gives a sacred value to food, which can easily be taken for granted. The act of limiting what is eaten points to the emptiness of overeating simply for pleasure, so common in the Roman Empire at that time. A habit of moderation builds an inner character that appreciates material goods and promotes stewardship of one's self and the fruits of the earth. Fasting also cools the undisciplined passions and, like limiting sleep, makes a person more open to depend on God. Amma Syncletica said, "Truly fasting and sleeping on the ground are set before us because of our sensuality."[35]

> A brother asked Abba Poemen, "Abba, how can I acquire the fear of God?" Abba Poemen said to him, "How can we acquire the fear of God when our belly is full of cheese and preserved foods?" . . . . He also said, "There are three things which I am not able to do without: food, clothing and sleep; but I can restrict them to some extent."[36]

Fasting in the desert was related, also, to the austere desert climate and the need to preserve food for long periods of time, especially for the hermits and hesychasts. Dried bread, water, olive oil and dried vegetables formed the basic diet, but even these were limited. The limitation of drinking water and use of dried vegetables was linked to an ancient designation of these foods as assisting in suppressing sexual desires. There were excesses in austerity, yet Abba Cassian remained firm in his endorsement of fasting among the desert monks. They had chosen this way of life and their dietary praxis must be seen in the wider context of seeking the grace of inner transformation: ". . . .the chastity of the inner person is discerned by the perfection of this virtue (of dietary restraint)."[37] Fasting was essential, but never more important than love of neighbor:

Abba Cassian related the following: "The holy Germanus and I went to Egypt, to visit an old man. Because he offered us hospitality we asked him, 'Why do you not keep the rule of fasting, when you receive visiting brothers, as we have received it in Palestine?' He replied, 'Fasting is always at hand but you I cannot have with me always. Furthermore, fasting is certainly a useful and necessary thing, but it depends on our choice, while the law of God lays it upon us to do the works of charity. Thus, receiving Christ in you, I ought to serve you with all diligence, but when I have taken leave of you, I can resume fasting again.'"[38]

In Conferences 12 and 13 Abba John Cassian promotes the essential values of fasting because he includes fasting, along with vigils and labor, as the three most fundamental parts of monastic life.[39] Their purpose, like all praxis, is the transformation of the heart. Columba Stewart, O.S.B., points out that "to deal only with the physical aspects of monastic asceticism is to miss the heart of the early monastic endeavor, which was to take human potential to its limits in order to show those limits to God who alone could surpass them."[40] The praxis of the desert elders was a collaboration of human effort with God, knowing that only God's grace can fulfill the monk's desire for authentic human life.

The Interior Dimension of Desert Praxis

The Whole Person Is the Venue for Grace: An Incarnational Anthropology

When the work of God is the principal aim, the needs of the body are put in proper perspective. "But strive first for the kingdom of God and his righteousness, and all these things will be given to you as well" (Matt 6:33, NRSV). Praxis puts the desires and needs of the body in the perspective of the realm of God and transforms the **body** into the venue for God's grace and love. The desert elders embodied this truth by developing an ascetic discipline designed to help the monk have **easily satisfied needs.**

In his youth Abba John the Eunuch questioned an old man, "How have you been able to carry out the work of God in peace? For we cannot do it, not even with labor." The old man said, "We were able to do it, because we considered the work of God to be primary, and bodily needs to be subsidiary; but you hold bodily needs to be primary and the work of God to be secondary; that is why you labor, and that is why the Saviour said to his disciples, 'Seek first his kingdom and his righteousness, and all these things shall be yours as well.'"[41]

The elders knew that when personal desires and needs are foremost, praxis is really hard work and a difficult intervention. The difficulty of praxis lies in the unwillingness of a person to let go of control of his or her life. Even the desire for "record-breaking" austerity adds one more personal need that is difficult to satisfy and misses the point of asceticism, through pride. This type of pride was called *vain-glory.* The "hard work" of praxis is necessary, but self-sufficiency is not the goal. The struggle is toward the limitation of a person's needs and desires so that they do not obstruct the formation of humility.

> Abba Ammonas was asked, "What is the 'narrow and hard way?'" (Matt 7:14) He replied, "The 'narrow and hard way' is this, to control your thoughts, and to strip yourself of your own will, for the sake of God. This is also the meaning of the sentence, 'Lo, we have left everything and followed you.'"[42]

This "narrow" or "violent" way calls for **self-care** through letting go of the self's will (the ego's desire to control the self). This sacrifice of control of the self through praxis invites God to provide a person's **true and authentic needs.** As long as "worldly" needs and work are the dominant force in a person's life, he or she risks losing the grace to find the needs that are real. Unlike the Greek philosophical praxis of their day, the desert elders learned that the fruit of their praxis is not to transcend the self and achieve a "spiritual" or non-corporal state of being. Monastic desert praxis sought a **transformation** of self, the inner being (the heart), by relying on God's grace.

Daily Life Is a Venue for God's Grace

The desert elders sought a never-ending growth and expansion of heart. Their happiness and joy was experienced in having easily satisfied needs that opened them to newness of life. "Abba Moses asked Abba Silvanus, 'Can a man lay a new foundation every day?' The old man said, 'If he works hard, he can lay a new foundation every moment.'"[43] Humility, through easily satisfied needs, brings the possibility of an ever new and renewed life, **a daily conversion.** The fruit of this constant renewal is progress in holiness, the embodiment of God through humility and love of neighbor. "Abba James said, 'We do not need words only, for, at the present time, there are many words among men, but we need works, for this is what is required, not words which do not bear fruit.'"[44] Praxis emphasizes living in the **present.** It serves the spiritual health of a person's soul as well as the common good of the community. As we saw in previous chapters, praxis transforms time by opening each act and intent to the presence of God. The backdrop of eternity sanctifies each task and desire with the fulfillment of a creation not yet completed. In this way praxis is not concerned with the past or with failure. God's judgment takes place in the present moment as each person seeks renewed life.

> It happened that when Abba Arsenius was sitting in his cell that he was harassed by demons. His servants, on their return, stood outside his cell and heard him praying to God in these words, "O God, do not leave me. I have done nothing good in your sight, but according to your goodness, let me now make a beginning of good."[45]

Rather than denigrating the body, praxis provides ever-new opportunities for the body's goodness to be consummated in humility and charity. The hard work of praxis confirms the sacredness of the body and the world.

> Abba Isaac came to see Abba Poemen and found him washing his feet. As he enjoyed freedom of speech with him he said, "How is it that others practice austerity and treat their bodies hardly?" Abba Poemen said to him, "We have not been taught to kill our bodies, but to kill our passions."[46]

When praxis is balanced it becomes a pattern of ascetic discipline that prevents bodily desires and the control of the self-centered ego from denying the soul its proper influence and, at the same time, keeps the soul aware of the sacred nature of the body.

A Psycho-Somatic Understanding of the Human Being.

"Abba Elias said, 'If the spirit does not sing with the body, labor is in vain. Whoever loves tribulation will obtain joy and peace later on.'"[47] As we have seen, the lives and sayings of the desert elders do not reflect the Greek philosophical or Gnostic understanding of dualism current in their day. There is no doubt that some of the elders, especially Abba Evagrius, were influenced by neo-Platonist and Stoic thought. Yet the anthropology of the desert elders is rooted in their reflection on the Bible and its clear affirmation that humans have the seed of goodness within them, even when they choose to flaw their nature. The tribulations of life, rather than being something to escape, can become opportunities for maturation and transformation. The goal of praxis, therefore, is not to free the soul from the body or the difficulties of human living. Salvation is transformation of the whole person through a process of growth leading to purity of heart, rather than liberation of the soul from the "limitations and unreality" of bodily life.

The goal of praxis is the expansion, the renewal of the **whole person** through openness to a relationship with God and cooperation with God's grace.

The desert elders did not think the body was a separate entity under the control of the unrestrained ego.[48] The body is part of the whole person who is a social being. The body is influenced by all aspects of the person and does not owe its significance to the limited desires of the ego. The body can be influenced by the ego in a manner that puts the focus of life on self-centered passions as if they were separate from the whole person. But this is not an authentic expression of human life. Praxis seeks to overcome the body's dependence on the unrestrained ego and its attachment to the physical passions and restore the integration of the body to the whole person. Praxis, then, serves the **whole person** by forming a relationship in which the soul and body, as integral dimensions of a human being, are "embodied" or "made perfect" in God's will.

This process of sanctification is predicated on the awareness that each human being is created in the image of God and does not take his or her identity from the limited desires of the unrestrained ego. The grace present in praxis can harmonize the soul and body within the divine will. The body and its passions are not to be destroyed to free the person from the "limitations" or "illusions" of history. On the contrary, the desert elders declare by their actions and wisdom that the sanctification of the whole person to its authentic being takes place **within history** in the context of a "heavenly city" (politeia) in the desert. The heavenly city is a place where new life is experienced every moment. God responds to each person's desire for repentance and new life in a unique way and no person is beyond God's reach:

Pseudo Macarius said:

> If there are those because of their spiritual immaturity cannot yet commit themselves entirely to the work of prayer, they should fulfill obedience in other matters, serving as they are able. They should work gladly, serving diligently with joy, not out of reward of honor, nor for human glory nor thanks of men. Let them shun negligence or sluggishness.
>
> Let them not be servants of the bodies and souls of others, but as servants of Christ and of us, let their work appear pure and sincere before God. Let no one believe that by zeal for good works he cannot do the things which will bring salvation to his soul. For God does not enjoin upon his servants, but he shows abundant and great love and divine goodness, so that of his own good will he rewards each one by giving him some good work to do. Therefore, no one who sincerely seeks salvation will lack power to do good. The Lord says, "Whoever will give even a cup of cold water to someone simply in the name of a disciple, amen, I say to you, that he will not go unrewarded" (Matt 10:42).

What can be more powerful than this commandment? Heavenly reward follows upon a cup of cold water. And look at the immense love for mankind! He says, "As long as you did it to one of these, you did it to me" (Matt 25:40). Indeed it is a small commandment, but when obeyed it brings forth from God a great and abundant gain.[49]

The Syrian author of Pseudo-Marcarius's *Great Letter* mirrors the wisdom of the Egyptian elders. Salvation is sought and found **on the earth** in simple work and in the giving of a cup of water. Human life and love are the venue for God's grace and human wholeness!

Praxis and Love of Neighbor

Praxis is never an end in itself. "Amma Sarah said, 'If I prayed that all men should approve of my conduct, I should find myself a penitent at the door of each one, but I shall rather pray that my heart may be pure towards all.'"[50] The desert elders looked at morality or moral obligations in a different way from conventional modern thought or theology. Modern morality is usually based on a personal obligation to the dicta of a set of external values usually articulated by a faith community or social institution. The result of not obeying this moral "high road" is personal guilt which the offender cannot eliminate because he or she has been judged a failure. Stelios Ramfos demonstrates that the desert elders had a more "utilitarian" approach to moral behavior.[51] They saw morality as something which, after repentance, is a genuine struggle along each person's chosen path to holiness. This struggle "that my heart may be pure to all" (in the words of Amma Sarah) is based on the **new life the person has chosen** rather than an exterior obligation. The desire for moral behavior is internal rather than in response to an external law or value.

The desert elders saw no distinction between a person's inward nature and the outside world. Therefore, **every action is related to the spiritual growth and inward nature of the monk.** Since the monk has chosen a path of holiness, what is spiritually desirable is now a source of pleasure and forms the monk into a better person. What is spiritually desirable becomes a great source of freedom, joy and pleasure (rather than the self-centered material pleasures of the ego). **Personal sacrifice and moral behavior become part of each person's identity and cease to be an obligation.** This does not eliminate the possibility of sinful behavior, but places each person's repentance in the context of his or her desire to renew the path he or she has chosen in every moment and in every action. Contrition is real and the sorrow and tears which often accompanied what the elders called *compunction* or *penthos* represented genuine sorrow for sins. Compunction is not only sorrow for sinful actions or omissions and their consequences, but also a person's sadness for being unfaithful to the path he or she had chosen. The grace present in genuine compunction initiates a person's desire for repentance that opens the possibility for a new beginning each moment of each day.

In modern faith communities, morality is usually rooted in external dicta or rules which represent the specific religious values of a faith tradition. An individual either fails or succeeds in fulfilling them. Failure brings guilt and judgment. This is a different mindset from the desert elders whose inner praxis leads to transformation of the ego and the will (purity of heart). This transformation produces an internal motivation to love others (moral behavior) rather than a response to an external law of love. In the praxis of the desert elders, morality is a natural desire. As a person moves toward the grace of humility he or she freely chooses charity and love of neighbor because that is their **vocation**. When a person fails to fulfill this inner desire, the guilt or sorrow that follows is an awareness that he or she has failed in the vocation they have chosen and not because some external law has been broken.

Christian churches are often criticized for an emphasis on human sin. They are stereotyped as being overly judgmental and the cause of a modern malaise of guilt-induced anxiety, fueled by a belief that the nature of humankind is depraved. God is often perceived as a judgmental creator who demands punishment. Sadly, this negative perspective is present in some Christian faith communities. It affects theology, preaching, moral imperatives and personal prayer. It is predicated on a negative anthropology. It is a tempting explanation of and response to the failures of humankind. The wisdom of the desert ammas and abbas is overwhelmingly different because it reflects a positive Christian anthropology rooted in the Bible and their life experiences. The desert elders were honest about their sins and the consequences, but they never lost sight of their original goodness. Guilt and compunction led them to a restored commitment to their true nature, always depending on God's grace. Their path to transformation, through praxis of prayer, emphasized the development of humility and charity.

> A brother questioned Abba Poemen saying, "Give me a word." And he said to him, "The Fathers put compunction as the beginning of every action." The brother said again, "Give me another word." The old man replied, "As far as you can, do some manual work so as to give alms, for it is written that alms and faith purify from sin." The brother said, "What is faith?" The old man said, "Faith is to live humbly and to give alms."[52]

Notes

1. *The Sayings of the Desert Fathers,* trans. Benedicta Ward, S.L.G. (Kalamazoo: Cistercian Publications, 1984) John the Dwarf, 34, 92.

2. Ward, *Sayings,* Syncletica, 1, 230–31.

3. I am indebted to Stelios Ramfos for these insights into the meaning of kopos and praxis. See *Like a Pelican in the Wilderness* (Brookline: Holy Cross Orthodox Press, 2000) 79–84.

4. From the author's class notes in *Early Monastic Studies,* taught by Columba Stewart, O.S.B., at St. John's School of Theology, Collegeville, Minnesota, 2002.

5. *The Syriac Fathers on Prayer and the Spiritual Life,* trans. Sebastian Brock (Kalamazoo: Cistercian Publications, 1987) "Evagrius, Admonition on Prayer," 66.

6. Dorotheos of Gaza, *Discourses and Sayings.* trans. Eric P. Wheeler (Kalamazoo: Cistercian Publications, 1977) "On Consultation," 128–29.

7. Ward, *Sayings,* Gerontius, 1, 50.

8. Brock, *The Syriac Fathers,* John the Solitary, 16, 86.

9. Dorotheos of Gaza, *Discourses,* On Renunciation, I, 77.

10. Ibid., 79.

11. Ibid., 81.

12. Ibid., 101.

13. Ibid., 83–84.

14. For a full description of Abba Dorotheos' analogy see *Discourses,* 86–87.

15. Evagrius Ponticus, *The Praktikos and Chapters on Prayer,* trans. John Eudes Bamberger (Kalamazoo: Cistercian Publications, 1981) Praktikos, ch. 54, 31.

16. *The Lives of the Desert Fathers,* trans. Norman Russell and intro. Benedicta Ward, S.L.G. (Oxford: Cistercian Publications, 1981) ch. viii, 50, 77.

17. Charles Cummings, O.C.S.O., *Monastic Practices* (Kalamazoo: Cistercian Publications, 1986) 137.

18. Ward, *Sayings,* Arsenius, 15, 11.

19. Massimo Capuani, *Christian Egypt* (Collegeville: Liturgical Press, 2002) 75.

20. Brock. *The Syriac Fathers,* "Evagrius, Admonition on Prayer," 70–71.

21. Columba Stewart, O.S.B., *Cassian the Monk* (Oxford: Oxford University Press, 1998) 74.

22. Pseudo-Athanasius, *The Life & Regimen of the Blessed and Holy Syncletica,* trans. Elizabeth Bryson Bongie (Toronto: Peregrina, 1999) 26–27, 22–23.

23. John Cassian, *The Conferences,* trans. Boniface Ramsey, O.P. (New York: Paulist Press, 1997) conference 10: On Prayer, VII.3, 376.

24. Douglas Burton-Christie, *The Word in the Desert. Scripture and the Quest for Holiness in Early Christian Monasticism* (Oxford: Oxford University Press, 1993) 134.

25. Ward, *Sayings,* Joseph of Panephysis, 7, 103.

26. Ward, *Sayings,* Poemen, 168, 190.

27. Columba Stewart, *Cassian the Monk,* 102.

28. John Cassian, *The Conferences,* conference 9: On Prayer, XI.1; XII. 1, 2; XIII, XIV, 337–38.

29. Ibid., conference 10: On Prayer, X.2, 3. 379.

30. John Cassian, *The Conferences,* conference 14. X. 4, 514–15.

31. It is possible to see the roots of a much later praxis called *lectio divina* in the simple *lectio* and *meletē/meditation* of the desert elders. Lectio divina became the norm in Benedictine monastic praxis and is now a common practice among laity as well, but should not be confused with its earlier roots.

32. Joseph Milne, *The Ground of Being: Foundations of Christian Mysticism* (London: Temenos Academy, 2004) 15.

33. Ward, *Sayings,* Theodore of Eleutheropolis, 2, 80.

34. Pseudo-Athanasius, *The Life of Blessed Syncletica,* 95, 60.

35. Ward, *Sayings,* Syncletica, 8, 232.

36. Ibid., Poemen 181, 185, 192–193.

37. Columba Stewart, *Cassian the Monk,* 72.

38. Ibid., 113.

39. Ibid., 72.

40. Ibid., 72.

41. Ward, *Sayings,* John the Eunuch 1, 105.

42. Ibid., Ammonas 11, 28.

43. Ibid., Silvanus 11, 224.

44. Ibid., James 4, 104.

45. Ibid., Arsenius 3, 9.

46. Ibid., Poemen 184, 193.

47. Ward, *Sayings,* Elias 6, 71.

48. The author is indebted to Stelios Ramfos for his discussion of this topic in ch. 7, "Ascetic Praxis" in *Pelican,* 83–88.

49. Pseudo Macarius, *The Fifty Spiritual Homilies and the Great Letter,* trans. George A. Maloney, S.J. (Mahwah, N.J.: Paulist Press, 1992) "The Great Letter," 270–71.

50. Ward, *Sayings,* Sarah 5, 230.

51. For a more thorough discussion of praxis and morality, see Stelios Ramfos, *Pelican,* 84–88.

52. Ward, *Sayings,* Poemen 69, 176.

8   Praxis and Labor

The Sanctification of Daily Life

Abba Pachomius said, "For I have truly seen the treasure of God hidden in human vessels"[1]

Seeking God Embraces All of Life

Someone asked Abba Agathon, "Which is better, bodily asceticism or interior vigilance?" The old man replied, "Man is like a tree, bodily asceticism is the foliage, interior vigilance is the fruit. According to that which is written, 'Every tree that bringeth not forth good fruit shall be cut down and cast into the fire' (Matt 3:10). It is clear that all our care should be directed toward the fruit, that is to say, guard the spirit; but it needs the protection and the embellishment of the foliage, which is bodily asceticism."[2]

Abba Agathon realized that a person's desire for God must be seen as a life that accepts the necessity and goodness of both physical and spiritual labor. Each person offers God his or her mundane activities as well as thoughts, prayers and spiritual discipline. Physical labor and ascetic discipline are both necessary for an undivided human life. As Abba Agathon noted, praxis can result in "the fruit of life," the spiritual vigilance or openness that leads to the formation of a person's inner life and acts of charity. In like manner, kopos—physical labor—when it takes its meaning from praxis, provides a spiritual bonding to the tasks and activities of daily life. The desert lured men, like Agathon, and women to seek God through a life of both prayer and labor. It was "A place where they are separated in their cells but united in love."[3]

Integration of Praxis and Labor: A Creative Tension

"Abba Agathon was wise in spirit and active in body. He provided everything he needed for himself, in manual work, food, and clothing."[4] Labor and praxis are not in competition, nor should either be neglected. This necessary integration is the focus of a colorful incident from the life of John the Dwarf:

> It was said of Abba John the Dwarf, that one day he said to his elder brother, "I should like to be free of all care, like the angels, who do not work, but ceaselessly offer worship to God." So he took off his cloak and went away into the desert. After a week he came back to his brother. When he knocked on the door, he heard his brother say, before he opened it, "Who are you?" And he said, "I am John, your brother." But he replied, "John has become an angel, and henceforth he is no longer among men." Then the other begged him, saying, "It is I." However, his brother did not let him in, but left him there in distress until morning. Then, opening the door, he said to him, "You are a man and you must once again work in order to eat." Then John made a prostration before him, saying, "Forgive me."[5]

This incident is reminiscent of Jesus' visit to his friends Mary and Martha (Luke 10:38-42). Mary sits listening attentively to Jesus while Martha is busy with work. When Martha complained, Jesus reminded her that her work had distracted her from "the better part," which Mary had chosen. Abba Silvanus interprets Jesus' response to Martha as concern about her overemphasis on work rather than his giving sole preference to Mary's listening. When a monk used Jesus' comment to Martha as justification for his personal choice of study and prayer over physical labor, Abba Silvanus corrected him with these words: "Mary needs Martha. It is really thanks to Martha that Mary is praised."[6]

There is always the need to integrate the listening and inner growth of praxis with the physical labors that make human life possible. Yet labor should never seek benefits that become distractions to the monk's ascetic discipline or be exercised at the expense of the welfare of other monks or their neighbors.

> At one time, when the Abbot Silvanus had left his cell for a little while, his disciple Zachary and other brethren moved the fence of his garden and made the garden bigger. But when the old man came back and saw it, he took up his sheepskin to go away. And they cast themselves at his feet and asked him to tell them why he did thus. And the old man spoke, "I shall not go into this cell," he said, "until the fence be brought back into its place." Which being speedily done, he returned.[7]

Zachary and his brother monks saw an opportunity to increase the productivity of Silvanus's garden. It would provide them with more food and perhaps additional income to meet other needs, including offerings for the poor. The response of Sivanus was stern, yet not ungrateful. He discerned that the additional crops would require labor that went beyond their needs.[8] He recognized that when labor is disconnected from spiritual praxis there is an opportunity to develop a passion for physical benefits and security. This can lead to greed and suppression or denial of the spiritual dimension of life and work. Abba Silvanus was guarding the inner life of his small community by firmly correcting his brothers. The purpose of their community was not abundance. It was to become open to God's presence and grace.

The integration of labor and praxis was always a tension for the monks of the desert, as it is in our lives. They had come to the desert for solitude with their eyes turned toward heaven. But they learned quickly that they had not left the earth and that their lives could never be lived without concern for others. How can a person be totally devoted to seeking God and the welfare of his or her soul and at the same time be concerned with the mundane activities of daily life? One response to this dilemma is to understand both labor and praxis as integral dimensions of **a single vocation.**

There came to the abbot Lucius in Enna certain monks of the kind called Euchitae, that is, Men of Prayer, and the old man asked them saying, "What kind of handiwork do ye do?" And they said, "We touch no kind of handiwork, but as the Apostle says, we pray without ceasing." The old man said to them, "So do ye not eat?" They said, "Yea we eat." And the old man said, "Now while ye are eating, who prays for you?" And again he questioned them saying, "Ye do not sleep?" And they said, "We sleep." And the old man said, "And while ye sleep, who prays for you?" And they could find no answer. And he said to them, "Forgive me, my brethren, but behold ye do not do as ye have said: but I shall show you how working with my hands, I pray without ceasing. For I sit, by the help of God, steeping my few palm leaves and from them I weave a mat, and I say, 'Have mercy upon me, O God, according to thy loving-kindness: according to the multitude of thy tender mercies blot out my transgressions.'" And he said to them, "Is this a prayer or no?" And they said to him, "Yea." And he said, "When I abide all the day working and praying with heart and mouth, I make sixteen denarii more or less, and out of them I leave two at the door, and I spend the rest on food. But whoso finds the two denarii prays for me while I eat and sleep: and so by God's grace there is fulfilled in me as the Scripture saith, 'Pray without ceasing.'"[9]

Abba Lucius refused to let the other monks' emphasis on constant prayer and study disconnect them from the necessity of physical labor. But he went even further. He demonstrated, from his own experience, that labor and prayer are embodied in each other and ennoble each other. Daily labor contributes to the welfare of the soul and is the venue for "the fruits of the soul" to manifest God's presence in the world. Every task, no matter how simple, is an opportunity to bring prayer to life and contribute to the welfare of others. **This means that labor, itself, is a spiritual activity.** Like prayer it is a venue for the flow of God's energy for the life of the world.

Stelios Ramfos outlines three dimensions of the wisdom of the desert elders concerning labor. Labor is a "spiritual work," labor is a "self-offering," and labor takes place in "eschatological time."[10] These three dimensions of labor integrate prayer and labor to form **an undivided life.** Ascetic praxis helps a person see the spiritual dimension of all of life, including labor. In the context of that vision, the materiality of labor becomes an opportunity for each person to offer his or her life to God and neighbor. Thus, the chronological time of both prayer and labor becomes filled with the eternal purposes of God and contribute to the coming of the Kingdom. Labor and time are transformed. In the words of Abba Lucius: "Is this a prayer or no?"

Labor Extends the Boundaries of Self-Interest and Embodies Prayer

"Abba Poemen said, 'Life in the monastery demands three things: the first is humility, the next is obedience, and the third which sets them in motion and is like a goad is the work of the monastery.'"[11] Just as the cell is the place of the monk's transformation, work is the venue for the monk's charity, the fruit of God's presence. In both cases a person must let go of the boundaries created by his or her ego. Abba Poemen identifies three fundamental requirements of monastic life:

The first requirement, **humility,** is genuine self-knowledge, recognizing one's limitations and accepting total dependence on God. Dorotheos of Gaza said:

> Among the seniors it used to be told how a brother asked one of the elders, "What is humility?" And the elder replied, "Humility is a great and divine work and the road to humility is labor, bodily labor, while seeking to know oneself and to put oneself below everyone else and praying to God about everything: this is the road to humility, but humility itself is something divine and incomprehensible" . . . Abba Dorotheos continued, "A man standing in need of everything from God is ready to make progress: he knows how he will make progress and cannot be puffed up. He does not rely on his own abilities but attributes to God everything he does right and always gives thanks to him."[12]

The second requirement, **obedience,** is listening to the needs of the community and placing the common good above personal desire and need. Discerning the common good was rooted in meditation on the Scriptures and prayer.

Abba Dorotheos said:

> In the Book of Proverbs it says, "Those who have no guidance fall like leaves but there is safety in much counsel." Take a good look at this saying, brothers. Look at what Scripture is teaching us. It assures us that we should not set ourselves up as guideposts, that we should not consider ourselves sagacious, that we should not believe we can direct ourselves. We need assistance, we need guidance in addition to God's grace.[13]

In the monastic communities guided by the rules formed by Pachomius, obedience was also found in the wisdom of the elders and superiors of each monastery.[14] In giving instruction to a monk who prayed and fasted excessively, Pachomius said: "The Lord says, 'I have come down from heaven, not to do my own will, but to do the will of the one who sent me.' Therefore listen also to him who says this through me."[15] John Cassian, in a visit to Abba Poemen near the village of Dioclos in the Nile delta, heard important advice about trusting and practicing the advice and teachings of the elders:

> But whoever begins to learn by discussion will never enter into the reason for the truth, because the enemy will see him trusting in his own judgment rather than in that of the fathers and will easily drive him to the point where even things which are beneficial and salutary will seems useless and harmful to him. The clever foe will so play upon his presumption that, stubbornly clinging to his own unreasonable understandings, he will persuade himself that only that is holy which he considers to be correct and righteous, guided by his erroneous obstinacy alone.[16]

But humility and obedience are not isolated virtues to be studied and discussed. They come forth from the crucible of life in the community. Abba Dorotheos said, "Let work humble the body, and when the body is humbled the soul will be humble with it, so that it is truly said that bodily labors lead to humility."[17]

The third fundamental requirement of monastic life, **the labor of the monk or anchorite in his or her cell and the common tasks necessary for community life,** is the "goad" which brings forth humility and obedience.

> Another old man had finished his baskets and was putting handles on them, when he heard his neighbor saying, "What shall I do, for the fair day is near,

and I have nothing to make handles for my baskets?" And the old man un-
fastened his own handles and brought them to his brother, saying, "Look, I
have these to spare, take and put them on thy baskets," and so for the great
love that he had he saw to it that his brother's work was rightly finished, and
left his own imperfect.[18]

The same is true in the monks' relationships with visitors and people
in surrounding communities:

The abbot Agatho, coming into the city to sell his work, found a stranger
lying in an alley sick, and with none to care for him: and the old man stayed
there and hired a cell for himself, and tended the sick man and supported
him with the work of his own hands. For four months he stayed there, till he
had healed the sick man: and so returned again to his own cell.[19]

Labor, regardless of its venue, is an opportunity for a letting go of self.
When labor and praxis are integrated, the work accomplished becomes an
offering to God and, at the same time, an offering of one's self and whole
life to God and neighbor. **Thus, to work is also to pray.** Agatho's labor on
behalf of the sick man in the city becomes filled with grace because it is an
occasion wherein God is present as a collaborator. Praxis without love of
neighbor is not genuine.

Abba Poemen said, "The will of a man is a brass wall between him and God
and a stone of stumbling. When a man renounces it, he is also saying to himself, 'By my God, I can leap over the wall' (Ps 18:29). If a man's will is in line
with what is right, then he can really labor."[20]

Labor, intertwined with praxis, becomes a process in which each person learns to make his or her will congruent with God's will. The "playing
field" of that congruence of will is daily work. A person's disciplined life of
prayer gradually releases the ego's desire to control one's life. Labor becomes dedicated to God's desires for us and the world around us. Labor
becomes an opportunity both to be **supported** by God's love and to **embody** God's love in the work, itself.

In the district of Arsinoë we also visited a priest named Sarapion, the father
of many hermitages and the superior of an enormous community number-
ing about ten thousand monks. Thanks to the labors of the community he
successfully administered a considered rural economy, for at harvest time all
of them came as a body and brought him their own produce, which each
had obtained at his harvest wage, filling each year twelve artabas, or about
forty modii (about 400 bushels), as we would say. Through Sarapion they
provided this grain for the relief of the poor, so that there was nobody in

that district who was destitute any longer. Indeed, grain was even sent to the poor of Alexandria.

As a matter of fact, none of the fathers whom we have already mentioned throughout Egypt ever neglected this form of stewardship. On the contrary, from the labors of the brothers they dispatch whole ship-loads of wheat and clothing to Alexandria for the poor, because it is rare for anyone in need to be found living near the monasteries.[21]

These monks linked their labor, the material reality of their agriculture and weaving, with the interior reality of their life of prayer. They experienced an undivided life, a wholeness of being. In contrast, when labor is limited to a material reality dominated by the ego it is separated from God's desires, becomes selfish and can bring hardship and injustice.

Labor becomes deeply spiritual, no matter how mundane or routine it may seem, when it becomes an act of self-offering. Alexandra was a young woman who left the city and shut herself up in a tomb. She received the necessities of life through an opening and did not see a man or woman for ten years. When Amma Melania asked her how she spent her time, Alexandra replied:

> From early morning until the ninth hour I pray hour by hour, spinning the flax all during that time. During the remaining hours I meditate on the holy patriarchs and prophets and apostles and martyrs. And having eaten my bread I remain in patience for the other hours, waiting for my end with cheerful hope.[22]

When labor is released from a person's control it becomes **more than what is accomplished.** Such self-giving labor is authentic human work and authentic personhood. It is an act of manifesting God's likeness in a human being's life. It is becoming a vessel of God's presence in time and space. Toward the end of the fourth century Rufinus, a friend of St. Jerome, visited the Egyptian desert and in his additions to the *Lives of the Desert Fathers* describes the monks in this way: "What can I say that would do justice to their humanity, their courtesy, and their love. . . .Nowhere have I seen love flourish so greatly, nowhere such quick compassion, such eager hospitality."[23]

Labor Is a Vessel for Grace in Time and Space

As we saw in earlier chapters, the desert abbas and ammas saw their lives in the context of the end, or fulfillment of time (the eschaton). They looked at each day and each activity against the backdrop of eternity. This released them from the anxieties of time and space, even though they lived within time and space. God filled every moment of life. Although they were conscious of themselves as individual human beings, they did not see their lives as their own possessions. Each human life was seen as a gift of God.

Abba Moses said to Abba Poemen. "If a man's deeds are not in harmony with his prayer, he labors in vain." The brother said, "What is this harmony between practice and prayer?" The old man said, "We should no longer do those things against which we pray. For when a man gives up his own will, then God is reconciled with him and accepts his prayers." The brother asked, "In all the affliction which the monk gives himself, what helps him?" The old man said, "It is written, 'God is our refuge and strength, a very present help in time of trouble'" (Ps 46:1).[24]

Abba Moses had learned that his experience of God in prayer must be present in his labor. When he let go of control of his will, there was room for God to be present in the work Moses was doing. This transformed both the deed and the elapsed time for its completion. Even in a battle with temptation God is present and although the monk has not overcome the struggle, his future transformation is present in his dependence on God in the present. Abba Elias articulates this truth in a poetic way: "If the spirit does not sing with the body, labor is in vain. Whoever loves tribulation will obtain joy and peace later on."[25]

As we discovered in earlier chapters, the desert elders were also aware of the fragility of life and the reality of their own death. This enabled them to be fully alive, experiencing a freedom and gratitude for life not limited by the crunch of time and the fear of death. John the Solitary said:

This is how your life will be preserved in good works: by constantly having before your eyes the picture of your death; for when someone does not live in expectation of the next day, then fear induced by having just the present day acts as his guide. For what sins or laxity will a person let himself get involved in, when he considers that his life will last but a single day, and he does not rely on the morrow.[26]

When life is viewed only from a chronological perspective it focuses on the limitations of time and the fact that resources are perishable. This generates anxiety that leads to a perception of labor as primarily a utilitarian **means** to an end. This imprisons labor in time and space. It separates the labor from the prayerfulness of the task. This is why the monk must keep his death in mind and condemn the vanity of the world. When time is experienced as **both** chronological and eternal, a person's ego is freed from the anxiety about longevity and decay and experiences his or her labor as contributing to salvation and not survival. This gives a new value and dimension to both labor and time. Each task becomes a "place" for the fulfillment of God's ultimate purpose for life.[27] Each moment becomes a sacrament and life is experienced as sacred, even when still heavy, often mundane and sometimes painful. We labor in peace because our view of life has been transformed.

This monastic understanding of the relationship between labor and time lies behind the practice of "mindfulness" and "the practice of the presence of God." It prompts us to ask, "How does the presence of God in each moment and activity help us with the tedious and repetitious responsibilities of our lives?" In the twenty-first century we have many anxieties about the "use" of time. In fact, we never seem to have enough time. We have replaced mindfulness with multi-tasking. The sacrament of the present moment is hidden so easily in the frenzy of efficiency and results. This is true in all sectors of our lives, including life in faith communities and their outreach ministries. Who are we becoming as we save time? What is lost when we separate our prayer from our work?

> Abba John said, "I think it best that a (person) should have a little bit of all the virtues. Therefore, get up early every day and acquire the beginning of every virtue and every commandment of God. Use great patience, with fear and long-suffering, in the love of God, with all the fervor of your soul and body. . . . Renounce everything material and that which is of the flesh. Live by the cross, in (spiritual) warfare, in poverty of spirit, in voluntary spiritual asceticism, in fasting, penitence and tears, in discernment, in purity of soul, taking hold of that which is good. Do your work in peace."[28]

Abba John and the other elders learned from experience that the end or fulfillment of all things is not only something that will be realized in the future, beyond time. In a mysterious way, it is present in every activity of daily life. This means that survival is not the goal of human life.[29] When survival becomes a person's goal, his or her life is limited to the boundaries of time and the resources of the material world. Time and material goods are holy gifts of God, but they are not given as ends in themselves. "Renounce everything material and that which is of the flesh." They neither create human life nor do they determine what is of greatest value. A new understanding of time evolved from the cells, the solitude and the ascetic practice of Abba John and the other elders. Their offerings of time, prayer, and labor were transformed by the presence of the eternal. Time was filled with grace through a spiritual intertwining with eternity. "Live by the cross, in (spiritual) warfare, in poverty of spirit, in voluntary spiritual asceticism. . . ."

Their time became **full** because it participated in a timeless dimension which brought awareness of **completion** and **authenticity** to what was happening within the hours and activities of their daily lives.[30] They were experiencing what St. Paul called *"the fullness of time."* Each moment became filled with the completion of creation, even though that process was not yet finished. Each act of labor or praxis was a *foretaste* contributing to the fulfillment of the cosmos. "Abba Theophilus, the archbishop, at the point of death, said, 'You are blessed, Abba Arsenius, because you have always had this hour in mind.'"[31]

Praxis and Labor Form the "Work of God"

> In his youth Abba John the Eunuch questioned an old man, "How have you been able to carry out the work of God in peace? For we cannot do it, even with our labor." The old man said, "We were able to do it, because we considered the work of God to be primary, and bodily needs to be subsidiary; but you hold bodily necessities to be primary and the work of God to be secondary; that is why you labor, and that is why the Savior said to the disciples, 'Seek first his kingdom and his righteousness, and all these things shall be yours as well.'"[32]

The abbas and ammas took seriously Jesus' exhortation to seek the realm of God before all else. When the work of God was their principal aim, the needs of their bodies were not ignored, but were **put in perspective**. The grace of praxis is the vision it provides for discerning the priorities of daily life.

> They said of Abba Megethius, that if he left his cell and it occurred to him to leave the place where he was living he would go without returning to his cell. He owned nothing in this world, except a knife with which he cut reeds and every day he made three small baskets, which was all he needed for his food.[33]

The wisdom of Abba Megethius's poverty is not that his only possession was a knife. The wisdom of his life was that he had all he needed to be faithful to the work of God. Megethius had learned how to integrate praxis and work. Yet he would never have assumed that his specific manner of poverty should be required for others. In the desert there was no single pattern for doing the work of God.

> Abba Isaac came to see Abba Poemen and found him washing his feet. As he enjoyed freedom of speech with him he said, "How is it that others practice austerity and treat their bodies harshly?" Abba Poemen said to him, "We

have not been called to kill our bodies, but to kill our passions." He also said, "There are three things which I am not able to do without: food, clothing and sleep; but I can restrict them to some extent."[34]

Each person must discern an appropriate relationship between praxis and labor. But it is the vision gained in praxis that gives a person the grace of having needs which are easily fulfilled and proper to his or her manner of life. If we place our own needs and desires in control of our lives we risk losing awareness of the spiritual dimension of life and the sacredness of our work. In our society aggressive advertising caters to materialism and it is difficult to have "easily satisfied needs" like Megethius or Poemen. How does our desire for material possessions influence our work and our use of natural resources? The desert elders remind us that personal prayer will help us discern what is proper for our lives, not as a "requirement," but as a personal desire for our possessions and our work to be "places" for God's presence in our lives.

> Amma Theodora said that a teacher ought to be a stranger to the desire for domination, vain-glory, and pride; one should not be able to fool him by flattery, nor blind him by gifts, nor conquer him by the stomach, nor dominate him by anger; but should be patient, gentle and humble as far as possible; he must be tested and without partisanship, full of concern, and a lover of souls.[35]

Amma Theodora recognized that pride, personal power and material pleasures will deflect a person from doing the work of God. When this happens praxis will become an unwelcome and difficult intervention. We will begin to see life as a dualism—sacred and secular—rather than experiencing the work of God as a unity of praxis and labor. The fruit of praxis will enable us to let go of these selfish desires and be satisfied with whatever is necessary to be a "lover of souls." This is the "work of God."

The work of God is not easy. One of its fruits is wisdom, but wisdom recognized through active living, rather than reading or talking. Praxis, too, is a difficult path, one which the ammas and abbas called a narrow and violent path. In spite of our modern aversion to the images of war and conflict, these desert men and women knew that praxis calls for a **care of the body and soul** that requires a conquering, or letting go, of our thoughts and will. Speaking to women who had gathered around the family tomb which became her cell, the anchorite Amma Syncletica said:

> Consequently the mind must become painstakingly diligent with respect to its thoughts. For when the enemy wants to destroy the soul as he would a build-

ing, he engineers its collapse from the foundations, or he begins from the roof and topples the whole structure; or he goes in through the windows, ties up the master of the house first and thus wins control of everything. "Foundation," then, signifies good works, "roof" faith, and "windows" the senses. And through all of them the enemy wages war. And so the person wishing to be saved must be very watchful. We do not have something to be careless about; for Scripture says: "Let the one standing firm take care lest he fall."[36]

A person's true self emerges from this violent struggle. By caring for ourselves through praxis we make space for God to provide our **true** needs. If we abandon this ascetic discipline we risk letting go of God's care and substituting *worldly* needs and work as the dominant force in our lives. Praxis transforms our labor into "the work of God" and sanctifies our daily lives.

Notes

1. *The Lives of the Desert Fathers,* trans. Norman Russell and intro. Benedicta Ward, S.L.G. (Kalamazoo: Cistercian Publications, 1981) Prologue, 3, 49.

2. *The Sayings of the Desert Fathers,* trans. Benedicta Ward, S.L.G. (Kalamazoo: Cistercian Publications, 1975) Agathon 8, 21.

3. Russell and Ward, *Lives,* 36.

4. Ward, *Sayings,* Agathon 10, 22.

5. Ibid., John the Dwarf 2, 86.

6. Ibid., Silvanus 5, 223

7. *The Desert Fathers,* trans. and intro. Helen Waddell (New York: Vintage Books, 1936), "The Sayings of the Fathers," trans. from the Greek by Paschasius, v. 2, 155.

8. Stelios Ramfos, *Like a Pelican in the* Wilderness (Brookline: Holy Cross Orthodox Press, 2000) 66. I am indebted to Stelios Ramfos for this insight into Zacharius' actions.

9. Waddell, *The Desert Fathers,* Book XII, ix, 117–18.

10. See Ramfos, *Pelican,* 66–71, for more details.

11. Ward, *Sayings,* Poemen 103, 181.

12. Dorotheos of Gaza, *Discourses and Sayings,* trans. Eric P. Wheeler (Kalamazoo: Cistercian Publications, 1977) 101.

13. Dorotheos of Gaza, *Discourses,* 122.

14. Philip Rousseau, *Pachomius: The Making of a Community in Fourth-Century Egypt* (Berkeley: University of California Press, 1999) 101.

15. Rouseau, *Pachomius,* The Greek Life of Pachomius, ed. F. Halkin, 69, referred to on 101.

16. John Cassian, *The Conferences,* trans. Boniface Ramsey, O.P. (New York: Paulist Press, 1997) 18:3:1, 2; 636–37.

17. Dorotheos of Gaza, *Discourses,* 102.

18. Waddell, *The Desert Fathers,* 150–51.

19. Ibid., 151.

20. Ward, *Sayings,* Poemen 54, 174.

21. Russell and Ward, *Lives,* 102.

22. *The Lausiac History of Palladius,* (Willits, Calif.: Eastern Orthodox Books, no date) book V, 1, 2, 3. 27–28.

23. Russell and Ward, *Lives,* 35.

24. Ward, *Sayings,* Moses 4, 141–42.

25. Ibid., Elias 6, 71.

26. Sebastian Brock, *The Syriac Fathers on Prayer and the Spiritual Life* (Kalamazoo: Cistercian Publications, 1987) 97.

27. See Ramfos, *Pelican,* 70.

28. Ward, *Sayings,* John the Dwarf 32, 92.

29. See Ramfos, *Pelican,* 74.

30. This understanding of time is at the heart of the spirituality of the Eastern Orthodox churches. I am grateful to Stelios Ramfos for the way he relates sacred time to labor. See Ramfos, *Pelican,* 69–74.

31. Ward, *Sayings,* Theophilus 5, 82.

32. Ibid., John the Eunuch 1, 105.

33 Ibid., Megethius 1, 149.

34. Ibid., Poemen 184, 193.

35. Ibid., Theodora 5, 83–84.

36. Pseudo-Athanasius, *The Life of Blessed Syncletica,* trans. Elizabeth Bryson Bongie (Toronto: Peregrina 1999) para. 46, 33.

9 Humility

Making Christ Tangible

Abba Antony said, "I saw the snares that the enemy spreads out over the world and I said groaning, 'What can I do to get through such snares?' Then I heard a voice saying to me, 'Humility.'"[1]

Amma Syncletica also said, "Just as one cannot build a ship unless one has some nails, so it is impossible to be saved without humility."[2]

"Amma Theodora also said that neither asceticism, nor vigils nor any kind of suffering are able to save, only true humility can do that."[3]

The desert elders are unanimous. There is no virtue greater than humility. It is fundamental for authentic life with God and other people. If this is true, what does it mean to be humble? Is it still practical for the complexities, dangers and challenges of twenty-first-century life? In this chapter we will seek responses to these questions in the words and actions of the desert mothers and fathers. Although we look for clarity and specific instructions, humility refuses to be confined within the boundaries of rational definition and mastery. The following words of Abba Dorotheos of Gaza are worth repeating:

> Among the seniors it used to be told how a brother asked one of the elders, "What is humility?" And the elder replied, "Humility is a great and divine work and the road to humility is labor, bodily labor, while seeking to know one's self and to put one's self below everyone else and praying to God about everything: this is the road to humility, but humility itself is something divine and incomprehensible."[4]

Humility's dynamic presence is embodied in the human heart and becomes incarnate in speech and behavior. In previous chapters we saw an initial aspect of humility in the threefold path of anachoresis: (1) a personal response to an inner desire for God by withdrawal from the inhabited world to the desert, (2) an acceptance of intentional solitude in a cell, and (3) a faithful commitment to a discipline of prayer. This first aspect of humility is a willingness to go beyond one's self, "Abba, give me a word," coupled with acceptance of patient vulnerability, "Go to your cell and your cell will teach you everything." It calls for total reliance on the mercy and power of God rather than development of personal abilities and self-reliance. Humility begins with a letting go of the agendas we have set for our lives. This sets the stage for what Jesus called abundant life.

Jesus of Nazareth as the Exemplar of Humility

Abba John of Thebaid said: "Above all things a monk ought to be humble. In fact, this is the first commandment of the Savior who said: 'Blessed are the poor in spirit, for theirs is the kingdom of heaven.'"[5] The desert elders always kept the example of Jesus' humility before their eyes because they believed it was the fundamental value exemplified in his life. Their ideal was to make Christ **tangible**. Images from the New Testament, particularly in the gospels, are mirrored in their words and actions. Their rejection of unnecessary pleasures, influence and status for the sake of others was directly related to St. Paul's awareness of the self-emptying vocation of Jesus ". . . who, though he was in the form of God, did not regard equality with God as something to be exploited, but emptied himself, taking the form of a slave, being born in human likeness. And being found in human form, he humbled himself and became obedient to the point of death—even death on a cross" (Phil 2:6-8, NRSV).

Amma Syncletica said:

> Because humility is good and salutary, the Lord clothed himself in it while ful-filling the economy (of salvation) for humanity. For he says, "Learn from me, for I am gentle and humble of heart" (Matt 11:29). Notice who it is who is speaking; learn his lesson perfectly. Let humility become for you the be-ginning and end of virtues. He means a humble heart; he refers not to ap-pearance alone, but to the inner person, for the outer person will also follow after the inner.[6]

The desert elders longed to incarnate Christ's self-emptying. "Abba Agathon said, 'If I could meet a leper, give him my body and take his, I should be very happy.' That indeed is perfect charity."[7] Self-emptying is a vessel of love for others. It embodies God's love for us. Rather than denying a person's worth, humility demonstrates a human integrity that is rooted in God and exemplified in Jesus, the Christ.

The crucifixion of Jesus became a metaphor and model for self-giving and obedience to Christ's primary commandment to "love one an-other." Abba Moses taught Abba Poemen, "The monk must die to everything before leaving the body, in order not to harm anyone."[8] The desert elders believed that Christ's commandment to love was their **primary vocation**. It was the only way to make Christ tangible in their lives. Submitting their lives to the needs of others united them to the self-giving of Christ.[9] "Abba Poemen said that a brother asked Abba Moses how some-one could consider himself as dead toward his neighbor. The old man said to him, 'If a man does not think in his heart that he is already three days dead in the tomb, he cannot attain this saying.'"[10] This direct link between the self-giving of a monk and the death of Jesus implies, also, that humility unites a person to Jesus' resurrection as well. As Jesus said, it is in laying down our lives that we shall be given life. Abba Moses' challenge to his mo-nastic brother indicates that his words are to be put into action, rather than savored as a theological insight. The following incident is worth repeating because it shows how Abba Ammonas practiced what he preached:

> It was also said of him (Abba Ammonas) that, coming to the town one day to sell his wares, he encountered a sick traveler lying in the public place with-out anyone to look after him. The old man rented a cell and lived there, work-ing with his hands to pay the rent and spending the rest of his money on the sick man's needs. He stayed there four months till the sick man was restored to health. Then he returned to his cell.[11]

Every human encounter is an opportunity to meet God and to empty one's self. A modern desert elder, Abba Matta El-Meskeen (Matthew the Poor Man) a Coptic monk of the ancient monastery of Deir el Makarios near Cairo, points to another powerful image of Jesus' humility: his bap-tism. In a sermon Abba Matta exhorts his fellow monks to embody Jesus' stature of bowing his head as he did when he submitted himself to the bap-tism of John ". . . . because it is fitting for us to fulfill all righteousness" (Matt 3:15). The one "in whom the fullness of God was pleased to dwell" (Col 1:19, NRSV) empties himself in order to offer humankind the mystery of humility through which our lives may embody God's presence.[12]

Self-Knowledge Leading toward Transformation

As we have seen, while still in a palace, Abba Arsenius prayed, "Lord, lead me in the way of salvation." A voice answered, "Arsenius, flee, be silent, pray always, for these are the source of sinlessness."[13] The challenge of this

threefold path would lead Arsenius nowhere without personal transformation. As long as he was in control of the journey, even for the best of inten-
tions, it would be an incomplete journey.

> It happened that when Abba Arsenius was sitting in his cell that he was ha-
> rassed by demons. His servants, on their return, stood outside his cell and
> heard him praying to God in these words, "O God, do not leave me. I have
> done nothing good in your sight, but according to your goodness, let me
> now make a beginning of good."[14]

This is a hard lesson for all of us. The path toward God begins with
the recognition of our own limitations and an awareness of our total dependence on God. In order to take the first step, we must know who we are
in relation to God. The words of ammas Syncletica and Theodora at the
beginning of this chapter could not be clearer, "Just as one cannot build a
ship unless one has some nails, so it is impossible to be saved without humility," and ". . . neither asceticism, nor vigils nor any kind of suffering are
able to save, only true humility can do that." Our spiritual practices, learning, and works are powerless to transform our lives without the stature of
humility. If we truly seek God we must come to terms with who we are.
Humility is physical, psychological and spiritual realism about one's self.

Jesus' Jewish spiritual heritage may be summarized as "knowing who
we are." The Hebrew Scriptures declare that humans are created in God's
image and at the same time bear witness to the struggles and failures we
encounter in trying to manifest God's likeness in the way we live. The psalms
are strikingly honest about the human desire for God and how helpless we
are if we depend on ourselves. The Psalter became a centerpiece of monastic
worship and meditation because it is a lens through which we glimpse honest views of human life, from one extreme of vengeful self-centeredness to
virtuous self-offering. The Psalms display our genuine desire for God,
"As the deer longs for flowing streams, so my soul longs for you, O God"
(Ps 42:1, NRSV), and acknowledge that we stray from the path we desire,
"For I know my transgressions and my sin is always before me" (Ps 51:3,
NRSV). The desert elders believed that knowing who we are, with this same
honesty, extends the boundaries of who we may become. "Abba Poemen
said to Abba Joseph: 'Tell me how I can become a monk.' And he replied, 'If
you want to find rest here and hereafter, say in every occasion, "Who am
I?" and do not judge anyone.'"[15]

The elders experienced self-knowledge in two ways. First, they became aware of their own limitations, weaknesses, and sins through their
solitary vigils and openness in prayer. As we have seen, these temptations

and memories of past sins often came in what they experienced as assaults by demons. It was difficult to discipline their natural passions and to confront the self-created world of their unrestrained egos. Discipline and self-restraint often failed when they were self-generated and led to the listlessness and despondency of accidie.

> When the holy Abba Antony lived in the desert he was beset by accidie, and attacked by many sinful thoughts. He said to God, "Lord I want to be saved but these thoughts do not leave me alone, what shall I do in my affliction? How can I be saved?" A short while afterwards, when he got up to go out, Antony saw a man like himself sitting at his work, getting up from his work to pray, then sitting down and plaiting a rope, then getting up again to pray. It was an angel of the Lord sent to correct and reassure him. He heard the angel saying to him, "Do this and you will be saved." At these words, Antony was filled with joy and courage. He did this, and he was saved.[16]

Antony was honest about his inability to control his sinful thoughts and the despondency caused by his powerlessness. He was afflicted by his own failures, but his **honesty about himself** led to his prayer for assistance from God. In going beyond himself, in humble recognition of his limitations, he learned to root his own efforts in God through constant prayer. He was willing to accept the Lord's correction and reassurance. Antony, like us, was striving for an ideal. He wanted to "get it right." Yet his own weakness stopped him in his tracks. He never abandoned the ideal of giving his entire being to God, but he was able to set that goal in the realistic context of knowing both his limitations and his need for God's grace. As Antony accepted what he learned about himself he opened himself to God's presence. He discovered that not only was God present in his weakness, but also that God desired to correct and reassure him. How many times have we, like Antony, crippled ourselves by striving for a perfection imposed by ourselves or others, while ignoring the reality that we must depend on God to complete the work in us?

Our culture worships productivity and high expectations and at the same time is filled with anxiety and afflictions that often lead to depression or addiction. The desert elders exhort us to "downsize" inauthentic images of ourselves. Ideals give us necessary vision, but we must live where we are—in community with God and other people—as we collaborate with God's grace in working toward what we desire. In our hyper-striving for results it is easy to forget who we are and leave our true selves behind. When that happens we lose our authenticity and become lost. Knowing who we are is a first step toward humility.

The desert elders were open to self-knowledge in a second way. As they were able to transcend the boundaries erected by their own egos they became free **to see themselves through the eyes of God**. Through their patience, praxis, worship, labor and charity to others (as we discovered in earlier chapters) they experienced a personal transformation and resurrection as they moved from the limited and inauthentic selves they had created to a fullness-of-being made possible by the grace and love of God. The abbas and ammas realized that their true identities could be found only in God. They learned to see themselves through the eyes of God. This expanded self-knowledge included realism about their limitations as well as openness to the transformed-self God saw in them. A glimpse of this transformation is present in some instructions given by Abba Moses the Robber to Abba Poemen:

> The monk must die to everything before leaving the body, in order not to harm anyone. If the monk does not think in his heart that he is a sinner, God will not hear him. The brother said to him, "What does that mean, to think in his heart that he is a sinner?" Then the old man said, "When someone is occupied with his own thoughts, he does not see those of his neighbor. If a man's deeds are not in harmony with his prayer, he labors in vain." The brother said, "What is this harmony between practice and prayer?" The old man said, "We should no longer do those things against which we pray. For when a man gives up his own will, then God is reconciled with him and accepts his prayers." The brother asked, "In all the affliction which the monk gives himself, what helps him?" The old man said, "It is written, 'God is our refuge and strength, a very present help in trouble.'" [17]

Abba Moses knew that dying to the old self must take place before "harmony between practice and prayer" could take place. Such authenticity is born in the heart, through a self-knowledge that one is a sinner. This freed Moses to see beyond the sins of other people in the same way that God saw beyond Moses' sins. As Moses saw himself through God's eyes he experienced the freedom to avoid judgment of his brothers. In this way he let go of control of his own will and became reconciled with God and what God desires. Moses experienced transformation of self. When Abba Poemen asked Abba Moses how it is possible to move beyond afflictions to transformation Abba Moses reminded him to depend on God as his only refuge and strength. This became a source of great confidence in God and inner peace for Abba Poemen who said to his disciples, "If you take little account of yourself, you will have peace, wherever you live." [18]

Abba Moses had learned that awareness of his authentic self was necessary to embody the fundamental monastic virtue of humility. His words speak to our modern age that stresses self-help programs and individual achievement. In our modern afflictions of conflict, injustice, poverty and materialism what will help our deeds be in harmony with our prayers? To be humble is to know that our very being is a gift from God. We are creatures of God. We are not complete in ourselves. We rely on God for authenticity of life. Reflecting on this monastic truth, St. Augustine of Hippo said, "If I am not in God then I am not at all." Paul Evdokimov, a twentieth-century Eastern Orthodox philosopher, social activist and mystic said, "Where there is no God there is no humanity either."[19]

Gratitude: The Gateway to Humility

Humility is the foundation of the house of love. Yet even that foundation sits on the firm earth of gratitude. "Abba Peter (the Pionite) said, 'We must not be puffed up when the Lord does something through our meditation, but we must rather thank him for having made us worthy to be called by him.' He used to say it is good to think about each virtue in this way."[20] Abba Peter's comment brings to mind a similar statement by Jesus, "I can do nothing on my own. As I hear, I judge; and my judgment is just, because I seek to do not my own will but the will of him who sent me" (John 5:30, NRSV). When the fruits of our prayer are evident it is tempting to become self-satisfied. It is possible to feel a sense of personal power. "My faithfulness in prayer is paying off! I'm getting wiser! I'm able to do great things for God!" Abba Peter reminds us that, like Jesus, we can do nothing on our own. In the same way that Jesus was called to embody the work of God, our faithfulness in prayer is a response to God's desire to work in us. Abba Peter points out that this openness to collaborate with God is consummated by gratitude. Humility dissolves without gratefulness. Gratefulness is the floodgate of all the virtues. It is both recognition of what God makes possible in us and a demeanor of life that continually opens us to God's presence and power. As he was dying, Abba Benjamin said to his disciples, "If you observe the following, you can be saved, 'Be joyful at all times, pray without ceasing, and give thanks for all things.'"[21]

Living a Transparent Life

Humility is not a characteristic formed through personal effort and then practiced at will. It requires constant openness for and discernment of God's spirit in one's daily behavior. A monk's praxis of prayer never guaranteed humility.

Amma Snycletica said, "There are many (monks) who live in the mountains and behave as if they were in the town, and they are wasting their time. It is possible to be a solitary in one's mind while living in a crowd, and it is possible for one who is a solitary to live in the crowd of his own thoughts."[22]

The desert abbas and ammas became aware of humility in the actions and words of humble persons.

A brother at Scetis committed a fault. A council was called to which Abba Moses was invited, but he refused to go. Then the priest sent someone to say to him, "Come, for everyone is waiting for you." So he got up and went. He took a leaking jug, filled it with water and carried it with him. The others came out to meet him and said to him, "What is this, Father?" The old man said to them, "My sins run out behind me, and I do not see them, and today I am coming to judge the errors of another." When they heard that they said no more to the brother but forgave him.[23]

The desert elders realized that humility is not a commodity. It is not the acquired skill of a "humble person." Humility is embodied in specific actions. It is transparent if a person is willing to drop the defenses of the ego. Abba Moses did not have to lecture his fellow monks. Their lack of humility became transparent through the humility of Moses. Their judgmental behavior was transformed into humility when they acknowledged their weakness and practiced forgiveness. In this case humility pointed to the weaknesses shared by all and the positive task of restoring wholeness to the monk who had sinned. The judgmental attitude of the monks on the council had narrowed their vision.

Desert monks learned, also, from the trials and errors of their own experience:

There was an old man who had a good disciple. One day he was annoyed and drove the disciple out. Yet the disciple sat down outside of the cell and waited. When the old man opened the door, he found him sitting there, and repented before him, saying: "You are my abba, for your humility and patience have overcome my narrow-mindedness. Come inside! From now on you are the old man and the father, for sure, and I am the young one and the disciple. For your good works have surpassed my old age."[24]

And again,

One day Abba Arsenius consulted an old Egyptian monk about his thoughts. Someone noticed this and said to him, "Abba Arsenius, how is it that you with such a good Latin and Greek education, ask this peasant about your thoughts?" He replied, "I have indeed been taught Latin and Greek, but I do not know even the alphabet of this peasant."[25]

An elitist blindness had infected the monk who criticized Arsenius for confiding in an Egyptian peasant. His contempt for a monk whose culture and experience were different from his own cut him off from wisdom that Arsenius, the famous scholar, recognized in awe. By labeling the Egyptian a "peasant" the contemptuous monk hardened his heart to the presence of the Spirit in another person. Yet Arsenius realized that his substantial learning would not be diminished in any way by his need for the peasant monk's wisdom. Although Arsenius was learned, he was able to look beyond himself in a time of need.

The desert elders always perceived themselves as novices. Embodying humility was a life-long experience and not something that could be "mastered." The anonymous "old man" in the narrative quoted above became impatient with his disciple yet did not let his status as "abba" stand in the way of learning from the persistence and humility of his younger novice. "Abba Poemen said about Abba Pior that every single day he made a fresh beginning."[26] They had what Buddhists call a "beginners mind."

> An old man said, "Every time a thought of superiority or vanity (pride) moves you, examine your conscience to see if you have kept all the commandments, if you love your enemies and are grieved at their sins, if you consider yourself as an unprofitable servant and the greatest sinner of all. Even then, do not pretend to great ideas as though you were perfectly right, for this thought destroys everything."[27]

Humility does not keep score, nor can our humble behavior in the past minimize the consequences of acting in a heedless way in the present. Every act and every word is a new opportunity to embody humility. Humility is a way of seeing that includes the horizon of the needs of others and the community that surrounds us. As we mature and gain wisdom we never lose the need for constant growth and transformation. If we become self-satisfied about our behavior and knowledge we risk "destroying everything." "The old men used to say: 'If you see a young person climbing up to heaven by his own will, hold him by the foot, and pull him down to the ground, for it is just not good for him.'"[28] We, too, are always beginners.

The Nature and Value of Humility: Abba Moses, the Robber

Arsenius was open to the wisdom of an Egyptian peasant because he refused to judge the monk in reference to himself. He would not label him.

Modern society is full of labels and stereotypes: poor, rich, enemy, ally, good, evil, conservative or liberal. Labels can inhibit humble openness to others. They point a finger at the "other" and in the process make it almost impossible for us to listen to each other and value each other as persons. Even worse, labels create divisions and stifle accountability and honesty about our own weaknesses and self-interests. In today's society humility seems unrealistic in this context because it asks for mutual responsibility and inter-dependence in a world that values hegemony and self-interest. This is true for individuals as well as nations. It is true within communities of faith as well as the marketplace. The opposite of humility is not arrogance. It is indifference and heedlessness. To become heedless is to assert one's life at the expense of the lives of other people. The desert mothers and fathers exhort us not to act in a heedless manner lest we forget who we are and cause unnecessary harm to others.

"Abba Pambo asked Abba Antony, 'What ought I to do?' and the old man said to him, 'Do not trust in your own righteousness, do not worry about the past, but control your tongue and your stomach.'"[29] Humility stands in stark contrast to self-centeredness. That is why it is so difficult. In his insightful book on the desert elders Stelios Ramfos calls humility "withdrawal from being." He says, "The definitive form of ascetic withdrawal, I would say, is a withdrawal from every kind of self-assertion, that is, holy humility. My life acquires value through my being something, or thinking that I am something. Humility is a voluntary withdrawal precisely from this 'being something.'"[30]

Humility as "withdrawing from being or self-assertion" is confirmed by another incident in the life of Abba Moses the Robber. He was an Ethiopian slave with very dark skin who, after his release, became a robber committing many crimes, including murder, in the vicinity of the monastic sites at Nitria. Brigands like Moses were the pirates of the desert and a constant danger to pilgrims, monks and merchants. Late in his life he embraced Christianity, became a monk and was ordained a priest. Under the influence of Abba Isidore and Abba Macarius he settled at Scetis (Wadi al-Natrun) in the late fourth century in the monastery of Al-Baramus where he became known for his high degree of asceticism. He was martyred there around 410 C.E. during a raid by the Massic Berber tribes. His relics are still in the monastery where, currently, there are fifty monks.[31]

> It was said of Abba Moses that he was ordained and the ephod was placed upon him. The archbishop said to him, "See, Abba Moses, now you are entirely white." The old man said to him, "It is true of the outside, lord and father, but what

about him who sees the inside?" Wishing to test him the archbishop said to the priests, "When Abba Moses comes into the sanctuary, drive him out, and go with him to hear what he says." So the old man came in and they covered him with abuse, and drove him out, saying, "Outside, black man!" Going out, he said to himself, "They have acted rightly concerning you, for your skin is as black as ashes. You are not a man, so why should you be allowed to meet men?"[32]

At first glance modern readers may find this incident offensive, perhaps cruel, because of the archbishop's need to "test" Moses and the priests' blatant racial slur. But if we look at the incident in its context, rather than make judgments as if it had happened today in our own culture, we will discover its wisdom. The ephod was a garment symbolizing the authority of the Jerusalem Temple High Priest at the time of Jesus. Only the High Priest was permitted into the Holy of Holies, and just once each year on the Day of Atonement. The ephod represented the whole community of Israel, the people of God, as did the High Priest who wore it. On the Day of Atonement the High Priest stood in the presence of the Holy One on behalf of the people of Israel. On the Day of Atonement the sins of the entire community were remembered and offered to God for forgiveness. It was a restoration of the purity of God's people. The color white became a biblical symbol of purity and in the book of Revelation the Lamb of God washes away the sins of the people. The inner garment worn by the priest is white and called an "alb."

The power and authority vested in Abba Moses as a newly ordained priest was truly awesome. The archbishop, knowing Abba Moses' past life very well, tells him that he is now pure, "entirely white," and empowered to enter the sanctuary and consecrate the bread and wine that will become the Body and Blood of Christ. The consecration takes place on the altar in the sanctuary, separated from the nave by a wooden wall with swinging doors. Since lay persons were not permitted in the sanctuary, the priest receives the Sacrament first and then brings the chalice and paten through the doors to the people saying, "Holy things for the holy!"[33] The chapel where Moses' ordination took place no longer exists but its fifth-century replacement reflects the basic design of the nave and sanctuary described above.[34] In addition to his liturgical and spiritual authority, Moses' new priestly authority included being a member of a council that presided over the communal affairs of the monastic community and made decisions regarding the discipline of monks who committed offences.[35]

"See, Abba Moses, now you are entirely white." The white garment and the black skin of Moses' hands and face demonstrate a vivid contrast between his former life as a bandit and his new life as a monk and priest. Using a play on words, the archbishop assures Moses that he has been fully cleansed and is now as pure as the garment he wears. Yet Moses is not so sure. He knows himself too well. Echoing a statement Jesus made when he was criticized for eating from unclean vessels, Abba Moses humbly expresses doubt that he is entirely clean. "It is true of the outside, lord and father, but what about Him who sees the inside?" Then the archbishop plots with the priests present to "test" Abba Moses. The purpose of the test is not stated, yet a clue is given in the instructions to the priests. Moses has never been in the sanctuary. "When Abba Moses comes into the sanctuary, drive him out, and go with him to hear what he says." The archbishop wants to discover what is "inside" Abba Moses. The priests, knowing Moses is Ethiopian and they are Coptic, decide to insult Moses because his origin and skin color is different from their own. They, also, use a play on words, only this time to infer that Moses is unworthy rather than pure. They drive him out saying, "Outside black man!"

Abba Moses responds in a manner that appears to reflect weakness and defeatism. It seems to ignore the rudeness and injustice of the insult. He says to himself, yet audibly, "They have acted rightly concerning you, for your skin is as black as ashes. You are not a man, so why should you be allowed to meet men?" Moses, a former slave, is well aware of how difficult it might be for Coptic priests to accept him as a peer. He assumes their anger is authentic (not knowing it was contrived). Yet he is able to look at their point of view, whether or not it is just. Then, in a moment of honest self-awareness, he remembers his own unworthiness. He does not allow the perceived rudeness of the priests to convince him that their behavior makes them less worthy than he. Unfortunately we do not know what happened next. But we do know that the incident (there is no reason to believe that it is fictional) was remembered as an example of humility in the life of one of the most revered abbas in Egypt.

The archbishop's "test" was not to prove anything about Abba Moses. It was a wisely conceived opportunity for Moses to discover the goodness he had on the "inside," despite his doubts, and at the same time became an opportunity for others to benefit from Abba Moses' humility. Both Moses and the priests learned from this experience, as difficult as it may have been. What can we learn from this incident? The response of Abba Moses was not aggressive or assertive. By withdrawing from self-assertion Abba Moses displayed humility. He withdrew from an opportunity to respond with either anger or judgment. Both would have limited his vision and made responding with further insults or violence seem appropriate options. It would

have been difficult, if not impossible, to resolve the situation without alien-
ating himself from the priests. "Abba Nilus said, 'Whatever you do in revenge against your brother who has hurt you will appear all at once in your
heart at the time of prayer.'"[36]

By withdrawing from contentious confrontation Moses opened the
possibility for the operation of God's grace. Here we see a congruity between Abba Moses' ascetic praxis and his behavior with other people. It
was he who said, "Go sit in your cell and your cell will teach you everything." There must be a link between our prayer and our outward behavior.
When Moses said to himself, "You are no man. . . ." he was acknowledging that his self-directed ego was powerless. He was nothing without God.
The desert elders demonstrate that when we recognize ourselves as creatures of God we make room for the activity of the Spirit in us. This humility before God makes it possible to manifest humility with each other.

It is essential to see that Abba Moses did not avoid the situation. **Humility is not weakness or avoidance of conflict**. It enables us to respond to a
situation without becoming the central feature. It extends our vision beyond
ourselves and our needs to a resolution that reconciles and serves all concerned. By withdrawing from self-assertion, humility makes honest communication possible. When we let go of our desire to be in charge or claim
superiority we make it possible for God's spirit to be present in a relationship
or action in a way that would not have been possible otherwise. "Where there
is deep humility thither comes the Holy Spirit; when the grace of the wor-
shipful spirit comes, the person under its influence is filled with all purity."
These words of St. Simeon the New Theologian echo the archbishop's awareness that Abba Moses was, indeed, pure. But his purity was not the result of
his own efforts to overcome his sinfulness. His purity was demonstrated in
letting go of his self-assertion toward God and his brother monks.

Monastic humility assumes that **purity is not moral perfection**. It
begins by accepting our own limitations and imperfections. This self-
knowledge expands our heart and invites the love and grace of God to
transform our thoughts and desires. This congruity between our will and
God's will is what the archbishop recognized in Abba Moses when he said,
"Now you are all white." This authentic human living is what the desert elders called "purity of heart." It is our vocation as well. Yet modern conventional wisdom and theology have a difficult time allowing purity and
imperfection to co-exist. The desert elders had no such problem. Purity
comes from awareness of sin that makes an inner transformation possible
through repentance. Abbas Elias said, "What can sin do where there is repentance? And of what use is love where there is pride?"[37] The elders expressed

sorrow for their sins through genuine compunction and tears. Yet they discovered that repentance is not only regret for sinful behavior or a desire for forgiveness. It is the awareness of human weakness and a desire for a completely new life. Repentance is an inward change of the heart and is less concerned with the failures of the past than with the transformation of the present. "Repentance is a change at the center of one's desire."[38]

> One day, Abba Issac the Theban went to a monastic community and he saw a brother doing wrong, and he condemned him. As he returned to the desert, an angel of the Lord came and stood in front of the door of his cell and said, "I will not let you in." He asked: "What is the matter?" And the angel replied: "God has sent me to ask you where he should cast the sinner on whom you passed judgment." Immediately he repented and said: "I was wrong. Forgive me." And the angel said: "Get up, God has forgiven you. In the future be sure not to judge someone before God passes judgment."[39]

Abba Isaac's repentance was made possible through acknowledgement that he was wrong to pass judgment on another monk. His humble request for forgiveness opened the possibility for a change in his life. In that moment he experienced transformation or purity of heart. Purity takes place in the present, not in the past or the future. Issac was pure even though he might sin again. In modern usage, the word perfection is often equated with moral purity. We might say, "How could Issac be pure when he was not perfect?" In fact, perfection, from the Latin *per-factio,* means to proceed toward completion or wholeness. Abba Isaac was, indeed, moving toward completion in God! The same freedom is ours today.

Humility Embodies Simplicity

Abba Moses' behavior during his ordination demonstrates that humility is incarnated through simplicity. "Foremost among the monastic values is humility, which is inseparable from simplicity, and which aims to cultivate a right sense of one's role within God's creation."[40] Moses' behavior was not naïve or self-negating. Neither was Moses weak or ineffective. His monastic formation guided him to regard himself, his needs and his behavior with simplicity. Fr. Columba Stewart, O.S.B., emphasizes this aspect of humility as a way of understanding the meaning of "monk", taken from the Greek *monos.* A monk is one who has voluntarily limited his or her life in order to live in an "uncomplicated, undistracted, single-minded" way.[41] In this context humility becomes an uncluttered way to look at all of life. It is a worldview, a form of consciousness. Jesus said, "If your eye is single, your whole being will be filled with light" (Matt 6:22, author's trans.). This means humility is not passive. On the contrary, humble behavior can be proactive and effective without being attached to personal power, status or desired outcome. Humility does not diminish a person but, rather, gives access to his or her authentic power and self. It begins with intentional listening and awareness that lead to action.

"Abba Hyperichius said, 'The person who teaches others by actions, not words, is truly wise'"[42] If a person is honest about her or his limitations and not personally assertive, that person may be amazed at what becomes possible. Amma Syncletica said, "Choose the meekness of Moses and you will find your heart which is a rock changed into a spring of water."[43] Humility enables us to speak and act from our hearts rather than the less reliable surface of life. It manifests our inward wholeness and integrity rather than our ego-centric exterior façade. Rather than being naïve, humility depends on what is truly real and not on what is unreal. It causes us to reflect the glory of God present in our true self. "Abba Poemen said, 'Teach your mouth to say that which you have in your heart.'"[44] Humility will flow from an awareness of what our hearts need. Poemen also said, "Do not give your heart to that which does not satisfy your heart."[45]

The desert elders are firm in declaring that humility cannot be grasped, yet is the fruit of intentionally seeking God. We have seen in previous chapters that this "intentional way" first includes isolation from the conventional distractions and comforts of the inhabited world, and then commitment to the praxis of prayer, labor and charity toward others. Humility does not appear from a vacuum. Abba Poemen's words must be repeated again, "Life in the monastery demands three things: the first is humility, the next is obedience, and the third which sets them in motion and is like a goad is the work of the monastery."[46] He also said, "These three things are the most helpful of all: fear of the Lord; prayer; and doing good to one's neighbor."[47]

Humility is learned from the crucible of living with other people and its primary purpose is "doing good to one's neighbor." A humble person is not a museum piece in a spiritual theme park. Humility is embodied in relationships and although it is simple, it is the fruit of what Abba Poemen calls "the work of the monastery." And that is often very difficult work. The same may be said for we who do not live in a monastic community. We, too, are called to "fear God" (knowing who we are and being honest about ourselves), to practice a life of prayer, and to serve our neighbors. Poemen is telling us that humility flows from both prayer and the hard work of living with other people.

Living Humble Lives: Matoes, Motius, and Poemen

If humility embodies simplicity, how does it happen? What does it look like?

Avoiding judgment

A brother questioned Abba Matoes saying, "What am I to do? My tongue makes me suffer, and every time I go among men, I can't control it, but I condemn them in all the good they are doing and reproach them with it. What am I to do?" The old man replied, "If you cannot contain yourself, flee into solitude. For this is a sickness. He who dwells with brethren must not be square, but round, so as to turn himself towards all." He went on, "It is not through virtue that I live in solitude, but through weakness; those who live in the midst of men are the strong ones."[48]

Abba Matoes knew himself well. His life of solitude was not a source of personal pride; it was recognition of his own weakness and desire for transformation. Being judgmental was a problem for him, too. The brother monk must have been terribly disappointed! He wanted an answer from a "master" and discovered that the abba had the same problem. Perhaps he was disappointed, too, that the abba turned out to be so ordinary. But wait. Embedded in Matoes's response is wisdom about living in community. "He who dwells with brethren must not be square, but round, so as to turn himself towards all." Matoes's "answer" is not a prescription for discipline of the tongue. It is advice about the difficulty of living in community. Be flexible, not rigid. If you want to live in community you must be willing to listen and learn from others. It is not easy to consider the opinions and needs of "the brethren." It requires the powerful virtue of humility.

Prayer, labor, common worship and learning are to be experienced beyond the boundary of personal need and opinion. This truth is the foundation for the monastic virtue of obedience. Amma Snycletica said, "As long as we are in the monastery, obedience is preferable to asceticism. The one teaches pride, the other humility."[49] A person can be formed by the community as well as one's personal life with God. It is essential to honor one another and serve the common good. To do this we must be round, not square. Humble and listening hearts are needed in families, the workplace, government, international diplomacy, and faith communities. The "answer" to modern conflicts and a just sharing of the world's resources requires a change in human consciousness. We are being called to replace rigid self-assertion and hegemony with humility. This will require learning to become round so that we can move freely among each other without the unnecessary harm caused by square, rough edges.

Resisting Anger

The desert elders struggled, also, with the demon of anger. "Abba Poemen heard of someone who had gone all week without eating and then had lost his temper. The old man said, 'He could do without food for six days, but he could not cast out anger.'"[50] Living alone or in very small communities is not easy. We can develop "short fuses." A short fuse is a sign of an undisciplined and self-centered view of life. It is a contradiction of the monastic virtue of patience. Patience is necessary for listening to a person or a situation. Anger can destroy a community by creating a collection of people who prefer listening to their own voices. It is a source of pride and control. Anger is an aggressive assertion of one's self and in a moment can neutralize a week's fasting! Abba Poemen knew that it is better to shorten a fast than to feast on anger. His disciple, Agathon, said "A man who is angry, even if he were to raise the dead, is not acceptable to God." This is stern teaching because so much is at stake. Agathon continues, "I have never offered agapes (love feasts); but the fact of giving and receiving has been for me an agape, for I consider the good of my brother to be a sacrificial offering."[51] Anger creates a barrier between God and other people and its emotional environment limits one's vision and leads to injurious behavior. Abba Isaiah said, "When someone wishes to render evil for evil, he can injure his brother's soul even by a single nod of his head."[52] Anger is the opposite of "withdrawal from self." In contrast, "the good of my brother" becomes an opportunity for an offering of self rather than assertion of self. This is humility.

Resisting Pride and Vainglory

It is easy to romanticize the desert fathers and mothers. They attracted thousands of people from cities and towns who came for advice, answers and prayers. John of Lycopolis described them as "the treasure of God hidden in human vessels . . . and through them the whole world is kept in being." At the same time he discovered some spiritual "keeping up with the Jones's." John commented, "Those in the remotest places make strenuous efforts for fear anyone else should surpass them in ascetic practices. Those living near towns or villages make equal efforts, though evil troubles them on every side, in case they should be considered inferior to their remoter brethren."[53] Some biographers, theologians, church councils and historians have held the desert elders up as ideal models of Christian living. There is truth in what they describe, but the desert elders, themselves, would have been surprised to hear such praise. They knew themselves too well. "It was revealed to Abba Antony in his desert that there was one who was his equal in the city. He was a doctor by profession and whatever he had beyond his needs he gave to the poor, and every day he sang the Sanctus with the angels."[54]

As we have seen, spiritual praxis was not an end in itself. The goal was never "perfection." Yet there was always the temptation to compare one's self with others and become proud about personal achievements. Abba Isidore said, "If you fast regularly, do not be inflated with pride, but if you think highly of yourself because of it, then you had better eat meat. It is better for a man to eat meat than to be inflated with pride and to glorify himself."[55] Isidore had learned that taking credit for one's achievements deflects awareness that we depend on God for everything. His psychological realism deflates the ego. It is better to eat than become spiritually obese with pride. Vain glory is a shadow of reality. It is a false start and to keep running will lead nowhere. Abba Motius sees the danger of comparing ourselves to others:

> A brother questioned Abba Motius, saying, "If I go to dwell somewhere, how do you want me to live?" The old man said, "If you live somewhere, do not seek to be known for anything special; do not say, for example, I do not go to the synaxis (common prayers); or perhaps, I do not eat at agape (a common meal after the Eucharist). For these things make an empty reputation and later you will be troubled because of this. For men rush where they find these practices." The brother said to him, "What shall I do, then?" The old man said, "Wherever you live, follow the same manner of life as everyone else and if you see devout men whom you trust doing something, do the same and you will be at peace. For this is humility: to see yourself to be the same as the rest. When men see you do not go beyond the limits, they will consider you to be the same as everyone else and no one will trouble you."[56]

Motius is saying that the purpose of praxis is not to rise above others, but to trust God's grace. We are all on the same path and no person, regardless of their position, is better or worse than anyone else. Wearing the same monastic habit in a community is a visible sign that all members of the community are equal in God's sight and all depend on God and each other. When a person purposely calls attention to himself or herself by unique praxis, the ability of the community to help form the person is compromised. At the same time the community's life is directed away from itself and its common life. The faithful presence of God will be discovered in the life of the **community**. A person will not find peace rushing around trying to be different or exceptional. It will create conflict, jealousy and harm to others. It is possible to be an individual and exercise unique talents without being exclusive. Humility is willingness to trust that we are all fundamentally alike and worthwhile. Humility bows to grace in our common life.

This may seem naïve in our modern culture of high expectations. It may smack of belittling the value of the individual. But the desert elders are saying that our personal integrity does not depend on being different. We are not defined by what we do. Calling attention to our accomplishments and importance makes it difficult to honor one another and serve the common good. In our culture of upward mobility the desert elders are recommending "downward mobility."[57] Abba Arsenius left his influential position in the Emperor's court to find his authentic self in the desert. His example does not contradict the need for institutional leaders and scholars. His example points to the need to discover **where we truly belong and on whom we truly depend**. Abba Poemen said, "If you think little of yourself, you will have peace wherever you live."[58]

Both abbas discovered that unless we are rooted in God, nothing we do will have genuine worth. Arsenius realized that his cushy influential position had lost meaning. It was empty. It was all about him. When he let go of himself and followed his heart to the desert he found his root. One day his servants overheard him praying in his cell, "O God, do not leave me. I have done nothing good in your sight, but according to your goodness, let me now make a beginning of good."[59] As he was dying Abba Pambo said, "Since I came to this place of the desert and built my cell and dwelt here, I do not remember having eaten bread which was not the fruit of my own hands and I have not repented of a word I have said up to the present time; and yet I am going to God as one who has not yet begun to serve him."[60]

The self-emptying and self-abnegation of the desert elders should not be seen as a fixation on denying the goodness of human life or as a form of self-hatred. It is true that some monks were obsessive to the point of self-abuse. Others took pride in their perceived humility. But they were corrected by the wiser and more experienced abbas and ammas. "Abba Isaac came to see Abba Poemen and found him washing his feet. As he enjoyed freedom of speech with him he said, 'How is it that others practice austerity and treat their bodies hardly?' Abba Poemen said to him, 'We have not been taught to kill our bodies, but to kill our passions.'"[61] The wisdom of self-discipline and voluntary material poverty is reliance on God. This opens a person to inner powers and resources that are far beyond the measure of his or her personal abilities and wisdom. The key is to balance what leads toward purity of heart with disciplines that guard our souls from anything that leads us away from our life with God. Amma Syncletica said, "There is an asceticism which is determined by the enemy and his disciples practice it. So how are we to distinguish between the divine and royal asceticism and the demonic tyranny? Clearly through its quality of balance."[62]

There Are Many Ways to Salvation:
The Monk Zossima and Amma Mary of Egypt

The *Life of St. Mary of Egypt* demonstrates that humility can lead to repentance and transformation through a deep psychological and spiritual honesty about one's self.[63] Mary probably lived in the fourth or fifth century because her *Life* was already being circulated by the sixth century C.E. At the age of twelve she left home in Alexandria and began a period of seventeen years "tarrying in the fires of lust."[64] She earned a living begging and spinning wool. Her passion for sexual pleasure led her to join a group of men bound for Jerusalem to celebrate the Exaltation of the Holy Cross. Although her desire for this pilgrimage was not worship, "I wanted to go so that I might soon have more lovers for my lust," she found herself desperate, but unable, to enter the Church of the Holy Sepulcher. After trying to enter three or four times she withdrew from the threshold and let go of her intense desire to enter. Then "a salutary understanding touched my mind and the eyes of my heart and shewed me that it was the sinfulness of my actions that prevented me from going in." Seeing an icon of the Virgin Mary she begged the Virgin to permit her to enter and to see the wood of the cross on which Jesus died. "As soon as I have seen the cross of your Son, holy Virgin, I will go wherever you as the mediator of my salvation shall order and lead." Mary entered the basilica in fear and trembling and fell on the floor near the cross in repentance. On leaving the basilica Mary stood by the icon of the Virgin and said, "Now therefore, lead me wherever you please; lead me to salvation, teach me what is true, and go before me in the way of repentance." Mary was led into the desert beyond the Jordan and remained a hermit, in complete solitude and constant prayer, for forty-seven years.

The *Life* of Mary, like all hagiography, is meant to inspire its readers and therefore contains some major themes present in the lives of other desert mothers and fathers. The primary theme in her life is the power of humility. It is easy to understand why she became one of the most important saints in the eastern churches who celebrate her feast on the Fifth Sunday of Lent. Mary is an icon of the path from a sinful life to repentance and transformation. Her hedonistic behavior never destroyed the image of God within her. The power of unrestrained sexual pleasure could not overcome her latent desire for God to lure her heart to "listen." "But I think my God was seeking my repentance, for He does not desire the death of sinners."

Like Arsenius, Antony, Syncletica and Theodora before her, Mary **listens** to the spirit present in her heart and **acts**. Faith (putting one's life in God's hands) leads to action. But Mary cannot go where she desires, even with all her power and energy. As she withdraws, in frustration, from the threshold of the basilica, she withdraws from self-assertion. Her action reflects the need for letting go of control, even of our path to God. Seeing the Virgin, she experiences sorrow for her life of lust and desires to be somewhere else: "wherever you as my mediator of salvation shall order and lead." In the words of Sr. Benedicta Ward, Mary becomes an "icon of repentance."[65] Mary realizes she has been living a false life and desires her true self, even though she does not yet know who she is. Mary embodies the nature of repentance. She turns from the past, with genuine sorrow, and becomes open to transformation. She asks for help to walk the path toward her authentic self. "Now therefore, lead me *wherever you please* (what God desires for her); *lead* me to salvation (completion in God), *teach* me what is true (authentic), and *go before me* in the *way* of repentance." (Italics and additional words in parens mine.) Seeking God is an open-ended journey! Mary becomes an icon of humility, submitting herself to God's desires and relying on God's help. Her repentance is not only in the moment of her prostration before the cross in the basilica, but also in embracing the *way* that will lead to her transformation.

Mary's path to transformation stands in stark contrast to what is recommended in our age of self-help programs and "pulling our own strings." She demonstrates that the power of self-emptying becomes the womb of **collaborating with God.** Mary's humble awareness of her weakness expanded her heart to listen to God's desires for her. Her listening was the source of her action to follow the path to her authentic self. Mary's humility made it possible for God's grace to be active in her and open her to possibilities that were beyond the boundaries of her former self.

But this is not the end of the story. As Mary's life was unfolding, a monk in Palestine was following another path to God. Zossima "was an old man renowned for his way of life and gift of words; from his infancy he was nourished in the monastic way of life and its works." His faithful commitment to the ascetic life was so well known and admired that many monks submitted to his teaching and disciplines. Yet Zossima "became tormented by the thought that it seemed as if he had attained perfection in everything and needed no teaching from anyone." He said to himself, "Is there a monk on earth capable of affording me anything new?" Zossima, in spite of his "success" as a monk, was not sure that it was enough. Was there more he should be doing? Then in a vision he was told that "no-one can attain perfection" and advised to leave his monastery for a "greater ordeal" that would teach him "how many and varied are the ways to salvation." Zossima travels to a monastery near the Jordan River and tells the abbot of his dilemma. The abbot's response summarizes monastic teaching on humility. He said, "God alone who heals human infirmity will reveal, brother, His divine will to you and teach us how to do what is right. Man cannot help man, unless, soberly and constantly, each brings attention to bear on what is right and proper and has God as his fellow worker in his labour."

Zossima, like Mary, responds to an inner calling from God. His affliction is **another kind of lust:** the desire for perfection. His barrier is not at the threshold of the Basilica of the Holy Sepulcher, but in his desire to reach the summit of monastic praxis. He will not relax in that pursuit.

During Lent the abbot sends all the monks into the desert where each is to remain in complete solitude "to fight against himself" before God. Zossima's hope is to find a hermit who will "fulfill his longing." Then he meets Mary, a fearsome figure who at first terrifies him. She is naked, her body blackened by decades of desert sun and her hair bleached white, coming down to her neck. Mary flees from Zossima who pursues her crying out, "Why are you running away from an old man, a sinner?" Zossima's pursuit of Mary seems to parallel his affliction in running after the goal of perfect monastic praxis. He realizes that he is exhausted by a race he cannot finish by himself. In that moment he, like Mary on the floor of the basilica, is overcome by sadness for the incompleteness of his life and its vainglory. Zossima shouts, "Stop and grant me, an old man, a prayer and blessing, for the sake of God who despises no-one." Mary declines, for he is a priest. She desires his blessing, having been separated from the sacraments of the church for forty-seven years. In an almost humorous interplay, mirroring a similar meeting between Abba Antony and Abba Paul of Thebes, they beg each other for a blessing. When Mary calls Zossima by name even though they have never met, he entreats Mary in the same manner that she prayed to the Virgin in the basilica. "O Mother in the spirit, it is plain from this insight that all your life you have dwelt with God and have nearly died to the world . . . . since grace is recognized not by office but by the gifts of the Spirit, bless me, for God's sake, and pray for me out of the goodness of your heart."

Zossima recognizes in Mary the grace he desires. He humbles himself and asks for help. This is his moment of repentance and the first step toward the transformation he could not grasp for himself. Mary is struck to the heart by his humility and responds, "Blessed is God who cares for the salvation of souls." She becomes, in Amma Theodora's words, "a lover of souls." She withdraws from her own needs and perception of what should be done and becomes a vessel of grace for another human being.

At Zossima's request, Mary continues to love him by, very reluctantly, telling him her story. She is honest about her continuing struggle to resist being drawn into the images and malign powers of her former life and emphasizes her dependence on God. "When I think from what evils the Lord has freed me, I am nourished by incorruptible food, and I cover my shoulders with the hope of my salvation." She is still a beginner after forty-seven years! Humility remains the source of her hope.

When Zossima leaves Mary she asks him to return the following year to bring her the life giving sacrament of the Body and Blood of Christ. She asks him not to speak of her to anyone as long as she is alive. When Zossima returns, Mary asks for his blessing and the sacrament. Zossima responds with words that mirror his inner transformation. "Indeed God does not lie when he promised that we shall be like him, insofar as we have been purified. Glory to you, Christ our God, who has shown me by your handmaiden here how much I should consider myself below the measure of true perfection."

Zossima returns to his monastery by the Jordan with a promise that he will bring the sacrament to Mary again the following year. He keeps his promise, but has difficulty finding her. Eventually he finds her body with hands folded and her face turned toward the east. Above her head, written in the sand, is her request that Zossima "bury in this place the body of Mary the sinner" and pray for her. In his grief Zossima begins to dig a grave, but cannot finish because of the hard desert soil. He is exhausted. He raises his eyes to see a huge lion standing by the body of Mary. The lion finishes digging the grave and Zossima buries Mary, beseeching her prayers for everyone. The preparation of the grave, itself, becomes a metaphor for his need for God because the lion, a symbol of Christ in the eastern churches, has made the completion of Zossima's work possible. Then, "The lion went off into the depths of the desert as meekly if it were a lamb, and Zossima went home, blessing and praising God and singing hymns of praise to our Lord Christ." God's presence in Mary had, indeed, been an oasis of wisdom.

Notes

1. *The Sayings of the Desert Fathers,* trans. Benedicta Ward, S.L.G. (Kalamazoo: Cistercian Publications, 1975) Antony 7, 4.

2. Ibid., Syncletica 26, 235.

3. Ibid., Theodora 6, 84.

4. Dorotheos of Gaza, *Discources and Sayings*, trans. Eric P. Wheeler (Kalamazoo: Cistercian Publications, 1977) "On Renunciation," 101.

5. *Desert Wisdom: Sayings from the Desert Fathers*, trans. Yushi Nomura (Maryknoll, N.Y.: Orbis Books, 2001) 8.

6. Pseudo-Athanasius, *The Life of Blessed Syncletica*, trans. Elizabeth Bryson Bongie (Toronto: Peregrina 1999) v. 57, 39–40.

7. Ward, *Sayings*, Agathon, 26; 24.

8. Ibid., Moses, Instructions, 2; 141.

9. I am grateful to Douglas Burton Christie for this insight. For more detail see *The Word in the Desert* (Oxford: Oxford University Press, 1993) 240–45.

10. Ward, *Sayings*, Moses, 12; 141.

11. Ibid., Ammonas, 27; 24.

12. Matthew the Poor, *The Communion of Love* (Crestwood, N.Y.: St. Vladimir's Seminary Press, 1984) "The Righteousness of Humility," 79–84.

13. Nomura, *Desert Wisdom*, Arsenius, 2;9.

14. Ibid., Arsenius, 3; 9.

15. Ibid., Joseph 2, 102.

16. Ward, *Sayings*, Antony, 1; 1–2.

17. Ibid., Moses the Robber, Instructions 1–4; 141–42.

18. Ibid., Poemen, 81; 178.

19. Paul Evdokimov, *Ages of the Spiritual Life* (Crestwood, N.Y.: St. Vladimir's Seminary Press, 1998) 91.

20. Ward, *Sayings*, Peter the Pionite, 4; 201–2.

21. Ibid., Benjamin, 4; 44.

22. Ibid., Syncletica, 19; 234.

23. Ibid., Moses, 2; 138–139.

24. Nomura, *Desert Wisdom*, 61.

25. Ibid., Arsenius, 6; 10.

26. Ibid., 1.

27. *The Wisdom of the Desert Fathers*, trans. Benedicta Ward, S.L.G. (Oxford: SLG Press, 1981) no.166, 47.

28. Nomura, *Desert Wisdom*, 35.

29. Ward, *Sayings*, Antony, 6; 2.

30. Stelios Ramfos, *Like a Pelican in the Wilderness* (Brookline: Holy Cross Orthodox Press, 2000) 183. Once again I am grateful for the influence of the scholarship and wisdom of Stelios Ramfos.

31. Massimo Capuani, *Christian Egypt* (Collegeville: Liturgical Press, 2002) 101–02.

32. Ward, *Sayings*, Moses, 4; 139.

33. Reverend Nikolaus Liesel, *The Eucharistic Liturgies of the Eastern Churches* (Collegeville: Liturgical Press, 1963) 36–37.

34. Capuani, *Christian Egypt,* 102–03. See O. Khs-Burmester, *A Guide to the Monasteries of the Wadi 'N-Natrun* (Le Caire: Societe D'Archeologie Copte-Editions Universitaires D'Egypte, 1954) 1–13.

35. Capuani, *Christian Egypt,* 75

36. Nomura, *Desert Wisdom,* 94.

37. Ward, *Sayings,* Elias, 3; 71.

38. Ramfos, *Pelican,* 228. I am grateful to Stelios Ramfos for this insight.

39. Nomura, *Desert Wisdom,* 86–87.

40. Columba Stewart, O.S.B., *The World of the Desert Fathers* (Oxford: SLG Press, 1995) 19.

41. Ibid., 19.

42. Nomura, *Desert Wisdom,* 38.

43. Ward, *Sayings,* Syncletica, 11; 233.

44. Ibid., Poemen, 63; 175.

45. Ibid., Poemen, 80; 178.

46. Ibid., Poemen, 103; 81.

47. Ibid., Poemen, 160; 89.

48. Ibid., Matoes, 13; 145.

49. Ibid., Syncletica, 16; 234.

50. Ibid., Poemen, 203; 94.

51. Ibid., Agathon, 19 and 17; 23.

52. Ibid., Isaiah, 8; 70.

53. *The Lives of the Desert Fathers,* trans. Norman Russell and intro. Benedicta Ward, S.L.G. (Oxford: Cistercian Publications, 1980) 49–50.

54. Ward, *Sayings,* Antony, 24; 6.

55. Ibid., Isidore, 4; 106-107.

56. Ibid., Motius, 1; 148.

57. I am grateful to Douglas Burton-Christie for this insight. See *The Word in the Desert,* 245–46.

58. Ward, *Sayings,* Poemen, 81; 178.

59. Ibid., Arsenius, 3; 9.

60. Ibid., Pambo, 8; 197.

61. Ibid., Poemen, 184; 193.

62. Ibid., Syncletica, 15; 233.

63. See Benedicta Ward, S.L.G., *Harlots of the Desert: A Study of Repentance in Early Monastic Sources,* (Kalamazoo: Cistercian Publications, 1987) 26–56.

64. All quotations in the narrative of Mary of Egypt and Zossima are taken from Ward's, *Harlots of the Desert,* ch. 3, 26–56, passim.

65. Ibid., 26.

10   Two Deserts

The Two Deserts: Searching for Authentic Human Life

Throughout *Oasis of Wisdom* I have spoken of the "heavenly society" the abbas and ammas created in the Egyptian desert. That desert was the place of their withdrawal to seek God. They longed for heaven, but God's response was the desert. Its lonely, dark nights were full of struggles with tempting old memories and self-knowledge. The desert's nakedness stripped away layers of human pride and self-reliance. Living water flowed throughout its arid emptiness. The surprising gift of the desert was renunciation, because its endless horizons baptized the elders in a new vision of human life. Its searing silence embraced the elders with the presence of God, their only source of life. The immense canopy of the desert's starry nights kept them from taking themselves too seriously. As they gave themselves to the desert and each other, the risen Christ became their constant companion in the work of love.

But there was another desert. That desert was the futility of the inhabited world. It was the emptiness the elders had experienced in a society whose over-abundance of activities, possessions, and irresponsible pleasures left little room for God and mocked the sacredness of life. The emptiness of the second desert was superficiality of life, the child of human pride and self-reliance. It was a consequence of losing sight of God. The horizons of this desert were short and its boundaries produced anxiety, greed, competition, and conflict. The desert elders left that desert to seek God in the desert of Egypt.

The desert elders did not leave the emptiness of the inhabited world because they believed the world, itself, is evil. They left a society that had become tarnished and profaned by human behavior. The motion picture

The Mission is a true story that depicts the two deserts. It documents the mid-eighteenth century struggle between a South American indigenous tribe to sustain its life and economy and protect its land from European slave traders and land barons. After contact with Jesuit missionaries they develop a rich Roman Catholic religious life. The Jesuits assist with their resistance to the land barons, who represent the economic interests of two monarchies loyal to the church. A representative of the pope visits the area and in the interest of political alliances that benefit the church, decides, with great personal anguish, in favor of the land barons, who then decimate the tribe. In the closing scene, one land baron comments on the outcome by saying, "Thus is the world we live in." The papal representative responds, "No, thus have we made the world! Thus have I made the world!"

Like the worlds of the desert fathers and mothers, the twenty-first century is experiencing international conflicts, terrorism, economic instability, clashes between religious ideologies, materialism, and major transitions within well-established institutions. Although we struggle to resolve differences and meet these challenges, there seems, also, to be great satisfaction with the surface of life driven by materialism and irresponsible pursuit of pleasure. Hegemony and fear are producing anxiety, fear, frustration, and impatience. Too often solutions are found in the use of hideous weapons of destruction, torture, and economic and political coercion. These violent solutions to conflict are planting the seeds for future violence. Sadly, faith communities are not free from violence, injustice and ideological wars. Millions of humans are hungry, dying of AIDS, and have no permanent home.

At the same time, the earth remains a place of great beauty and fecundity. Science, technology, communications, industry, education, transportation, agriculture, and healthcare offer opportunities for fullness of life in all parts of the world. The ethnic and cultural diversity, art and religious wisdom of humankind bear witness to the integrity and variety of human experience. Millions of people around the earth live ordinary lives, caring for each other and taking risks to overcome injustice, disease, hunger and resolution of conflicts.

How can we live with such polarities? There is much in modern life that is futile and it is tempting to become cynical and lose hope. Not all of us can flee to a desert. The desert elders remind us that fleeing from our problems is NOT the answer! They did not simply flee the futility of their world. They withdrew TO a life of transformation and a change of consciousness about life, itself. They never lost sight of the indelible image of God in human beings and the sanctity of all creation. We still have monastic communities in all the major world religious traditions. Their monastic lives call attention to the spiritual dimension of all forms of human life. They remind us not to lose sight of the beauty and resilience of life and to take the risks of responding to the challenges we face. They remind us, also, that when we depend solely only ourselves, our technologies, institutions, military power, and financial resources, the challenges we face will continue to overwhelm us.

The desert abbas and ammas can help us discern whether "Thus is the world we live in" or "Thus have we made the world" is a more accurate perspective on the source of life's tragedies and injustices. Their wisdom exhorts us to choose between the two deserts. One desert is like a maze. We enter seeking the center, but encounter repeated dead ends and false centers. As we try to recover our way we encounter further dead ends. The other desert is like a labyrinth, whose single path always leads to the center. There we experience God's presence and are empowered to return to the world.

One desert is an empty world of our own creation. It is a house of fear dominated by three weapons of mass destruction: self-reliance, self-interest, and self-centeredness. These weapons blaspheme the sanctity of life. They rely on human power and give birth to fear, anger, injustice, greed, vengeance, and war.

The wisdom of the desert fathers and mothers lures us to another desert where the monastic virtues of humility, purity of heart, and love of neighbor offer more lasting solutions to the challenges we face than weapons of mass destruction. They rely on God's power. Life in this desert is a difficult struggle as we learn to accomplish the work of love. It is not without risks, failure, and casualties. How is it possible to live in this second desert? The abbas and ammas call us to a change of consciousness: a change in our attitude about ourselves and human life. As Christians, they exhort us to take on the mind of Christ and through this Christ-consciousness look honestly at ourselves and the society we have created. We cannot be forced to enter this desert. Like the elders, we must leave the first desert and choose the second. Our work in the second desert will begin by slowing down and listening to God and each other. We will say, "Give me a word." And "What should I do?" The response will be as hard for us to accept as it was for the novices who came to the desert elders: "Go to your cell and your cell will teach you everything."

We cannot rely on the desert elders to solve our problems. Like them we must learn to rely completely on God. They can be our companions, but we must walk our own path to transformation. We are always beginners. But their legacies can help us know ourselves better and guide us along the path we choose.

The Legacies of the Desert Fathers and Mothers

The legacies of the desert fathers and mothers are diverse. Here are eight that relate their wisdom to the complex challenges we face today. We can begin with ourselves, one day at a time, close to home.

The Great Commandment

The foundation of the monastic culture of the desert elders was the great commandment of Jesus: "This is my commandment, that you love one another as I have loved you" (John 15:12, NRSV). The worlds of the desert fathers and mothers formed a crucible that shaped their wisdom from the raw materials of their interactions with those worlds. It was a constant struggle to make the law of love tangible in their lives because they took the great commandment very seriously. It was not a simplistic attitude reflected in generalities and rhetoric. The place where monks became lovers of souls was in specific interactions with other monks and the public worlds that surrounded them. This legacy reminds us that the great commandment is the foundation of the Christian path and should be the identifying characteristic of our lives within the Christian community. It should be the primary motivation for our relationships and actions in the venues of our daily lives.

The Inside of Life

The desert elders remind us that it is possible to spend our days living on the surface of life. They withdrew from a society that mocked the sacredness and integrity of human life and was filled with anxieties and emptiness. They protested a society whose frenzy, greed, conflicts and values were futile and heading nowhere. They took the risk of looking for God and formed a society committed to the inside of life. They discovered how their desires to control their lives limited their vision and were the causes of the futility they experienced. By opening themselves to God's presence, power, and desires they experienced a transformation and a new vision of life. The transformed vision did not deny the goodness of human life or material creation. It recognized the interior sacredness of what society had profaned and created a desire to see all people and things with divine values and a sense of stewardship. This legacy of the desert elders reminds us of the constant need to discern the values of our society, to reject influences that degrade and profane the sacredness of life, and risk the consequences and hard work necessary to replace what is futile with more just and authentic alternatives. That wisdom already lies within us.

A Commitment to Continual Prayer and Transformation

The desert fathers and mothers call us to our own forms of the hard work of love. They are clear about two things. The hard work of love is not our work; it is God's work in us. And, secondly, the venue for God's work in us is prayer. We can learn from and adapt their methods, but must develop our own patterns, based on our manners of life. This legacy also includes the wisdom present in the ways they experienced transformation. Here is an attempt, knowing that words are very limited in this context, to summarize what they experienced (I write in the first person because this is something I seek, as a beginner, in my own life.)

If I am to learn to love my neighbors and serve our common good, I must renounce everything that is futile and vain in me and my society. By withdrawing from what is unnecessary and profane in my life, I will begin to release my undisciplined ego from its desire to create and protect my self-interests.

As I let go of this "false self" and the personal power I need to sustain my self-image I will discover my true identity. I will encounter my true self and experience a readiness to seek God with my whole being. Through an awareness of my true self, in God, I will be able to develop easily satisfied needs (the needs that are fundamental in my life). As I continue to seek God, freed from dependence on unnecessary material resources and unrestrained passions, I will become more aware that everything in life is a gift. This change of consciousness, flowing from an attitude of gratefulness, will generate a sense of the wonder and sacredness of the earth, its creatures and all human beings . . . including my enemies.

As I begin to see that all things are held together in God I will begin to discover God's presence in all things. I will experience an expansion and flexibility of heart and be more accepting of God's presence and energy. I will become more aware of a unity with my neighbor. Rather than seeing him or her as a separate "other," with whom I must compete for survival, I will begin to desire the same goodness for my neighbor that I have learned God desires for me. I will begin to let go of my need to "take over" every situation. I will try to let go of my need to judge or label my neighbor or to see my neighbor primarily in terms of how useful he or she may be to me. I will begin to learn the dangers of anger and discern specific ways anger will limit my vision and perpetuate conflict. I begin to discover the power of being a forgiving person and my need to ask for forgiveness. I will value self-care, but not "look out for number-one."

When I am able to acknowledge that all life is a gift, I will begin to see life through the eyes of God's love. I will experience more freedom and openness for the expansion of my heart so that my words and actions may become more congruent with my true self. This purity of heart will become the source of what I desire and my freedom to love my neighbor. I will discover that this passion to love is not motivated by the need to fulfill exterior laws or expectations, but springs from a deep personal desire, with all my heart, to honor my neighbor and serve our common good. I will begin to realize that the primary virtues that guide me as I seek purity of heart are slowing down, honest listening through some form of contemplative prayer and meditation, patience, and total dependence on God. I realize, also, that this path to humility, purity of heart and love of neighbor must take place in and through my daily work and relationships. I will remember, too, that I am always a beginner and not above my neighbor.

Listening to the Word of God

The desert elders placed great emphasis on listening. They learned that listening requires intention, availability, watchfulness and focus. The central focus of their listening was the Bible. It was a source of both God's wisdom and experience of God. Their interest was not intellectual. It was formation. They looked to the Bible as the primary means of being formed by the God they believed in. The words of the Bible were indeed instructive and inspiring, but were recited primarily as a threshold to a personal encounter with the Holy One. As they listened "with the ears of their hearts" during meletē, meditatio, lectio, and their prayer they discovered that ". . . the word is very near to you; it is in your mouth and in your heart for you to observe" (Deut 30:14, NRSV). As they discovered God's voice and presence in Scripture they learned to recognize that same voice and presence in their work and relationships. Another aspect of the desert elders' legacy is the necessity of making a firm commitment to listen to God and experience God's presence in the Bible. They inspire us to renew the art of listening to God and to be committed to its disciplines. As we learn to listen to God, faithfully, we will value listening to each other and to the needs of the world.

Companions for a Journey That is Always Beginning

Very few of the desert elders were loners. Even the hermits were mentored by more mature abbas and ammas. The temptation to "go it alone" and concoct and control a personal spiritual path is tempting. God will be with us, but in a more limited way, when we are in charge. The image of the elders pulling a heaven-bound young novice down to earth by his feet is both humorous and all-too-true in our "quick-fix" and "fast-food" society. This legacy of the desert fathers and mothers includes awareness that walking the path is also the journey's destination and that we need help. We are like Zossima looking for new techniques and better results. The desert elders remind us that we are all beginners and must depend totally on God. At the same time they offer us the wisdom of their failures and experience. We do not have to travel alone. We can learn from mentors who already know the path. One of the greatest needs in Christian faith communities today is the need for mentors, companions along the way. In a society that worships being younger we do not pay attention to one of our greatest resources: our elders. An elder is not necessarily one who is older, well educated, or professionally trained as a religious leader. Remember that Arsenius sat at the feet of an "uneducated" shepherd. The abbas and ammas remind us of a pattern of spiritual formation that deserves more attention in our faith communities. The new interest in the lives, ministries, and writing of spiritual leaders throughout the Christian tradition is a great step toward renewing the role of mentors.

This legacy of mutual support for the journey is based not only on the role of the desert elders as mentors to individuals, but also reflects the mutual interdependence of monks in coenobitic monastic communities. Each monk is formed by the life of the community and, in turn, contributes to the formation of the community, itself. This "conversation" between the community and each member is an essential mentoring pattern that the legacy of the desert elders offers our modern faith communities.

Recovering Patience in Ourselves and Our Society

Personal calendars reflect the movements of our lives. Cell phones, the web, e-mail, and television bring us the world's joys, adventures, gruesome wars and crimes, innovations, art and beauty at the speed of light. The rapidity of images on a TV screen, the speed and volume of traffic, and the ever-increasing speed of computer operating systems are all icons of our fast-paced society. The legacy of patience as a virtue is very countercultural. The desert elders do not advise the avoidance of technology. They were glad to use the innovations of their day, such as punctuation in manuscripts. Patience is not avoidance of action. The virtue of patience lies in the stewardship of time and the influence of time on our lives. The elders remind us that time can be a source of anxiety because of its limited duration. The pressure of time affects the quality of decisions, productivity, and the discovery of innovative options. Patience allows space for the complexities of relationships to develop and for the crucial discipline of listening. The elders demonstrated how patience allows time for initial emotions to be tempered by reflection and makes space for God's presence and grace in a relationship or decision. The complex challenges of our world require both long-term vision and immediate actions, especially in resolving conflicts. Being patient with each other and ourselves is a sacred gift that makes mutual interdependence and compassion possible.

Stewardship of Our Souls and Our Society

The desert elders "guarded their souls." This legacy, rather than creating a spiritual ghetto, can remind us to form a personal pattern of prayer, study and solitude that will help sustain our life with God and make Christ tangible in our daily lives. This will require hard decisions about use of time, a place, and the "content" of our solitude. When we do not withdraw from our active lives we risk vulnerability to the treadmills of our society. The elders remind us that our "cell" is not only the place we pray and study, but also the person we become as we pray and open ourselves to growth and transformation. They exhort us to care for the person we become in our "cell" so that the pressures and futile influences of society do not scatter and distract us from the person we have become, in God. The elders remind us that we are a temple of God's Spirit and whatever we allow ourselves to experience, hear, eat, see, and do will influence who we are and how we influence those around us.

A second aspect of guarding our souls and remaining in the company of God is related to our vocation to listen to God and the world. When we listen faithfully to God's voice in prayer and the Bible we will be able to discern God's voice in all sectors of our daily lives. The presence of God in us will enable us to discern and support what is wholesome and serves the common good in society and to recognize and respond to malign and futile influences that profane the sacredness of people and the earth.

The Sanctity of Daily Life and Little Things

This legacy reminds us that human life is the venue for God's presence and grace. Each human life, every word, every task, every encounter can become a vessel of God's presence and love. Awareness that life is sacred invites responsible living and reminds us that anger, pride, and heedlessness divide and diminish our lives. The elders encourage us to see that our work, however mundane, contributes to the creation of the world. All work is a gift to someone and our enthusiasm, hopefulness, creativity, and relationships are interconnected. Every presence to another person recreates a broken world.

Arsenius: An Icon of Desert Wisdom

These eight legacies do not exhaust the oasis of wisdom we have explored in the previous nine chapters. But they offer specific ways to begin relating **the applied spirituality** of the desert elders to our Christian lives, faith communities, and the complex challenges facing our world. At the same time, the life of Abba Arsenius offers a simple, yet full image of how we may continually remember and begin drinking from the desert fathers' and mothers' oasis of wisdom. Their simple virtues speak directly to essential needs of twenty-first-century societies and our vocation to make Christ tangible through our words and actions.

Arsenius asked, "What must I do to find salvation?" It is the question of someone who lived on the surface of life and who desired the mystery of salvation. The word Arsenius used for salvation is the Greek "*soteria.*" Soteria refers, literally, to breathing deeply or having abundant health. As we breathe deeply, our lungs deliver more oxygen to our muscles, including the heart, and the heart is able to expand more fully. Salvation is abundant life; it is breathing in the fullness of human life. It is manifesting the image and likeness of God in our lives. God's response to Arsenius's desire required three actions: to flee, to become silent, and to pray always. These three actions, as we have seen, form the praxis of the desert elders. They are the spring of living water flowing from their oasis of wisdom into our lives.

Fleeing, or withdrawal, is a dual movement away from one thing toward something else. Anachoresis is an action, not a thought. It is the threshold of repentance as it leaves what is superficial, scattering, and futile behind and initiates a movement toward transformation. Fleeing, in this sense, is a form of discernment. It is waking up to what is missing, coupled with an action to move toward fullness of life.

Silence, within solitude, is a freely chosen willingness to let go of all that inhibits listening to God and knowing ourselves. The vocation of silent listening exposes the self-reliance, self-interest, and self-centeredness that have limited our lives. Silence is the first step leading toward transformation.

The desert elders called constant prayer "resting in God's presence." It is a freedom we experience when we are no longer attached to ourselves and the need to control our lives. Resting, or peacefulness, is the environment of grace we experience when our hearts have expanded with the presence of God's energies and love. It is what the elders called purity of heart and is the source of an awareness of our unity with all creation. It opens our eyes to the sacredness of every living creature. Inner peace gives birth to compassion because we have chosen to unite our desires with God's desires. When we are able to speak and act from this inner peace, humility becomes tangible. The great commandment is transparent in us.

The desert elders desired a peace that is beyond human understanding, yet is the foundation of authentic human life. They called this peace *eudaemonia*. It is the experience of living within the mystery of God's invisible and ineffable nature (the "kingdom of God"). *Eudaemonia* is a state of communion with God that is both a source of spontaneous joy and happiness and, at the same time, the source of compassion. It unites body, mind, and spirit and combines ecstasy with love of neighbor. *Eudaemonia* is a human vocation because we are created in the image of God and are called to manifest God's likeness in our manner of life. It was the unconscious motivation or yearning that led Arsenius, Syncletica, and the others to the desert. *Eudaemonia* is the raw material of the realm of God on earth. As Abba Dorotheos knew, it is the *natural state* of the human heart and the only reliable and lasting source of peace, justice, and compassion. It is our vocation, as well, to discern how we may experience *eudaemonia* in our busy and responsible lives today.

I am convinced that some of the greatest needs of twenty-first-century societies are the recovery of the desire to listen to each other, the practice of civility in conversations and relationships, a sharing of resources and wealth prompted by genuine compassion, and seeking the wisdom of the major world religious traditions. These virtues will help us discern between the two deserts. The life of the world depends on which desert we inhabit. One desert lacks water. The other leads to an oasis of wisdom.

Select Bibliography

For Basic Study

Burton-Christie, Douglas. *The Word in the Desert: Scripture and the Quest for Holiness in Early Christian Monasticism.* New York: Oxford University Press, 1993.

Chryssavgis, John. *In the Heart of the Desert: The Spirituality of the Desert Fathers and Mothers.* Bloomington: World Wisdom, Inc., 2003.

Forman, Mary, O.S.B. *Praying with the Desert Mothers.* Collegeville: Liturgical Press, forthcoming.

Palladius. *The Lausiac History.* Westminister, Md.: Newman Press, 1965.

Russell, Norman, and Benedicta Ward, S.L.G. *The Lives of the Desert Fathers: The Historia Monachorum in Aegypto.* Kalamazoo: Cistercian Publications, 1980.

Stewart, Columba, O.S.B. *The World of the Desert Fathers.* Oxford: SLG Press, 1995.

Swan, Laura. *The Forgotten Desert Mothers: Sayings, Lives, and Stories of Early Christian Women.* New York: Paulist Press, 2001.

Vivian, Tim. *Journey Into God: Seven Early Monastic Lives.* Minneapolis: Fortress Press, 1996.

Ward, Benedicta, S.L.G.. *The Sayings of the Desert Fathers: The Alphabetical Collection.* Kalamazoo: Cistercian Publications, 1975.

For More Thorough Study

Alfeyev, Hilarion. *The Spiritual World of Isaac the Syrian.* Kalamazoo: Cistercian Publications, 2000.

Athanasius. *The Life of Antony.* Trans. Robert C. Gregg. Mahwah, N.J.: Paulist Press, 1980.

The Syriac Fathers on Prayer and the Spiritual Life. Trans. Sebastian Brock. Kalamazoo: Cistercian Publications, 1987.

Cassian, John. *The Conferences.* Trans. Boniface Ramsey, O.P. New York: Paulist Press, 1997.

Chitty, Derwas J. *The Desert a City.* Crestwood, N.Y.: St. Vladimir's Seminary Press, 1995.

Cyril of Scythopolis. *The Lives of the Monks of Palestine.* Trans. R. M. Price. Kalamazoo: Cistercian Publications, 1991.

Dorotheos of Gaza. *Discourses and Sayings.* Trans. Eric P. Wheeler. Kalamazoo: Cistercian Publications, 1977.

Ephrem the Syrian. *Hymns.* Trans. Kathleen E. McVey. New York: Paulist Press, 1989.

Evagrius Ponticus. *The Praktikos and Chapters on Prayer.* Trans. John Eudes Bamberger, O.C.S.O. Kalamazoo: Cistercian Publications, 1981.

Goerhring, James E. *Ascetics, Society, and the Desert: Studies in Early Egyptian Monasticism.* Harrisburg: Trinity Press, 1999.

Early Fathers from the Philokalia. E. Kadloubovsky and G.E.H. Palmer, ed. London: Faber & Faber Ltd., 1953.

Writings from the Philokalia on Prayer of the Heart. E. Kadloubovsky and G.E.H. Palmer, ed. London: Faber & Faber Ltd., 1951.

Pachomian Koinonia 1: The Life of Saint Pachomius. Trans. Armand Veilleux. Kalamazoo: Cistercian Publications, 1980.

Pachomian Koinonia 2: Pachomian Chronicles and Rules. Trans. Armand Veilleux. Kalamazoo: Cistercian Publications, 1981.

Pachomian Koinonia 3: Instructions, Letters, and Other Writings of Saint Pachomius and His Disciples. Trans. Armand Veilleux. Kalamazoo: Cistercian Publications, 1982.

The Philokalia Vol. 1. G.E.H. Palmer, and others, ed. London: Faber & Faber Ltd., 1979.

Pseudo-Macarius. *The Fifty Homilies and the Great Letter.* Trans. George A. Maloney, S.J. New York: Paulist Press, 1992.

Ramfos, Stelios. *Like a Pelican in the Wilderness: Reflections on the Sayings of the Desert Fathers.* Trans. Norman Russell. Brookline: Holy Cross Orthodox Press, 2000.

Rousseau, Philip. *Pachomius: The Making of a Community in Fourth-Century Egypt.* Berkeley: University of California Press, 1985.

Stewart, Columba, O.S.B. *Cassian the Monk.* New York: Oxford University Press, 1998.

Theodoret of Cyrrhus. *A History of the Monks of Syria.* Trans. R. M. Price. Kalamazoo: Cistercian Publications, 1985.

For Study of Early Monastic Women

Clark, Elizabeth A. *Women in the Early Church*. Collegeville: Liturgical Press, 1983.

King, Margot. *The Desert Mothers: A Bibliography*. Saskatoon: Peregrina Publishing, 1983.

_____. *The Desert Mothers: A Survey of the Female Anchoretical Tradition*. Saskatoon: Peregrina Publishing, 1983.

Krawiec, Rebecca. *Shenoute and the Women of the White Monastery: Egyptian Monasticism in Late Antiquity*. New York: Oxford University Press, 2002.

Handmaids of the Lord: Contemporary Descriptions of Feminine Asceticism in the First Six Christian Centuries. Trans. and selected by Joan M. Petersen. Kalamazoo: Cistercian Publications, 1996.

Matericon, *Instructions of Abba Isaiah to the Honorable Nun, Theodora*. Safford, Ariz.: St. Paisius Serbian Orthodox Monastery, 2001.

Nichols, John A., ed. *Distant Echoes: Medieval Religious Women*. Kalamazoo: Cistercian Publications, 1984.

Pseudo-Athanasius. *The Life of Blessed Syncletica*. Trans. Elizabeth Bryson Bongie. Toronto: Peregrina, Co., 1999.

Ranft, Patricia. *Women and the Religious Life in Premodern Europe*. New York: St. Martin's Press, 1996.

Shaffer, Mary. *The Life of The Blessed and Holy Snycletica by Pseudo-Athanasius: Part Two, A Study of the Life*. Toronto: Peregrina, 2001.

For Personal Reflection on the Wisdom of the Desert Elders

Bondi, Roberta C. *To Love as God Loves*. Philadelphia: Fortress Press, 1987.

Cowan, James. *Desert Father: A Journey in the Wilderness with Saint Anthony*. Boston: Shambala Publications, 2004.

Gruen, Anselm, O.S.B. *Heaven Begins with You*. New York: Crossroad 1999.

Mayers, Gregory, C.Ss.R. *Listen to the Desert*. Liguori: Triumph Books, 1996.

Williams, Rowan. *Silence and Honey Cakes: The Wisdom of the Desert*. Oxford: Lion Publishing, 2003.

The labels within the map image include:

BLACK SEA

Constantinople
Chalcedon
• Nicaea

Site of household monastic community led by
Macrina the Younger, who influenced her
+ brothers, Basil the Great and Gregory of Nyssa

GREECE
• Nyssa

ASIA
MINOR

• Nazianzus

• Athens
• Ephesus
• Antioch
+ Female community of
virgins led by the
deaconess Publia

SYRIA

MEDITERRANEAN SEA

Caesarea
Jerusalem
PALESTINE

Gaza + DEAD SEA

Alexandria
Bethlehem
Site of monastic communities
of Jerome and Paula

Nitria +
Scetis + Cellia
Mt.
Sinai

Antony
Oxyrhynchus •
• Antinoë

ARABIA

EGYPT
Lycopolis •
Tabennesi   RED
SEA

• Town or city
+ Monastic site
• Thebes

Latopolis •

1. The Worlds of the Desert Fathers and Mothers

169

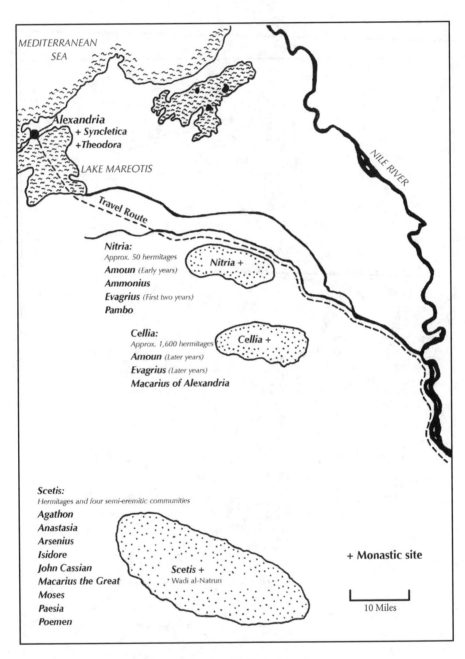

MEDITERRANEAN
SEA

Alexandria
+ Syncletica
+Theodora

LAKE MAREOTIS

NILE RIVER

Travel Route

Nitria:
Approx. 50 hermitages
Amoun (Early years)
Ammonius
Evagrius (First two years)
Pambo

Nitria +

Cellia:
Approx. 1,600 hermitages
Amoun (Later years)
Evagrius (Later years)
Macarius of Alexandria

Cellia +

Scetis:
Hermitages and four semi-eremitic communities
Agathon
Anastasia
Arsenius
Isidore
John Cassian
Macarius the Great
Moses
Paesia
Poemen

Scetis +
Wadi al-Natrun

+ Monastic site

10 Miles

2. Lower Egypt
Hermits and Semi-eremitic Sites

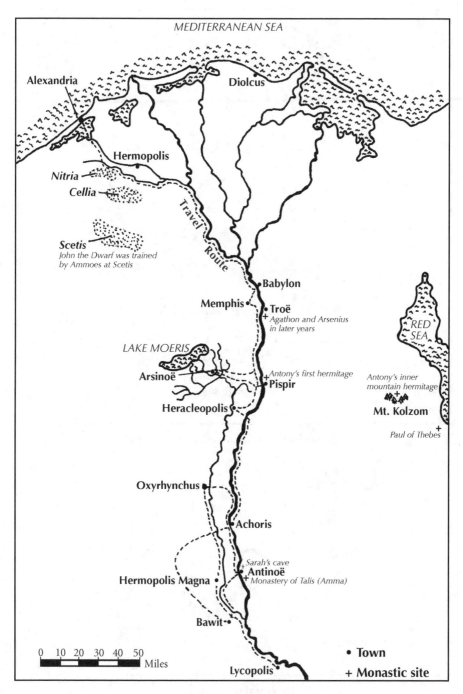

MEDITERRANEAN SEA

Alexandria

Diolcus

Hermopolis

Nitria

Cellia

Scetis
John the Dwarf was trained
by Ammoes at Scetis

Babylon

Memphis

Troë
+ Agathon and Arsenius
in later years

RED
SEA

LAKE MOERIS

Arsinoë

Antony's first hermitage
Pispir

Antony's inner
mountain hermitage

Heracleopolis

Mt. Kolzom

Paul of Thebes +

Oxyrhynchus

Achoris

Sarah's cave
Antinoë
+ Monastery of Talis (Amma)

Hermopolis Magna

Bawit

0 10 20 30 40 50
Miles

Lycopolis

• Town

+ Monastic site

3. Lower and Middle Egypt Monastic Sites

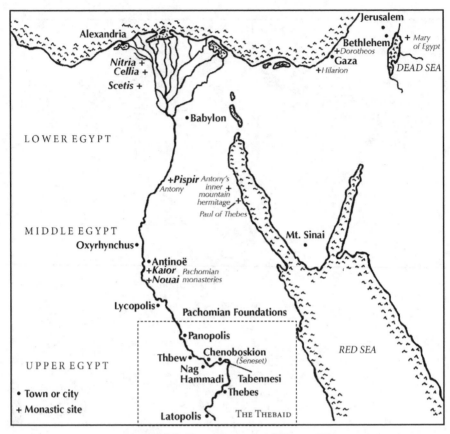

4. Coenobitic Foundations of Upper Egypt

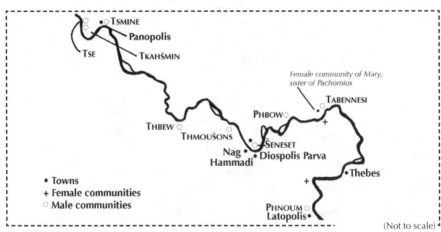

5. Pachomian Foundations

Source: Philip Rousseau. *Pachomius.* 56

Index of Names and Places

General Index

abbas, 2, 8
  teaching methods, 8–11
accidie, 34, 35, 135
active life, 81, 86–89, 98, 128
agapés, 84, 147–48
always a beginner, 139, 149, 153, 158, 160–62
amerimnesia, 48
amma, 2, 8,
  teaching methods, 8–11
anachoresis, 4, 49, 56–57, 62, 88, 131–32, 164 (*see also* withdrawal)
anchorite, 4, 10, 12, 50
anger, 147, 160, 163
apatheia, 24–25, 29–30, 34, 90
Apophthegmata Patrum, xvi
apotaktikoi, 6–7, 50
applied spirituality, 90, 92, 105, 164
ascetic life, 2, 24, 27–31, 35, 51, 58, 62, 96, 104
  combined with labor, 118–21
askesis (*see* ascetic life)
attachment, 83–84
authentic self/human life (true self), 49, 51–52, 54, 56–57, 63, 70, 80, 84, 90, 97, 100–01, 110, 124, 136, 143, 151, 156, 160, 165
awareness of death (*see* death)

Bible, 18–22, 27, 31, 37, 39, 41–44, 51, 54–55, 64–65, 68, 71, 88, 99, 101, 105–08, 112, 115, 122, 132, 161

body, 22, 35, 40, 54, 56–57, 73, 85, 89, 97, 101, 110
  goodness of, 112–13
  venue for grace, 111–12

cell, 47, 62–63, 71, 73, 79–80, 82, 90, 163
  physical environment of, 50
  significance of, 50–52
  as place of transformation, 52–53
  as place of discipline, 53–55
  as sacred space, 56–57
  as a manner of life, 56–57
  guarding the cell, 56–57
  and love of neighbor, 57–58
  and the world, 58–59
chanting the Psalms, 43, 103
chastity, 104, 108
Christ tangible in lives, 75, 132–33, 159, 163–64
church fathers, 18, 24
coenobite, 11, 27
coenobitic life, 11–12, 37, 50, 146, 162
collaboration with God's grace, 63, 110, 113, 123, 135, 151
community, 146, 148–49, 161
compunction, 115, 144, 150–52
conferences (*see* monastic teaching)
congruence between prayer and behavior (between words and action), 82–84, 87, 89, 90, 98, 105, 143, 161
consciousness, 87, 89, 146, 157–58, 160
  Christ consciousness, 158